DOWNSIZING FOR CLIENT/SERVER APPLICATIONS

This book is printed on acid-free paper. ∞

Copyright © 1995 by Academic Press, Inc.
All rights reserved.
No part of this publication may be reproduced or
transmitted in any form or by any means, electronic
or mechanical, including photocopy, recording, or
any information storage and retrieval system, without
permission in writing from the publisher.

All brand names and product names mentioned in this book are
trademarks or registered trademarks of their respective companies.

AP PROFESSIONAL
955 Massachusetts Avenue, Cambridge, MA 02139

An Imprint of ACADEMIC PRESS, INC.
A Division of HARCOURT BRACE & COMPANY

United Kingdom Edition published by
ACADEMIC PRESS LIMITED
24–28 Oval Road, London NW1 7DX

ISBN 0-12-402680-X

Printed in the United States of America
94 95 96 97 98 IP 9 8 7 6 5 4 3 2 1

DOWNSIZING FOR CLIENT/SERVER APPLICATIONS

PAUL KAVANAGH

AP PROFESSIONAL
Boston   San Diego   New York
London   Sydney   Tokyo   Toronto

For Danny and Allison

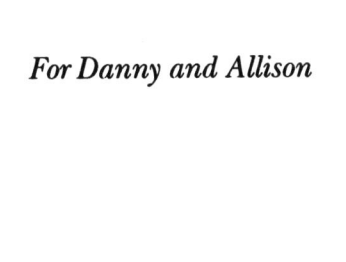

Contents

Acknowledgments xv
Preface xvii

1 Why Develop Open Client/Server Systems? 1

What Is Client/Server? 1

Client/Server and Open Systems 1 • Client/Server and Database Systems 2 • Client/Server and GUI Systems 2 • Client/Server and Networks 2 • Client/Server and Downsizing 2 • Client/Server and Development Methodologies 2

The Impact of New Technology 3
A Brief History of Business Computing 5
The Cost Advantage of the New Systems 9
Open Systems Advantages 10

Key Questions 13 • The Bottom Line on Standards 14

Improved Access to Enterprise Information 14
Improved User Interface 15

The Internet 18 • Ubiquitous Computing 19 • Ability to Respond to Changing Business Needs 19 • Are All Mainframes Going to Be Replaced? 19 • Summary 20

2 The Downsizing Strategy 21

Selecting the Downsizing Approach 21
Remove the System 22
Redesign the Business Process 23
Replace with Packaged Software 23
Rewrite the Software with New Tools 24

Rehost the Existing Software 24
    COBOL 26 • CICS Options 26 • Emulation or Conversion? 27 • Code Conversion 27

Refurbish the Existing Software 28
    Refurbishing the User Interface 28 • Refurbishing the Database 29 • Refurbishing the Business Rules 30 • Types of Code Recovery Tools 31 • Tools to Understand the System 32 • Tools to Improve the System 32 • Tools to Reengineer the System 32

Circumscribe 32
    Summary 33

3 Planning the Downsizing 35

Automation and Empowerment 35
Poor Candidates for Total Client/Server Architecture 37
    System Size and Complexity 38 • Large Centralized I/O Processing 38 • Centralized Control 39 • Tight Mainframe Integration 39

Good Candidates for Client/Server Architecture 39
    Professional and Analytical Work 40 • Special Situations 41 • Which Systems to Build First 43 • Strengths of the Old Environment 44

Business Assessment 45
Technology Assessment 47
    1. Assess Existing Applications 48 • 2. Assess Infrastructure 49 • 3. Assess Current Work and Staffing 50 • 4. Assess the Current Costs and Problems 50 • 5. Analyze the Results 51 • 6. Prepare Migration and Nonmigration Costs for Each Application 51 • 7. Determine a Basis for Migration 51

Risk Assessment 52
    An Example 54

Cost/Benefit Analysis 55
Client/Server Cost Analysis 57
    Moving One Application 58 • The Cost of the Second Application 59

Establishing Measurements of Payback 60
Calculating Workstation Cost 61
    The Cost of Moving to Windows 61 • Transition Costs 63 • Summary 64

Contents

4 Reengineering the Business Process 65

The Principles of Reengineering 65

    Organize around Outcomes, Not Tasks 66 • Have Those Who Use the Output of the Process Perform the Process 67 • Subsume Information-Processing Work into the Real Work That Produces the Information 67 • Treat Geographically Dispersed Resources As Though They Were Centralized 68 • Link Parallel Activities Instead of Integrating Their Results 68 • Put the Decision Point Where the Work Is Performed, and Build Control into the Process 69 • Capture Information Once and at the Source 69 • Recognize and Manage Processes 70 • Triage the Process Based on Customer Need 70 • Reduce the Cycle Time of Product Development and Delivery 70 • Anticipate, Measure, and Continuously Improve Your Product's Success on the Key Dimensions of Customer Satisfaction 72

Business Transformation 72

Business Process Selection 74

    Potential Benefits of Business Reengineering 74 • Transformation or Improvement 76 • Overview of the Approach 76 • The Selection Process 83

Business Modeling 84

Business Process Analysis 86

    Education and Scheduling 86 • Activity/Task Identification 86 • Detailed Analysis 88 • Process Flow Chart Guidelines 89

Business Process Design 89

    Design Alternatives Direction 90 • Benchmarking 90 • Brainstorming 91 • Action Prioritization and Scheduling 92 • Summary 93

5 Selecting the New Architecture 95

Definition of Client/Server Architecture 95

    Development of Languages and Interfaces 96 • Decomposing an Application 99 • Distributed Presentation 100 • Remote Presentation 101 • Distributed Processing 102 • Remote Data Access 103 • Distributed Database 104 • A Practical Approach to Architecture 104

Issues in Selecting Client/Server Tools 105

    Evaluating Tools 106 • Portability 109

Standards 110
    Standards Offer Choices 110 • What to Do about Standards 113
Selecting the Network 113
Network Hardware 114
    Ethernet 115 • Token Ring 116 • High-Speed LANs 116 • Wireless LANs 119 • Wide Area Network Choices 119
Communications Protocols 120
Network Operating Systems 121
    Network Operating System Features 121 • Peer-to-Peer LANs 123 • Summary 123

6 Server Hardware Selection 125

File Servers 126
Resource Servers 127
Database Servers 127
Application Servers 127
Classes of Server 128
Hardware Choices in PC-Class Servers 130
    Deskside 130 • Server 131 • Superserver 131
Issues in Selecting PC-Class Servers 132
    Processors 133 • Disk Storage 134 • Fault Tolerance 135 • Scalability 136 • Support 136
Processor Choices 137
    Processor Benchmarks 138 • Performance Trends 139
Operating System Choices in Servers 140
    Novell NLM 140 • OS/2 141 • Windows NT 142 • UNIX 142
H-P Server Line 143
IBM Server Line 144
SUN Server Line 144
DEC Server Line 144
Small UNIX Servers 145
Large UNIX Servers 145
General Issues with UNIX Systems 146
    Summary 147

Contents   xi

7 Selecting the Database   149

     The Advantage of Relational Databases   150

         Early Databases 150 • Relational Databases 151 • SQL 151 • Object Databases 152

     Comparing the Database Products   153

         Multiplatform Databases 153 • Single-Platform Databases 154 • Niche Suppliers 154

     Basic Statistics   155

         Commodity Trend 156 • Support 156 • Pricing 157

     Data Access   157

         The SQL Standard 157 • Database Objects 159 • Database Functions 159 • SQL Implementation 159 • Stored Procedures and Triggers 160 • Declarative Referential Integrity 161 • Front-End Software Support 162 • Data Dictionary 162

     Performance   162

         Design for Performance 162 • Benchmarking 164 • Transaction Processing Benchmarks 164 • Portability and Scalability 166 • Data Storage 167

     Manageability   167

         The Special Case of DB2 167 • Summary 168

8 Selecting Workstations, Development Tools, and Applications   171

     Selecting Workstations   172

         DOS Limitations 172 • X Terminals 173 • Windows/DOS 174 • Windows NT 174 • Macintosh 175 • OS/2 175 • UNIX 176 • Taligent 178 • Is There a Case against GUIs? 178 • Emulations 180 • Processor Choices 181 • GUI OS Choices for the Desktop 182

     Selecting Development Tools   182

         4GL Product Features 184

     Information Display Tools   189

         EIS and Decision Support 190 • Forest and Trees 191 • Lightship 191

Graphical Client/Server 4GLs 191

    PowerBuilder 192 • SQLWindows 193 • ObjectView 194 • Paradox for Windows 195 • Visual Basic and Access 195 • Tools from Database Vendors 196 • SmallTalk Tools 196 • AI Tools 197 • More Tools 198 • "Large System" Tools 198 • CASE 199 • C++ 200

Personal Workstation Applications 200

    Groupware 201 • Summary 203

9 Building a New Automated System 205

Overview 205

Establish Project Plan 209

    Project Business Case 209 • Development Environment 210

Establish Business Requirements 210

    Facilitated Session: Joint Requirements Planning 211 • The Structured Workshop Facility 213

Application Design 214

Prototyping Using JAD 215

    The Timebox 216 • Types of Prototype 217 • Content Prototype 217 • Advantages of JAD 218 • Facilitated Session: Joint Application Design 218 • Estimating the JAD Session 220 • Example JAD Estimate 221

Data Modeling 221

    Building a Data Model 222 • Data Normalization 224 • Example of Data Normalization 224

Team Composition 226

    Summary 226

10 The Old and the New: Porting and Bridging Systems 227

Mainframe Connectivity with SNA 228

Mainframe Connectivity with Open Systems 229

Using Middleware to Access Legacy Systems 230

    Legacy System Complexity 232 • Access to SQL Databases 234 • Access to Non-SQL Databases 235

Replication Strategies and Data Warehouses 237

    Summary 238

11 Implementing and Managing the New Systems 239

Technical Problems with Client/Server Systems 239
Performance Management 241
Configuration Management 242
Accounting Management 243
Security Management 243

    Identify and Authenticate Users 244 • Restrict Access to Resources 246 • Database Security 246 • Audit Access to Resources 247 • Physically Control Access 247 • Use Encryption to Secure Communications 248

Fault Management 248
Operations Management 249
Storage Management 250

    Backup 251 • Network Management Products 252 • SNMP 252 • DME 252

Mainframe Vendors Offering UNIX Tools 253

    Computer Associates' CA-Unicenter 254

How Practical Is UNIX? 257

    Security 257 • System Administration 258

Service and Support of Heterogenous Systems 258

    Summary 259

12 The Human Side of the New Technology 261

Costs 261
Functions to Centralize 262
Training 263

    Summary 266

Index 267

Acknowledgments

I would like to acknowledge Tony Stepanski, Al Franco, Rich Huntley, Sheldon Dansiger, and Jon Burley (AGS), and Jack Krasula (DCI), former employers who gave me the opportunity to learn different aspects of this business. Many former AGS colleagues contributed ideas and opinions, which have been incorporated here, to the consulting practice—notably John Hutchinson, Bob Kendrick, and Sid Wise (Keane), Steve Koning (Booz, Allen), Michael Spring and Bob Coughlin (independent), Stu Roth (CSC Index), Belinda Kaake (Meritus), Roel Mahatoo (Peat Marwick), and Nick Taylor (DCI). Last but not least, the ever-patient Alan Rose.

This book was written on my personal system, an Intel 486-based desktop, using Microsoft Word, Visio Shapeware, Microsoft Excel, and Microsoft PowerPoint. Software was tested and developed using PowerSoft PowerBuilder, Gupta SQLWindows, Microsoft Visual Basic and Visual C++, Watcom SQL and Microsoft SQL Server. Many other software products were used or reviewed, as discussed in the text.

Basking Ridge, NJ
Tampa, FL
San Jose, CA
Oak Park, IL

February 1993–May 1994

Preface

The challenge of redeveloping information systems to use the new technologies introduced over the last few years is the main one now facing computer professionals and business people alike. These technologies are driving all of the current challenges faced by our industry—for instance, reengineering, outsourcing, rightsizing, and client/server (Figure P.1). This book is intended to offer a roadmap to those challenges from a practical technical perspective, based on considerable experience consulting on systems integration in this area.

It is written first and foremost for computer professionals from traditional environments, who are moving to the set of new technologies popularly called open systems or client/server systems. This is a transition I have made personally. I was also a mainframe professional for some years, using MVS

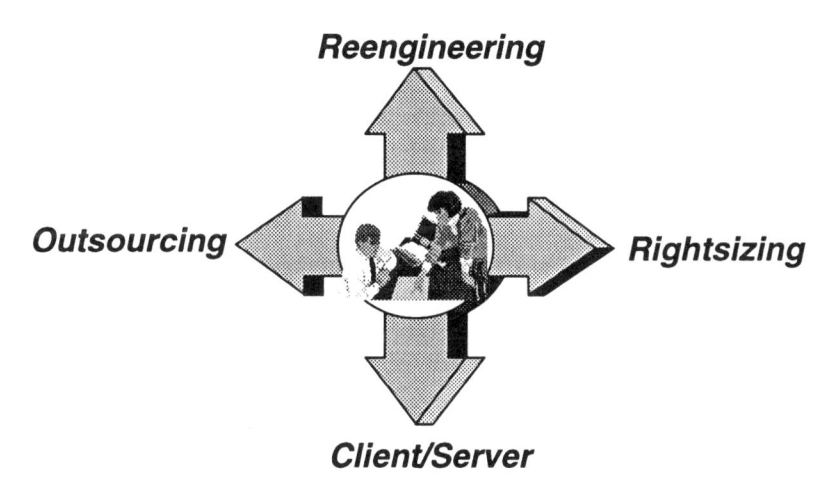

Figure P.1 Today's issues

systems and programming in PL/I and COBOL for CICS, IMS, and DB2. I taught classes on CICS performance and wrote a prior book on COBOL. When the first PC C compilers became available in 1982, I started to develop systems with them, while still focusing on IBM CICS. For 10 years I have used PCs, using PC networks when they were very immature. Then, six or seven years ago, I moved to development on networked UNIX systems; now, most of my work involves Windows-based client/server tools. Each of these environments has its strengths; our goal is to use them all appropriately.

The two companies I worked for while writing this book employ over two thousand computer professionals using new and old systems in a variety of industries. I was privileged to meet many of them and have access to information on those systems and the success and failure of the strategies employed to build and manage them. The themes for this book come from this experience and from talking to our employees and our customers about the issues involved and lessons learned in this transition to a new model of computing. I also had the opportunity to work with a number of hardware and software systems vendors in the course of a variety of projects. There is a common set of questions asked by those embarking on the journey, as well as issues encountered on the way. This book is intended to be a roadmap for the first part of the trip.

THE STYLE AND STRUCTURE OF THIS BOOK

I've attempted to keep the style and language used in this book simple. As a professional myself, I recognize that the demands on time in this industry are intense. Each chapter is quite long and contains complete treatment of a subject but is structured into segments so that useful information can be obtained in a short sitting. I have tried to include real-life examples where possible to illustrate the ideas introduced.

The book is intended as a self-teaching guide to the issues faced in transitioning to a new environment. It assumes an understanding of computer technology in general, but not of the latest buzzwords. Alternatively, the book can be used as the textbook for a seminar; I use it myself in that way.

THE APPROACH TAKEN BY THIS BOOK

There are many reasons to consider using the new technologies of inexpensive workstations, fast networks, and standard databases to build systems today. A perspective on these benefits and on the historical context and

Preface   xix

future developments within which they occur is important to using the systems well. The first chapter summarizes the benefits of these technologies and the reasons for adopting them.

After this, the book focuses on the types of systems most often met and the criteria for determining how to approach them; whether to outsource, reengineer, downsize, stabilize, replace, and so on. This includes cost/benefit and risk analysis as well as technical analysis of the systems themselves. Also, since changing the technology without examining the business it supports is never a good idea, this part introduces the concepts and methods for analyzing and redesigning the business processes of an area, a useful first step in much system development.

An important part of the book is focused on the design of an overall client/server architecture, the factors to weigh and the tools and technologies to consider, and the near-term trends in distributed computing. This includes sections on the competing products available for the server and client components of the system. Ironically, the choice of product may be one of the less important factors in overall success, but this information is often heavily focused on early in a downsizing project. To avoid obsolescence, this book looks at the criteria to use so that you can make good choices even though particular products seem to change rapidly.

The next part of the book introduces the recommended methodology for developing an extremely common type of application. It is a rapid evolutionary method based on structured prototyping with graphical tools.

The final part of the book covers the areas which are most complex and up to now most disappointing. One chapter covers the issues of connecting to and coexisting with legacy systems. The tools available in this area generally do less than promised; when they do what is promised, it is generally less than the user expectation. Another covers the technical issues of system cutover and the business issues of new system introduction. This is the area where hidden costs can mount up and unexpected problems can surface, leading to disappointments. It also covers the organizational and "people" issues of these changes on the IT support organization.

THE AREA COVERED BY THIS BOOK

The full life cycle of system introduction is covered, including selecting the systems to implement, choosing a technical architecture, and managing the introduction of new systems. While the issue of downsizing an application without change using emulation tools is briefly dealt with, the emphasis is on using the technology to achieve change in the business processes being supported.

The book recommends and assumes an approach that combines the newer techniques in system analysis and design with the newer technologies for system implementation and delivery. Accordingly, it stresses the subjects of business process reengineering, JAD, RAD, CASE, open systems, and client/server systems. The type of systems focused on are generally information-rich front-end systems, which enhance and surround the legacy systems, offloading function without replacing them wholesale. Figure P.2 illustrates this type of system from a physical point of view.

As an introduction and overview, this book does not present details of programming in the various languages discussed. There are numerous books and tutorials on each of these, and, since significant updates occur so frequently, they become obsolete within months. All of the products used in writing these books had upgrades released within the development period that significantly improved them while lowering their cost.

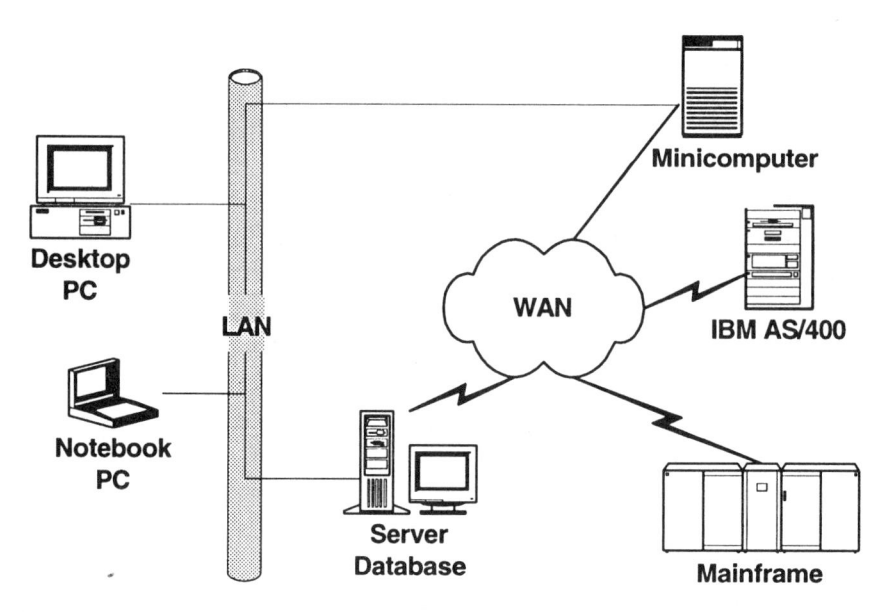

Figure P.2 Typical client/server system

1

Why Develop Open Client/Server Systems?

WHAT IS CLIENT/SERVER?

There are many definitions of client/server computing, and many similar terms, such as distributed or cooperative computing. Simply put, a client/server application system is one developed so that parts of it can be run on separate computers.

There are many concepts, which will be covered later, that overlap with client/server. Since they are often used interchangeably, I will try to delineate the relationships here.

Client/Server and Open Systems

An open system is a system that, to a greater degree, allows its owner choices in replacing, interfacing, or upgrading components. No system is wholly open or wholly closed; openness is desirable in general but may involve trade-offs with other good qualities, such as high performance. It is possible to build client/server systems using more or less proprietary databases, networks, and development languages.

Client/Server and Database Systems

One of the simplest ways to separate function between computers is to put the database on one system and the user interface on another. The majority of client/server systems today are based on a relational database as a core component, although that is not essential. In the future, more complex divisions of the application wil be commonplace.

Client/Server and GUI Systems

It is, of course, possible to develop a system with a graphical user interface (GUI) for a stand-alone PC. It is also possible to develop a client/server system without a graphical interface. However, all of the systems we discuss in this book will incorporate a GUI front end.

Client/Server and Networks

Most applications on networks today are not client/server. Many networks are running applications that were written for dumb terminals and do not use the workstation effectively. Other applications were written for the PC and use the server solely for data storage. Client/server applications use the network infrastructure to distribute processing appropriately.

Client/Server and Downsizing

Downsizing can refer to migration of all or some of an organization's applications to less costly platforms. Often, these less costly systems will be client/server; often, today, they are not. For example, an organization could move an application from a 3090 to a 9370, AS/400, or UNIX system, even replacing the terminals with PCs, but unless the code is altered, the application is not client/server because all processing occurs on the server.

When a new application is developed using client/server, it always involves some functionality being off-loaded from the mainframe, which can be viewed as downsizing. It also may raise the demand for mainframe data storage or access activities.

Client/Server and Development Methodologies

The tools of client/server, particularly relational database and GUI 4GLs, enable a rapid prototyping approach to application design. The type of system being built is also often suited to evolutionary development. As a result, some client/server systems can be developed entirely with rapid prototyping, and components of almost all systems can be built this way. On the other hand, client/server adds complexity to large systems development, particularly since today the tools are immature and the developers are often inexperienced. As systems that are larger and more transactional are developed with client/server architectures, they will need architecture and methodology at least as much as monolithic systems.

A client/server development strategy simply attempts to develop software that can be tuned to exploit the available systems so that the right parts are run in the right places. Since it is occasionally appropriate for the entire system to run on a single computer, we can see the client/server design as always the correct one, with the monolithic system simply being a degenerate case. In the past, it often was not acceptable for performance reasons to rigidly separate the user interface, business logic, and database manipulation portions of an application. That excuse no longer applies.

In this book, we will address the type of system that we see as typical for business applications. This is an application developed for a system that includes SQL-based relational databases with stored procedures and networked workstations with a graphical user interface, developed by a team using a mixture of graphical tools and conventional programming.

Because most large organizations are transitioning to this type of development from a monolithic mainframe philosophy, we address the issues in making such a move.

THE IMPACT OF NEW TECHNOLOGY

Computer professionals who have been in the field for some time have been through many changes regarding the systems used. These changes have often been introduced with great fanfare as being capable of solving the many problems we face but have generally disappointed. CASE tools, fourth-generation languages, AI, databases, even COBOL at one time, were thought to provide the answer to programmer productivity problems. Several generations of computers have offered cost savings. Some IT professionals are by now disillusioned with this pattern and inclined to dismiss all new developments as passing fads.

The new wave of open, client/server systems is not like these previous changes in some very important respects. It is grounded in the deep, long-running trend of price reductions and performance improvements achieved by the microprocessor-based components of the computer industry. It addresses real end-user demands for systems that are manageable and understandable. It is global and industry-wide.

Some professionals have compared this to the previous introduction of distributed computing in the 1970s. That effort was driven by the advent of the minicomputer, which did not have the powerful underlying cost trends of the microprocessor driving it. It was pushed by individual vendors, who used it to extend their proprietary architectures, rather than pulled by customers expanding their use. It was limited to a few manufacturers.

Figure 1.1 shows the well-known technology introduction S-curve. The graph represents the sales of a successful new technology over time. The left area of the figure is the experimentation and introduction area. The central area is the widespread adoption of the technology, and the area to the right is remaining enclaves of the old technology. Because people tend to assume linear change, this curve catches most people by surprise, even when they know about it. The first surprise is the first upturn. As a technology catches on slowly, we become comfortable with its niches and its growth pace. After the early adopters have proven it, the sudden pace of adoption is a surprise. A product that has taken 10 years to reach 20 percent of the market share may go to 80 percent in three years. The second surprise is the downturn at the top. The old technology has its adherents and may last for a generation because of that. It may also have strengths, which ensure its survival in some niche indefinitely.

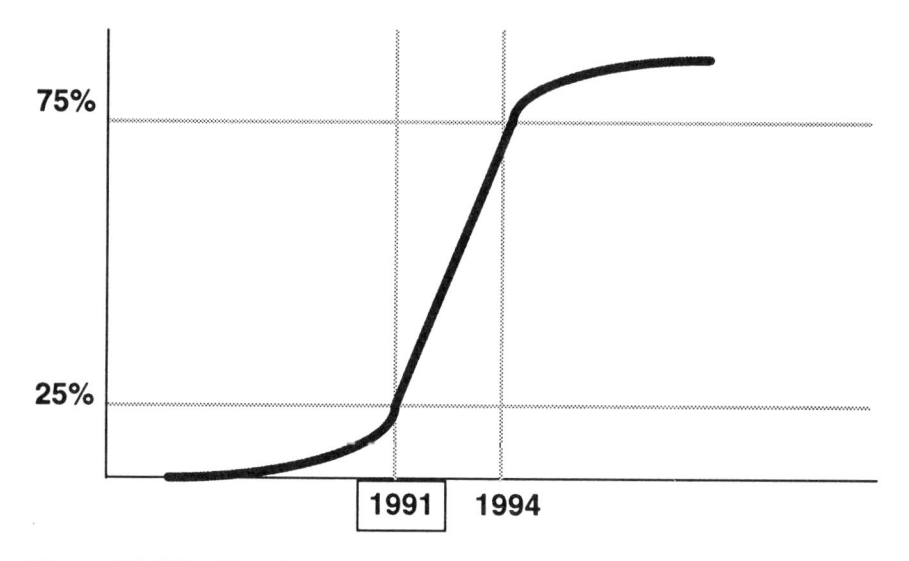

Figure 1.1 The client/server S-curve

Examples of this curve in the computer industry include the PC, the relational database, and many component introductions (386 or 486 processor, 3 1/2" disks, laser printers). With respect to client/server, we can put approximate dates and times on the curve: from 1991 to 1994. In 1991, less than 25 percent of development was client/server; by 1994, about 75 percent appears to be.

A BRIEF HISTORY OF BUSINESS COMPUTING

In the 1950s, the general-purpose computer was developed. These were very expensive devices used for government activities, such as the census, cryptography, and other defense work. There was a limited market because of the high cost.

In the late 1960s, the IBM System/360 and System/370 introduced the standard business computer. The systems pioneered a scalable, standard architecture. Previous computers had been custom-built by comparison. From that time to now, this architecture has matured and grown by accretion, while remaining fundamentally the same. The class of problems that it addresses has expanded greatly in an evolutionary way, but the price of the system, particularly software and maintenance, remains high, limiting its use.

In the 1970s, Digital Equipment Corporation and others introduced the minicomputer. These systems were much less expensive than the mainframe and found new uses. Although some commentators at the time expected downsizing, there was never a trend of any substance to downsize from mainframes to minis. Over time, the minicomputer software became mature enough to support general business systems, but the systems went into departments of large corporations, or smaller companies, that would otherwise not have had a computer.

In the 1980s, the IBM PC bestowed corporate legitimacy on a new class of computers. This was a machine based on the microprocessor, which reduced the cost of production by an order of magnitude. IBM built the system from standard, off-the-shelf, parts. This opened up the business of computer design to "garage shops," and this creativity opened up the price/performance even more. Even the IBM PC business itself was a "garage" type of operation. These machines found whole classes of new use—not so much in the home, as some had expected, but in personal business applications, notably the spreadsheet.

As these three waves were introduced, there was little competition between them. Some minis displaced time-sharing mainframes, and the mini-based dedicated word processing industry was chewed up by PCs in the mid-1980s. On the whole, however, each new wave addressed a fundamentally different market in terms of volume and price.

We are now experiencing a fourth wave, which we are calling open client/server systems. This is fundamentally unlike the other waves. Instead of delivering better price/performance in a lower-cost, higher-volume package, these new systems can offer dramatically improved performance and function. They can open new uses for the systems, solving new business functions. They can also replace the previous systems at a greatly reduced price. Figure 1.2 illustrates these waves.

The minicomputer manufacturers, rising stars in the 1970s, are all faced with severe problems responding to the new technology. Their product is closer to the threat, and they do not have the maturity of the mainframe companies, who have diversified into services.

In the future, the mainframe class of system will have a role as a corporate repository and network hub. The price of the machine will drop tremendously, owing to competition from new types of systems with equivalent power, and, with the loss in margins, the marketing and software advantages will disappear.

The role of the minicomputer has been usurped by microprocessor-based systems. As Hewlett-Packard and DEC have shown, the best minicomputer companies can be effective manufacturers of RISC/UNIX servers; the HP

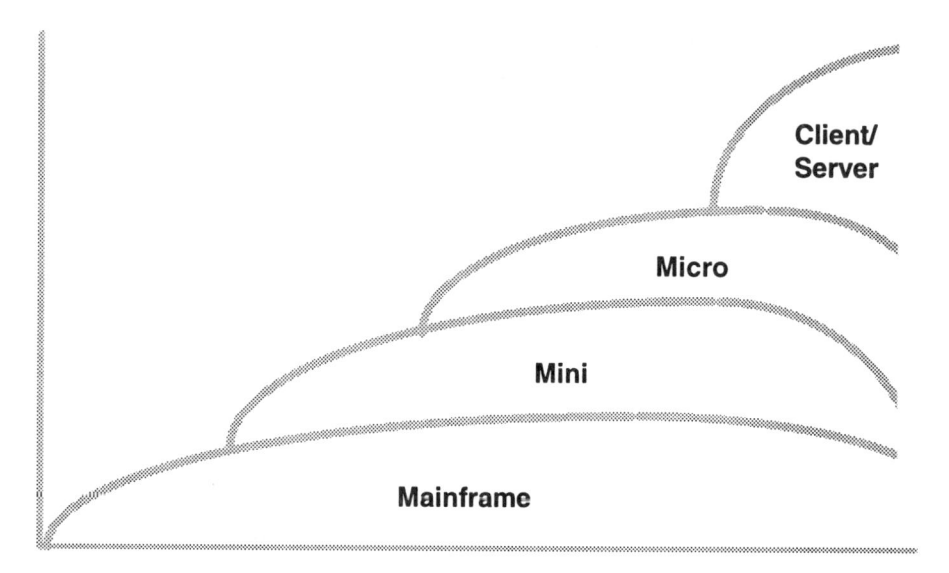

Figure 1.2 Four waves

PA-7100 and DEC Alpha are the best-performing machines of this type. However, the companies are being transformed from suppliers of proprietary systems to open systems vendors in the process.

The personal workstation continues to become more powerful and smaller, destined apparently to physically disappear soon in an era of personal digital assistants and wireless communication.

All of the major computer companies have committed to open systems based on microprocessor technology. The companies that did this first and have committed the most have experienced astonishing growth. Apple, Sun, Compaq, and Dell, in order, have set records as the companies to grow to a billion dollars fastest in the history of the world. The large numbers hide some important details; the divisions of IBM that produce PC and RISC/UNIX systems have also grown rapidly from nothing, masked by the poor performance of other operations.

The result of this new type of system is that the limiting factors of the systems we built from 1965 to 1990, which were computer processing power, the user interface, and the cost of the system, have disappeared. It is possible to buy a system with the power of a 1983 mainframe, with a graphical high-bandwidth user interface, for $500 to $1,000 from mail-order discount catalogs.

The new limiting factors today are network bandwidth, access to data, and the difficulty of changing business and people to take advantage of what is available (see Figure 1.3).

The network bandwidth issue is a technology problem that appears to be solved. New high-speed networks are being introduced very quickly. The other two problems are much more difficult to address and will be the focus of much of this book.

The data in corporations are locked up today inside a mixture of systems from the previous three waves. Many companies will have a mainframe for corporate and financial systems, minicomputers in manufacturing and distribution, and PCs for middle management and administrative employees in many places. Some data are still on paper, altough this is becoming rare in the United States. There is very little in the new technology that will solve this problem easily. It takes a great deal of hard work to access the data buried in "legacy" systems, and these systems are going to be around for a long time.

When a technology is introduced, it is initially adopted to replace a previous technology. It takes a long time for the specific advantages of the new technology to be exploited. Historically, this change in use has postdated the introduction by as much as centuries, generally not less than a generation.

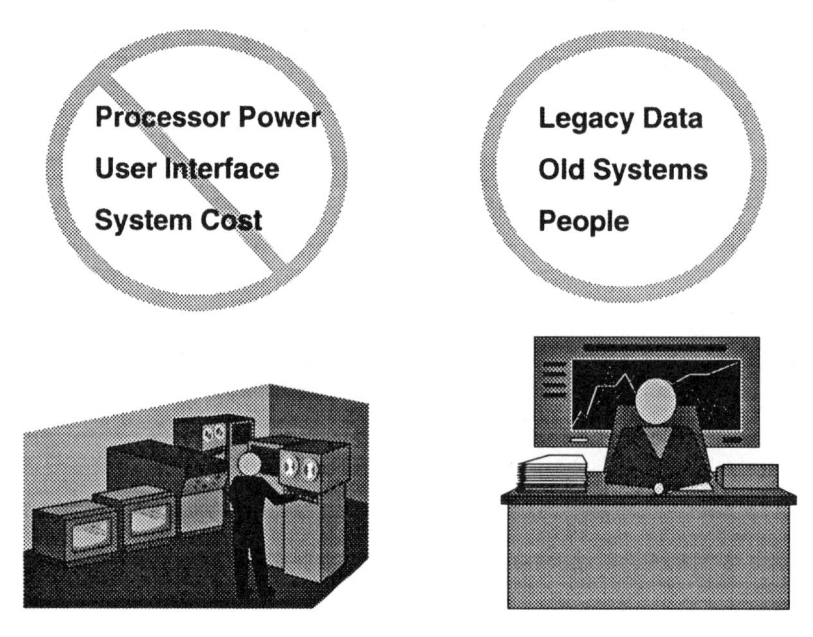

Figure 1.3 Limiting factors

This phenomenon is known as "paving over cow paths." Other examples include the "horseless carriage" and the early military use of artillery and tanks. For example, tanks were introduced in France in 1917. Their use led to a few tactical gains of a few miles. By 1940, new ways to exploit the mobility

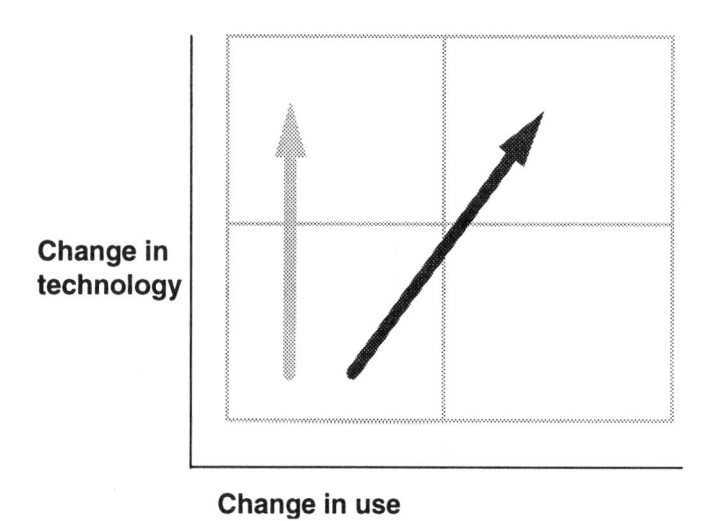

Figure 1.4 Second-order effects

Chapter 1 • Why Develop Open Client/Server Systems?

of the tank had been developed by Guderian and others. The German army gained hundreds of miles of territory in a few days and won a major strategic victory. The widely quoted 1953 Thomas Watson belief that the world market for computers was a couple of dozen is from this vein, also. The changes resulting from rethinking the use of a new technology are generally much more far-reaching than its early use as a replacement would suggest. (See Figure 1.4.)

THE COST ADVANTAGE OF THE NEW SYSTEMS

The underlying cause of the new client/server model is the convergence of trends in small computers, networks, and databases. The costs of the components of systems have followed an improving price/performance curve from the introduction of the transistor to today. This has clearly been the case in the silicon parts—processors and memory—where the advances are driven by improvements in manufacturing technology, leading to more and more function being placed on the same quantity of silicon. It is also true of the electro-mechanical parts, which have improved in price and performance partly because of technology improvements but largely owing to the higher volume of manufacture. Disk drives, printers, cathode ray tubes, and LCD panels have all improved substantially.

Table 1.1 shows the relative performance of professional, business, and home computers on a log scale. Each integer represents a tenfold increase in performance. The rate of improvement is increasing, and improvements move more rapidly from the professional level to general business.

The numbers in the table are approximate, since the categories are vague and tend to change. The systems are instrumental in redefining the role of a professional. A professional workstation is what was used by a physicist in the

Table 1.1 Processor Power of Typical Computers, 1956–1993

MIPS	Home	Business PC	Professional Workstation
.001			1956
.01		1965	1962
.1	1984	1980	1977
1	1992	1986	1982
10	1993	1992	1986
100		1995	1990
1000			1993

Table 1.2 Configuration of Typical Personal Business Computers, 1982–1994

Chip	PC	Speed	Proc	K Trans.	MIPS	Memory	Disk	Floppy	Video	Comm.
1978	1982	4.8	8086	50	.3–.7	.064	0	.3	64	.3
1982	1985	8	80286	150	1–2	.64	10	1.2	224	1.2
1985	1988	16	80386	300	5–10	1	40	1.4	307	2.4
1989	1992	33	80486	1200	20–50	8	200	1.4	786	14.4
1993	1994	66	Pentium	3000	100	16	500	500	1311	29

1950s, an aerospace scientist in the 1960s, a CAD professional in the 1970s, an architect or bond trader in the 1980s, or an animation professional at Industrial Light and Magic today. The business PC is the Apple II or IBM PC (1980), the Compaq Deskpro (1986), the 486 (1992), or Pentium and Alpha (1995). The home machine is the Super Nintendo in 1992 and MPC multimedia machines in 1993.

Because the chip plans and the performance of professional workstations are well known, we can predict that similar improvements in price/performance will continue for several years.

Table 1.2 shows the typical business configuration including memory, disk, and available peripherals. This represents five generations of Intel processors. The price has fallen slightly in a period where performance has improved about 100-fold.

The Intel P6 chip in 1996 will offer over 250 MIPS, using 9,000K transistors running at 133 MHz.

OPEN SYSTEMS ADVANTAGES

A major advantage of today's systems is the degree to which they are open. The meaning of "open" is certainly unclear; there are degrees of openness. A system is more open to the extent that it supports the available standards. In a truly open system, we could obtain any hardware and software component from the "best in class" vendor, at a fair price. We would deal in a market, rather than with a dedicated skilled sales force. The skills we need to work with the systems will also be available in a market.

The best practical example of open systems is the 386/486 PC market. We can assemble a system from component hardware and software and run it with reasonable confidence. Ironically, this market has grown on top of the historical near monopoly of Intel microprocessors and Microsoft operating

Chapter 1 • Why Develop Open Client/Server Systems? 11

systems. But this is a market situation earned by continuous innovation and price/performance improvement.

The UNIX market is somewhat open, in that application vendors and peripheral manufacturers have found it possible to move their wares between the different products in a cost-effective way. It is not, in practice, very open for the end users, who often find themselves locked into obsolete branches of the UNIX family tree, eventually discovering that UNIX portability can be very expensive if not designed in.

As opposed to proprietary systems, an open system gives its owner the freedom to change vendors and/or architectures if necessary. This is always possible, of course, but a more open system lowers the cost barrier substantially. For example, a system written in C and based on the UNIX operating system can be moved to another UNIX system by changing about 10 to 25 percent of the code. This work will be less if porting is considered when the code is first created. A system written in the assembler language of the processor must be rewritten line by line. At a higher level, a system written in SAS or FOCUS might need changes in 10 percent of the code, compared to CICS/IMS/COBOL, which might need a 50 percent rewrite. Appropriate systems can now be developed in I-CASE tools, or packages purchased, which can be ported to a variety of platforms completely without change.

History has shown that it is advisable to be prepared to move systems to new platforms and architectures. Figure 1.5 is a representative, not complete, list of obsolete computer systems, which are not now supported by their original manufacturers. (It may be unfair to include OS/2, which is still supported by IBM but not Microsoft, and NeXT hardware, which is now supported by Canon, but they meet this criterion.) Most have left orphan applications, which had to be migrated wholesale to new architectures. Some of these systems were purchased from the largest, most financially sound, most stable, or the most up-and-coming vendors at the time. Some of the systems were technically far better than their competition. There certainly will be additions to this list in the future, including some UNIX versions and some very new operating systems. It is impossible to reliably predict which systems will survive and thrive in the future.

The advantages of "open" systems are interoperability, portability, and scalability. If systems are "open," we should be able to share and really use data across systems. With today's businesses looking at support of cross-functional processes, within and between corporations, this is an increasing need.

With an open system, we should be able to get incremental growth of the system. In the past, the time came for a "forklift replacement"; the system was

- RCA, Control Data, Honeywell
- Wang, Prime, Interdata, Concurrent
- IBM Series/1, 8100, System/34-36
- DEC System 10, 20
- NCR mainframes, AT&T 7100, 3B2
- Unisys CTOS
- Data General Eclipse
- Apple III, Lisa
- Apollo, Stardent
- Sun 3, 386i
- Microsoft OS/2
- NeXT hardware

Figure 1.5 Obsolete systems: RIP 1970–1993

obsolete, or it had run out of capacity, or we had changed our development standard, or "we couldn't get there from here" because it supported proprietary networking and database standards.

Systems built with "open" standards should be scalable, so that we can upgrade the applications to larger volumes if we grow or downsize them to regional locations if we distribute. They should support interoperability standards, so that the data we keep on them can be accessed from other systems we may acquire or build. They should be portable to the greatest degree possible, so that we can move them to other architectures or systems.

A further benefit of portability is the freedom it gives us to negotiate with vendors. There is an inevitable temptation for hardware suppliers in particular to milk their installed base on maintenance contracts, peripherals, and other services to the captive market. If a system can run on competing platforms, this possibility is controlled.

Openness is not transitive. If vendors reap the benefits of open systems, they may not pass them on to you. For example, many suppliers of highly technical support systems, such as power system SCADA systems, are moving from the VAX/VMS operating system to the IBM RS/6000 or HP 9000 UNIX systems. This is promoted as a move to "open systems." In practice, the buyer of one of these systems is locked into that vendor. The systems are sufficiently complex and mission-critical that you will not attempt to add

Chapter 1 • Why Develop Open Client/Server Systems?

SCSI peripherals or access the operating code. In case you are tempted, the contract generally prevents it.

The openness of each component of an application can be considered. Certainly, we should measure the openness of:

- hardware
- operating system
- database
- development language
- application software architecture
- application data architecture
- application software

For example, an ideal open system might use all of the following:

- standard, scalable, computer hardware available from different vendors (Pentium, SPARC, PowerPC) and employing internal standard components
- widely available or standards-based operating systems (Windows, HP-UX, Novell)
- standard, well-supported SQL database (ORACLE, Sybase)
- nonproprietary development language (such as C++); unfortunately, there are no standards for 4GLs
- software architecture that allows addition of new components or replacement of components; it should avoid proprietary data access layers or unusual user interface standards, for example
- data architecture that allows external access; this is harder than it appears—if an SQL database is employed but the data need proprietary "massage" or are not accurately documented, it is not accessible
- software should be accessible, modular, documented, and free of license restrictions; alternatively, well-documented and sufficient user exits should be provided

Systems today can approach such an ideal to only a limited extent.

Key Questions

Questions to ask to test the openness of a system include:

For each vendor, what do I do if that vendor goes bankrupt, tries to overcharge me, or ceases to support the product?

What will it take to move the system to a platform several times smaller or larger?

How easily can I buy a package or build a new application to add or replace functionality?

Standards also play a part within hardware systems. The availability of third-party memory cards, disk drives, and utility software has reduced the price of these items considerably. Systems with EISA or ISA buses, in particular, offer these components for much less than systems of similar power that are proprietary. SCSI is another leveler.

The Bottom Line on Standards

We should take a pragmatic attitude to standards. De facto standards that work are better than theoretical standards that do not. For instance, the various standards based around the IBM PC have been very effective, whereas POSIX has not. So far, the pragmatic TCP/IP standard has been successful in supporting interoperability, and the better, theoretically founded OSI effort has not.

IMPROVED ACCESS TO ENTERPRISE INFORMATION

One pragmatic definition of "open system" is one that is accessible to its users, in that the information contained in it can be recovered with reasonable time and skills. In contrast, many companies feel that their data are "trapped inside" their legacy systems, unreachable except by an expensive, unresponsive group of MIS programmers.

Building systems that are accessible in this way is certainly not simple and has more to do with developing an information architecture than with using PCs. A few years ago, advocates of easy access to enterprise-wide information were forced to recommend time-consuming compilation of data dictionaries and enterprise-wide data models. These efforts have not appeared to bring much payback and seem to have been discontinued in most corporations.

There are some recent developments that have made this objective more practical. The most important is the proliferation of SQL as the lingua franca of data access. The widespread adoption of relational databases using SQL has been followed by the availability of gateways and translators for accessing file systems on all types of computers that are not relational, including IMS, VSAM, AS/400, VAX/VMS, dBASE, and spreadsheets.

Second, the connection of an arbitrary pair of computers is made simple by the widespread availability of TCP/IP and SNA networking standards and of relatively cheap modems running at 38 Kbps and LANs running at 10 Mbps.

Allowing users access to data used to require learning awkward commands and procedures of operating systems, such as MVS and VAX/VMS, or hiding the system behind prewritten menus that restricted use. Systems like Intellect, for example, offered native-language query capability but only after an elaborate dictionary had been constructed. More recently, systems like Metaphor were developed, which allow end-user data navigation using graphical metaphors. This type of system was expensive but gave some users access to data in real time, with the flexibility they needed.

We can now connect the PC tools that the end user of today (at least the younger ones) is familiar with with the legacy systems where the data are stored. This allows, for the first time, a large group of professionals and middle managers to access the information of the enterprise in a flexible, needs-driven way. Access to enterprise data in a more global way will be a characteristic of the modern corporation. The moves to user empowerment, and to reengineering the business to push information and decision making outward and down, build on and demand this trend. If the bulk of corporate information is to become more accessible, rapid application development using PC-based tools will become possible, leading to competitive advantage over those companies whose data are tied up inside inaccessible legacy systems.

As object technology becomes more available, this may improve on SQL access as a way of communicating with legacy systems. One can envisage an architecture where the old systems are sealed within a case of object code and accessed by message passing to obtain both data and embedded procedures. Needless to say, that situation is not yet upon us.

IMPROVED USER INTERFACE

Using client/server design, it is possible to place application function where it is most appropriate. This is covered in more detail later in the book, but the first cut is to place data management and storage functions, including data-intensive processing functions, on the server and the user interface, including interface-intensive processing, on the client. Other processing, such as business rules, could ideally be distributed to the lightest-loaded machine. Changes in the cost of components and the ability to place powerful processing close to the user have led to the evolution of multimedia computer interfaces.

Multimedia is the combination of text, data, voice, image, and video in appropriate ways to communicate between the person and the computer system. We are clearly in a transition phase at the moment. For 25 years, we interacted with the computer using text and data only. Today, most corporate business users access a graphical interface with images, formatted text, icons, and color. Home users experiment with multimedia systems playing back audio and video. Pen-based systems are on trial in selected applications. The fax machine has introduced a standard for electronic transmission of graphic images. Voice storage, voice mail, and text-to-speech conversion are in wide use but not well integrated. Speech recognition is on trial, as it has been for 20 years. Virtual reality is entering the mainstream at the battlefield and in the shopping mall.

Some excellent examples of the collision of product categories come from the word processing industry. Word processing machines from companies such as IBM (Displaywriter), NBI, and Wang, replaced the typing pool in the 1970s. PC-based word processing software companies, led by WordStar and MultiMate and then WordPerfect, were responsible for the destruction of the dedicated word processing industry within a few years around 1984. Around 1986, the desktop publishing industry, led by Aldus, Apple, and Adobe, created a large industry, replacing dedicated older typesetting equipment. By now, the desktop publishing business has become a suburb of mainstream word processing. Similar collisions appear to be on the way, as all storage becomes digital. A single machine can play audio CDs, photo CDs, and computer CD-ROMs. The fax, scanner, copier, and printer merge into a single networked device. These collisions affect very sizeable industries. Audio storage, for instance, has a 100-year history from Thomas Edison. Audio communication and data processing are two of the largest industries in the world. The collision of these product categories is creating opportunities for businesses. This is noticeable in merger and acquisition activity in the telecommunications, cable TV, entertainment, and computer industries.

As computers become more commonplace, we are beginning to see an upswing in the firms that are strong in consumer and industrial electronic equipment. As the electromechanical components (printers, screens) and rugged miniature packaging (LCD panels, miniature disk drives) become more of the added value, Toshiba, Sony, Matsushita, Canon, Texas Instruments, and Hewlett-Packard become leading vendors.

Chapter 1 • Why Develop Open Client/Server Systems?

The fax machine has introduced image transmittal to the workplace. The next step is document scanning and storage. This makes new kinds of work flow possible.

Examining the I/O devices used for human/computer interaction, we had a standard of a keyboard and text printer for many years. The touch screen, mouse, tablet, trackball, and pen have all been used to add analog (spatial) input.

Graphic printers (laser, LCD, or inkjet) became common around 1985, scanners somewhat later. Recently, affordable color scanners and printers have been available.

Text to speech has been in common use now for telephone operators and the disabled. This does not have the recognition problem. Voice recording with digital storage and playback is also commonplace. Speech recognition is not common yet, but home applications are available.

Video playback and video in a window are now available if desired. Video-conferencing between conference rooms is now common in corporations. Experimental setups offer desktop teleconferencing; the price of the built-in camera in every monitor is still too high.

Table 1.3 shows the video capabilities of the standard professional workstation and business PC. For reference, the professional standard is taken to be the standard Sun or H-P/Apollo machine of the time, the business standard the standard IBM or Apple of the time.

Application delivery on CD-ROM is now becoming a reality. In 1993, some home computer applications and a few operating systems were delivered this way. Within two years, it will be the standard for large applications. This

Table 1.3 Video Capabilities of Professional Workstations and Business PCs

	Business PC	*Professional Workstation*
Teletype		1956
Text CRT	1965	1962
320x200x2	1980	1977
640x480x8	1986	1982
800x600x8	1990	1983
1024x768x8	1992	1984
1280x1024x16	1994	1986
3-D 24-bit		1989
Virtual reality		1991

distribution medium allows any application to offer reasonable animation, bit-mapped graphics, and sound. We should look to the game user interface today to merge with the business application interface for 1995.

The CD-ROM allows effective distribution of information as a product. We first saw encyclopedias and atlases, then roadmaps and city guides, distributed this way. Microsoft is selling its developer support; other companies will begin to use CD-ROM as an alternative to wide area networks for distribution. In a sense, CD-ROM rivals client/server in making it possible to put the database on the workstation and eliminate the server for low-volatile information.

Multimedia capabilities allow several new uses of the workstation. The multimedia system allows the untrained user to access the system, so that information kiosks in public areas can be made available. This is used in transportation centers, lobbies, etc. It allows the lightly trained person to do the work of the more experienced or professional, as in support lines. It allows the trained user to access more information—for instance, offering just-in-time training.

The Internet

The next few years will see massive growth in the network resources available to business and the home. This will include existing technologies and new breakthroughs.

In the years leading up to 1994, there was a continuous rise in the size and throughput of the Internet, that loose conglomeration of networks based on TCP/IP networking technology. It continues to grow at double-digit rates every month. New advances in the user interface of this institution are encouraging more and more use. Also, in mid-1994 some new possibilities for commercial transactions on the Internet are being opened up, and the major online providers are rushing to offer full access to all this. We can also expect interactive television to become possible in increasing volume through the next five years.

The result is the availability of very large databases of information in a number of standardized ways. Workstation software can navigate this to create new opportunities which can be difficult to predict. The success of the WorldWide Web (WWW) and Mosaic software is a case in point. This protocol combines with an attractive multimedia interface to allow relatively unskilled people to access information on servers all over the world.

Ubiquitous Computing

The price/performance changes that have made the desktop computer so powerful have had another effect. The functionality and performance of a $5,000 desktop business PC from 1984 is now available in a $500 wallet-sized device weighing a few ounces. The HP 100LX is an example of this type of system, commonly called a Personal Digital Assistant (PDA); it includes a spreadsheet, database, e-mail, word processing, and powerful calculator functions and runs standard PC programs. There are portable systems available at intermediate points from this to the six-pound 486-color notebooks. Not only modems and network adapters but also cellular telephone and wireless network technology are available to connect these systems to others. Computer systems can effectively be made available at any place we want them.

Because of limitations in the network bandwidth, reliability, and speed, systems that employ portable systems, particularly PDAs, cannot be developed as unrestricted client/server applications yet. We can employ data downloading and e-mail to make components of application function available to field staff. Order entry, claims processing, job estimating, on-line catalogs, and repair tracking are examples of applications that can benefit from this approach.

Ability to Respond to Changing Business Needs

Less than 5 percent of applications developed on the mainframe are used as planned. Ninety-five percent are either abandoned during development or come on-line too late to be useful. Once installed, these systems are difficult to change in small ways and impossible to change in large ways.

Are All Mainframes Going to Be Replaced?

There is a small industry of consultants making speeches on the subject "the death of the mainframe has been overhyped." Let's look at the facts.

According to Computer Intelligence, there were 467,000 MIPS on 24,000 mainframes in the United States at the end of 1992. The power is up 14.6 percent since 1991; this is a reduction in the rate of growth. The number of systems has shrunk from a high of over 27,000 at the end of 1989. The IBM mainframe market peaked in 1991 and is now falling 8 to 10 percent per year. This is expected to continue. To sum up, the United States has more mainframe power each year, consolidated into slightly fewer systems, and pays less for it.

This is a contrast from the mainframe computer industry growth of an earlier age and the growth still enjoyed by client/server vendors. It does not mean the immediate abolition of the data center. Client/server computing has a role for the data center as a repository of important corporate information and standards.

The price/performance gap between mainframes and other systems is closing. The companies that make mainframes also make high-performance RISC systems and PCs. As they bring out new generations of their systems, they are incorporating the technology from the smaller machines. Mainframes are getting a lot less expensive and more powerful.

Summary

A client/server development approach allows us to take best advantage of the different types of computers available. We can place the user interface on small systems near the user that offer access to information in an efficient, intuitive manner. We can store databases on central machines with appropriate security and economies of scale. We can distribute business rules between systems for best efficiency of development, maintenance, and operation.

There are long-term underlying trends making systems more powerful, less expensive, and capable of a wider variety of functions. An open approach preserves our investment in software as these new developments are introduced, so that we can benefit from them without the need for wholesale replacement of our systems.

2

The Downsizing Strategy

SELECTING THE DOWNSIZING APPROACH

There are many approaches to downsizing. This chapter will describe seven basic approaches to an old application, their strengths and weaknesses, and how to choose between them. In most real situations, a mixture of these approaches will be used. The seven approaches are:

Replace the business system

1. Remove the system — Abandon or outsource function or do manually
2. Redesign the business process — Analyze the business and design new procedures and systems to support current needs

Replace the automated system

3. Replace with packaged software — If a function is not a core differentiator, others must have developed similar solutions
4. Rewrite the software with new tools — Build a replacement system with appropriate new tools

Keep and enhance the automated system

5. Rehost the existing software	Move the current software to a new platform without change
6. Refurbish the existing software	Keep the software on the current platform, improving its appearance or maintainability as appropriate
7. Circumscribe	Keep the current system, but do all new development in a new environment, accessing the old data as needed

The fundamental questions to ask are related to business goals. What is our approach to the business process under review? Is it to create a new business process, to solve problems in an existing process, or to leave the business process alone and replace the supporting technology? Simply stated, in order to decide on an approach, we examine the business processes, the application systems that support those processes, and the technology supporting those systems. For each, we ask:

Is the basic business process necessary?
Is it working well enough?
Is the application working well?
Is additional function needed?
Is additional ease of use needed?
Is the underlying technology working well?
Is the technology expensive or obsolete?

REMOVE THE SYSTEM

It is a well-known cliché among engineers that the most reliable parts in a system design are the ones that aren't there. As we look on software as a liability to maintain and recognize the cost of maintenance, it is worth considering whether systems should exist at all. Often, the purpose of a system is lost in the history of a company, continued because some long-forgotten manager started it. There are many cases of reports which, when examined, are never read. Some systems can be abandoned without pain. An inventory of the applications on most large mainframes will reveal some programs that are never used or have a single user who could just as well use something else. Others could be dropped at some cost, or outsourced.

We recently examined a system that tracked returned parts for automobile warranty claims. It became apparent that the returned parts, which had once been recycled, were now simply thrown away in almost all cases. The few parts being returned in a cost-effective manner could be handled manually. The parts were not needed, and the system was not needed either.

REDESIGN THE BUSINESS PROCESS

The goals and techniques of business process redesign are covered in a separate chapter. Many systems support business operations that are not necessary or efficient. By first examining the business process, we have the opportunity to discover streamlining ideas, which will reduce the scope of the automated systems.

REPLACE WITH PACKAGED SOFTWARE

In the past, most smaller businesses ran largely on packaged software, at time-sharing bureaus, on minis, and more recently on microcomputers. Large companies tended to build their own or to greatly customize the packages they acquired. Recently, two trends have occurred.

1. The packages have become more powerful, easily customized, and accessible from other applications. The biggest, most robust packages were once mostly available on mainframe and VAX platforms. They are now available for distributed systems.

2. The larger corporations have recognized that their accounting, manufacturing, H/R, and inventory functions are not so different that they require custom code. They are increasingly prepared to redesign their processes around a state-of-the-art package. After all, this is a form of benchmarking.

As a result, the common functions within many large companies are often candidates for replacement by packages. Leading packages for the generic functions of accounting, human resources, manufacturing, and distribution for client/server systems include:

- ASK ManMan, etc.
- Avalon Manufacturing
- Collier-Jackson
- D&B
- Fourgen

- Lawson
- ORACLE Financials and Manufacturing
- Peoplesoft
- Ross Financials
- SAP R3
- Western Data Systems
- Xerox Computer Services

As a rule of thumb, consider that all mainframe packages will be available in client/server versions by 1995.

REWRITE THE SOFTWARE WITH NEW TOOLS

If the current business function has changed sufficiently so that the existing system is obsolete, and a search has revealed no packages with adequate functionality, a new system appears to be indicated. Much of this book is devoted to the development techniques and tools that are appropriate to do this. It is a problem at the moment that the techniques and tools for client/server systems are not robust enough for a common class of large transactional systems. It would be best to delay rewriting these systems for two years, to avoid the "teething troubles" of new hardware and software. Some rules of thumb for this problem follow in this chapter.

REHOST THE EXISTING SOFTWARE

There are many software products in the fourth-generation language (4GL) category that can run the same application code on a variety of platforms. Some examples are:

CA	Datacom/Ideal
CA	IDMS/ADS
CGI	Pacbase
Cincom	Supra/Mantis
IBI	Focus
ORACLE	ORACLE
SAS	SAS
Software AG	Adabas/Natural
TI	IEF

These products are widely installed on mainframes, VAXes, and proprietary minicomputers. The analytical packages, such as SAS, can generally run

Chapter 2 • The Downsizing Strategy

with better performance and less cost on open systems. They are natural candidates for downsizing. Many other analytical, decision-support, and scientific packages currently on mainframes are candidates for transfer to UNIX workstations.

The database/transaction systems should be benchmarked carefully. Mainframes are good at database management and transaction handling, and many of the early ports of database and transaction products were intended for developers, not production situations.

CA-IDMS/PC is a version of the CA database for PCs. It can be run for a single user or based on a LAN using shared dictionaries and databases. It includes CA-ADS/PC, allows SQL access, and works with CA-Realia COBOL and CICS. CA-IDMS is based on an earlier product named TAB.

CA-Datacom is available as CA-Datacom/PC, which can be obtained as a LAN version, and CA-Datacom/UNIX, which is currently available for the HP 9000 series. The UNIX version delivers good performance.

There are two complicating factors in these migrations:

1. The migration generally depends on getting the code level up to the current product. If a product has been around for years, the version on a hot new workstation may be 9.0, and your legacy system may be on 5.3. You will have to go through the necessary upgrades before you can bring the code over. These problems can be severe. Early versions of Informix, for instance, were not even SQL-based. Upgrading to the current level is practically a rewrite.

2. All the application code may not be written in the 4GL. Many FOCUS systems were written for VM/CMS systems. They typically have embedded REXX or CMS EXEC calls on every page—for example, for file management. Earlier versions of the ORACLE 4GL SQL*FORMS were not a very complete language, and many programmers had to write a lot of C code to implement the functions they needed. Products for mainframes, particularly those which do not have a relational database underpinning, will have application logic for file access and run-time dependencies buried in IBM JCL.

Applications written in traditional languages can also be migrated to client/server systems. There are versions of COBOL, PL/I, FORTRAN, Business Basic, and other languages available for UNIX, DOS, and OS/2. There are some significant problems of compatibility. In addition to the two problems of versions and embedded platform-specific code mentioned above, there are often differences in the language features. The PL/I subset G, most common on smaller systems, does not support all IBM mainframe features. FORTRAN has gone through numerous changes in standards, and Pascal, FORTRAN, and BASIC dialects contain numerous proprietary extensions. It is necessary to analyze the code and prepare a migration plan. The big problems to watch for are in:

- screen management
- database and file management
- add-on function libraries
- access to system features

Assembler is obviously not portable between platforms, although there is an excellent IBM assembler emulator for PCs available as freeware.

COBOL

The COBOL language can be less of a problem than other languages, since the language definition has been quite stable and its core function is more or less the same between systems. The problems are in the same areas listed above, particularly screen and file management. Minicomputer COBOL environments, in particular, vary somewhat in screen and file management and need specific analysis. Tools for migrating mainframe COBOL applications are available and are well supported and tested.

The Micro Focus COBOL tools are the same products used for IBM's larger SAA platforms and support several versions of the language, including the 1974 and 1985 standards. Micro Focus offers emulation environments for CICS, IMS DB/DC, VSAM, and DB2. CA's Realia COBOL has similar offerings.

You can use products such as KEDIT (Mansfield Software) or ISPF/PC (Command Technology) to make programmers feel comfortable in the PC environment.

CICS Options

CICS emulations have been available for several years from Integris (Unikix), Infosoft (Conveyor), and VI Systems (VIS/TPS). Recently, IBM has launched its own range of CICS offerings for downsized platforms. CICS OS/2, CICS/400, and CICS/6000 offer a variety of migration choices. CICS/6000 is being developed by Hewlett-Packard and IBM for the IBM RS/6000 and the HP 9000 systems—the first time that IBM CICS could be run on another vendor's platform. Recent announcements of DB2/6000 and DB2/2 have strengthened this; an application written for CICS and DB2 now theoretically can be ported to OS/2 or the RS/6000 without code changes. CICS for OS/2 even supports DOS, Macintosh, and Windows clients on a LAN.

Emulation or Conversion?

There is a variety of software available to support other platforms on open systems. Several companies offer emulations of the IBM midrange System/36, System/38, and AS/400 environments on UNIX and PCs. There are companies that specialize in products for Unisys or Prime emulation or conversion, for example.

The fundamental question to answer is whether to emulate or convert. Emulation is generally quicker and cheaper but does not make the best use of the new platform. It almost always leads to poor performance. While some staff may initially feel more at home, emulation certainly leads to an eventual problem when the old platform is gone and the programmers have been retrained or moved on. Emulation is a partial solution.

It is sometimes difficult to tell the difference between emulation and conversion. A package that converts code from the VAX to UNIX, for example, will contain run-time libraries of VAX system calls. This is a partial emulation. You could not take that code and port it to OS/2, because you would be missing the run times.

Code Conversion

Code conversion, as opposed to rehosting when there is little or no code translation involved, is often best done with software to automate the conversion. The exception would be smaller systems, which would not justify the one-time cost of the tools. If tools are not justified or available, it is best to plan the conversions and develop simple tools, using shell scripts and macro languages, to automate the repetitive work. Sometimes, the compiler on one or the other systems can be induced to flag the code that will not operate.

There are basically two types of conversion tool—the point-to-point translator and the generalized translator. Generalized translators usually come with some specific source and target libraries loaded.

An example of point-to-point translation is the tool set from Accelr8 Technology of Denver, Colorado. They offer several tools for VAX/VMS to UNIX migration, including:

Open LIBR8	VMS system call library on UNIX
Open ACCLIM8	Translates VAX FORTRAN (including proprietary extensions)

Open TRANSL8	Data migration
FMS/UNIX	VAX forms management
Open MIGR8	C translation and VAX utilities, such as Submit

This toolset includes specific conversion aids for the language extensions, system calls, screen management, data management, job submission, job control language, and editors of the source environment, plus data conversion and real-time communication to assist the migration.

Software Translations offers similar VMS-UNIX migration. Transport, from B-iTech, migrates from HP 3000/MPE to UNIX.

An excellent example of a generalized translation technology is the Extract Tool Suite from Evolutionary Technologies, Inc. (ETI) in Austin, Texas. ETI is a spin-off from MCC, the computer research consortium. Its product, which runs on Sun SPARC or RS/6000, has two major components. The Master Set is a set of tools for defining a legacy environment. The Data Conversion Tool then automatically generates conversion programs. The tools maintain a database, which describes the source and target systems. This system can be used for one-time conversions or continuous periodic operation to support interoperability (circumscribe) strategies. A scheduler is available to run the periodic extracts. The IBM MVS and Datacom environments are already defined to this tool.

REFURBISH THE EXISTING SOFTWARE

It will often prove most cost effective to retain an existing application, particularly if the business logic embedded in it contains valuable information. Some firms derive a proprietary advantage from their information systems, and over time this knowledge is often buried in the system rather than the people who use it. This is an efficient way to operate but can create a dangerous dependency on the application system when it become obsolete. All of the major components of a legacy system can become obsolete:

- user interface
- database
- business rules

Refurbishing the User Interface

The user interface can be refurbished by using a tool that improves the appearance without changing the original application code. These tools exist for on-line and batch systems.

Chapter 2 • The Downsizing Strategy

For on-line systems, several tools use the IBM EHLLAPI interface to access the system as if they were a dumb terminal, allowing a programmer to develop graphical front ends. This allows old applications to conform to the standards that users of newer systems expect. Leading systems of this type are:

- Easel
- Mozart
- Knowledgeware Flashpoint
- Wall Data Rumba
- Micro Focus Application-to-Application Interface

Wall Data's Rumba can work with PowerBuilder and other client/server development tools to access mainframe screens, and, because it acts as a DDE server, it can be integrated into many applications.

Batch tools, such as Personics' Monarch and Access Paths' Access/RT, allow programmers or sophisticated end users to convert batch-printed reports into input for interactive tools, such as spreadsheets and PC databases.

This approach is known as "putting lipstick on the pig." Among the ways in which it is still a pig, you are still:

- paying for all the mainframe processor cycles
- maintaining all the legacy code (including redundant edits and displays)

This can be a good migration stage, as a component in a larger strategy.

Refurbishing the Database

The database can be refurbished by cleaning up the data and making it accessible to other applications. Making it accessible may involve migrating to a relational database, such as DB2, or using timed replication to copy the data to such a repository. The biggest problem is often cleanup. Most older data files have undocumented problems, which make access much more difficult than it appears at first. Among the problems data in legacy systems can have are:

- data can be missing or corrupt
- data items can be embedded in nonexplicit ways
- data can require business rules for interpretation

Many fields in old files are not actually used. Others may be used partially or used for noncritical purposes without editing. This may be clear by examining the field, or it may be a semantic problem. For example, in a warranty claims system, it was proposed to use the "reason for failure" information to drive new product design decisions. It was found that the information in that field had never been checked but was used to pay retailers for work done. The data were fraudulent—simply a function of the various pricing promotions offered, not actually reflecting product failures. When you buy a dozen cans of cat food in the supermarket, the clerk will scan the same can over and over. All the flavors are the same price, and no one at point of sale cares if the marketing decision support system is working off erroneous product information.

Object wrapping is the idea of encapsulating an existing system and then restricting its interface to a set of inbound and outbound messages. Arguably, this can be achieved with Easel or similar products. Unfortunately, none of the benefits of object-oriented development accrue to the maintainers or developers who work with the system. There are no reusable components, no inheritance. Maintenance changes must still be made the old way.

Refurbishing the Business Rules

An application seems to be subject to the laws of entropy. As time goes by, its structure decays. Additional rules and functions are added on, often without regard to the original architecture. Functions that were isolated in parameters or subroutines to allow change become disregarded and replicated. Code size becomes larger, making the esssential core of the system more difficult to grasp. The original developers either leave or become disinterested. The development techniques used become out of favor and ultimately arcane. Eventually, the system becomes "chaotic"; even small changes may produce unexpected results.

Problems with applications on legacy systems include:

- original specifications lost (or there, but inaccurate)
- system documentation missing, inadequate, or inaccurate
- original staff has left (or original staff still there, resisting change)
- accretion of changes has led to lack of integrity and consistency
- lack of maintenance, so software versions are obsolete (e.g., assembler, COBOL 68, Macro CICS, ISAM/BDAM)

These decaying systems are often important, even critical, to operation of the company. There is no simple answer to this problem. There are some tools that can help to analyze code, even drawing it into a CASE tool so that

Chapter 2 • The Downsizing Strategy

it can be understood. Study of an old application system is an interactive business, requiring skilled staff using these tools.

Automated approaches include:

- recover data descriptions (reverse engineer data model)
- recover process logic (reverse engineer process model)
- recover business rules (design recovery)

Further goals might be tactically useful:

- recover screen design (convert screens)
- recover transaction integrity (generate automated testing scripts)

Recovering a higher level of abstraction is difficult but signifies real reverse engineering. Once design intelligence is lost, one cannot get it back. If reusable modules are not used, you cannot find redundancies in code later.

As a practical matter, systems can be divided into those which have low or high complexity. Systems that have low complexity should be thrown away and rewritten. The user interface and data model are certain to be obsolete, and there is little else.

For systems that are complex, triage into different types of components is appropriate:

- throw away support code and reports, which will be redeveloped with a 4GL
- identify and eliminate redundant components
- recover the data model with tools
- recover the algorithms manually

Types of Code Recovery Tools

The items to recover for a mainframe system are typically:

- COBOL items
- Data files in copybooks or data division
- JCL
- BMS or MFS maps
- database catalogs

Tools can be categorized into those which assist in understanding the system, those which improve the system, and those which reverse engineer the system for replacement.

Tools to Understand the System

Tools that measure the code—for example, counting lines of code or function points or calculating measures of complexity—include those from Rubin and McCabe. Tools that analyze code, flagging "bad" statements or unexecutable code and cross-referencing access, include the Viasoft products, VIA/Insight and Renaissance; Compuware Navigator and Adpac; the David Black Explain COBOL analyzer; and the HP Advise tool, which advises on conversion to HP-UX.

Tools to Improve the System

Tools that clean up code—beautifying, typesetting, or restructuring—include Compuware XA and Knowledgeware LTI.

Tools to Reengineer the System

Tools that recover the design of a system into structure charts or data models are available from Cadre, ProCASE, Bachman Reverse Engineering, Software Rework, LBMS (reveng), and Interport (InterCASE). This is a very difficult job, and it is important to have the right expectations of what these tools can do. Data models are much more likely to be recovered than process models.

CIRCUMSCRIBE

Since it is cost effective to build most new applications on new platforms, and it is also cost effective to leave most old applications on the platforms they are currently on, we must expect to find that the best solution is often to combine a new system on a new platform with an old system on an old platform. We call this strategy "circumscribe," because that word has overtones of surrounding, or hiding, the old system and also of forbidding, as in preventing further development on the old system.

Circumscribing involves migrating to new technology incrementally:

- continue to use the existing hardware, software, and staff
- add new technology capabilities incrementally
- clean up and document the legacy system database and interfaces

- establish continuous or periodic data exchange between the new and old systems
- migrate components with the priorities and pace that suit the business
- build all new applications on the new systems

It is vital in a circumscribe strategy to have the right tools available for communication with the legacy system, since important data are being maintained there. There are several approaches. The Evolutionary Technologies toolset, described previously, Trinzic InfoPump, or the Prism Warehouse Manager can be used to perform the extracts. Note that these are all designed as one-way products from the mainframe to the distributed systems. If there are a smaller number of legacy databases, custom code can be written using any of several approaches.

Summary

In practice, it is common to combine several of these approaches. A single application may need multiple approaches and an application portfolio almost certainly will.

For example, a circumscribe strategy will probably require refurbishment of the old database, if some of the old screens are retained. At the same time, refurbishing the user interface will provide a standard appearance for the user. Rehosting often requires some refurbishing of the code—for instance, to bring obsolete versions of a language up to date or to identify unused application segments. It is common to purchase one or several application packages for standard functions and rehost some code that performs functions specific to the particular business.

Rehosting and refurbishing are much less attractive on close inspection than they may appear at first. Like an old building or an old machine, old software has many undiscovered problems. Whatever you do, it is still old, and it is becoming increasingly difficult to find people with the skills to maintain it.

3
Planning the Downsizing

AUTOMATION AND EMPOWERMENT

At this time, many applications are not well suited to client/server development on downsized platforms. Of those which are, not all are suitable to begin with for an inexperienced IT shop. In this chapter, we will discuss the rules for selecting systems to approach the new technology and avoid undue risk.

Particularly for the first few projects, it is a good idea to select from the type of application that delivers significant functional benefits in addition to cost savings. The idea is that if you move to a new system for cost benefits alone, and the cost benefits do not materialize because of delays or cost overruns in the project, you have nothing. If you aim for functional benefits and overrun on cost, the system is still worth delivering. We will look at the systems that deliver the best payback.

There are two basic strategies for computing: automation and empowerment. Automation replaces people with technology; empowerment augments people with technology. Mainframe systems are very good at automation, with their batch processing and automated job scheduling. Client/server systems are not very good at automation today. The client/server advantages of rich information display and availability any time, any place are not necessary to the "production line" situation, and the management of these systems is still immature. They are very good candidates for the empowerment strategies, building systems that are used by professional, managerial, sales, or customer service staff to increase their performance. (See Figure 3.1.)

By now, most corporations have automated their basic transactional systems, sometimes several times and sometimes in different places and different ways. It is rare to find a large corporation without an inventory system, for example. It is, however, very common to meet a company with several disconnected inventory systems. Such a company may not be able to answer the question, "How many parts do we have available?" and may be producing the wrong product. Such a situation could be caused by national boundaries, divisional lines, acquisitions, or any of a number of reasons.

Transaction, or automation, systems are, on the whole, poor candidates for a GUI/database client/server approach. They often have high transaction rates. Some are in difficult environments, such as the factory floor or delivery vehicle. They are staffed by employees who are performing rote work, and, therefore, the user interface is simple. Often, there is a high batch component, as in telephone billing.

There are exceptions in this layer—one is the area of order entry and customer service, where a client/server system as a front end to the trnsactional system can deliver great payoff. These systems often need to be

AUTOMATION	INFORMATION

◆ Transactional:
  – High volume
  – Transactional integrity
	◆ Provide information to empower

◆ Predictable transactions and response times	◆ Often low or no updates
	◆ Information sharing between areas
◆ System optimized for single purpose	◆ Ad hoc queries
◆ 24 by 7 availability	◆ Analytical support (DSS)
◆ Accurate (auditable)	◆ May offer standard reports (EIS)
◆ Data quality assured by "edit & validation"	◆ System optimized for usability
◆ Often automates rote work	◆ Data unstructured, historical, graphical

Figure 3.1 Automation and information

Chapter 3 • Planning the Downsizing

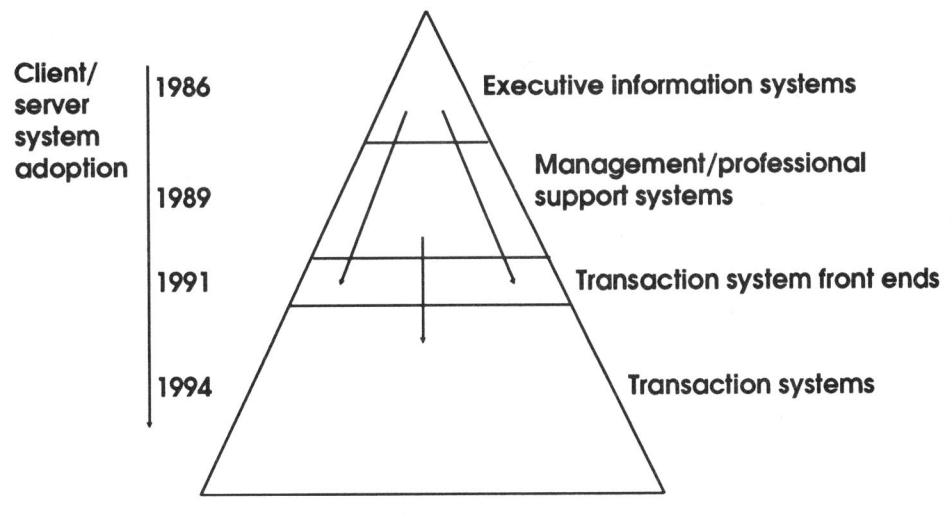

Figure 3.2 Systems pyramid

Client/server system adoption:
- 1986 — Executive information systems
- 1989 — Management/professional support systems
- 1991 — Transaction system front ends
- 1994 — Transaction systems

carefully designed with transaction managers and object-oriented methods. Replacing them is not cheap.

Executive information systems is one of the areas where client/server technology was pioneered. Companies such as Metaphor and Pilot produced graphical systems and database navigators as expensive custom systems before moving to the mainstream. Similar systems were built on Wall Street to support traders in stocks, bonds, and commodities. They combined expensive custom graphical workstations and custom filters and gateways to access the operational data and make it available to decision makers. Because the custom development was so expensive, the systems were confined to the higher reaches of the corporate pyramid.

Other informations systems support managers and professionals, usually working with data from the transactional systems and from outside the enterprise. This is the area that is ripe for client/server development today. Similar systems can be built for a fraction of the cost of five years ago, using off-the-shelf software components and graphical workstations, which are now mainstream appliances. (See Figure 3.2.)

POOR CANDIDATES FOR TOTAL CLIENT/SERVER ARCHITECTURE

The rules in this section are intended to help select the best systems to develop now in an enterprise that has not yet made a large commitment to the introduction of client/server technology. Every one of the rules in this section can be broken successfully. It would even be possible to successfully develop a client/server system that failed all of these tests, and there are companies doing this. They are very large, well-funded companies, which are planning to take the lead by employing these systems and are prepared to manage the risks they are taking.

System Size and Complexity

Very complex systems are not appropriate yet for wholesale adoption of this new technology, unless they can be broken into discrete components. At the moment, the client/server architecture adds complexity in itself and, most importantly, lacks the tools to control large system development projects. It is unusual to find such a system where user interface and information display components cannot be tackled with client/server tools, however.

Systems where thousands of users share a database should probably be left alone, despite the published open system transaction processing numbers. System management for these types of systems is better understood in the traditional "glass house," and the exposure of this type of move is very high. Again, we can benefit from new technology by circumscribing a core system with display tools. For example, airline reservations will remain on the mainframe, but an intelligent order-entry system can be added using PCs, and an analysis of seat usage can be performed on UNIX servers. Of course, when that is done, we read headlines such as "American Airlines downsizes."

Mission-critical systems in general should be considered carefully, because of the lack of professional expertise. Designing a fault-tolerant client/server system is possible, but this is a very different job from a departmental payroll update system, and in many parts of the world there is nobody with the skills to do it.

Large Centralized I/O Processing

High-volume database updates, whatever the number of users, must be carefully designed. The open systems mainframe replacements are not yet generally competitive with the traditional architecture in the disk farm business.

Large databases that cannot be partitioned should remain on the mainframe. "Large" might be 20 gigabytes, although this number changes every year. Some large enterprises, such as AT&T, are testing the limits of UNIX systems and relational databases on mainframe-class UNIX systems, such as the Pyramid and Sequent, and there are certainly far larger databases than this; most commercial companies, however, will prefer to stay well within the current envelope.

Systems with large batch requirements, such as telephone billing, should remain on mainframes. This is not a function that "mainframe alternative" vendors have been targeting. These systems are very good print servers at the high end, together with the software and support staff.

Centralized Control

Systems that require centrally managed security or other important services should be left on the mainframe. It is true that technically any level of security can be achieved on open systems, and this is done at, for instance, the Department of Defense. However, this often cuts across the grain of the culture, so that programmers and administrators for these systems do not take these things seriously. Over the years, we have learned how to perform effective security functions in the data center.

High availability is another case to be considered carefully. Twenty-four-hour availability is usually best arranged from a central data center, which can afford the staff coverage and the redundant systems to assure this.

Tight Mainframe Integration

If an application is tightly integrated with other mainframe applications, it is going to be difficult to move it without the others. It may be possible to off-load some processing, but if data have to be communicated or replicated, there may be no benefit.

Some applications would be ideal candidates for downsizing, if it were not for the large investment in existing equipment, particularly the network. An oil company, for instance, might want to move a field analysis application onto UNIX. Fast RISC processors outperform an IBM 3090-class mainframe running packages such as SAS and at a much lower cost. If the users are using 3270 terminals scattered on a widespread SNA network, the solution looks unappealing. You do not want to replicate that network, and most UNIX systems do not support 3270 terminals.

GOOD CANDIDATES FOR CLIENT/SERVER ARCHITECTURE

The following are all systems that have been successfully implemented with a wholesale client/server architecture or, where indicated, a "circumscribe" approach accessing legacy data. The general rule is that systems that empower their users are best built with a client/server approach. There are also some special cases where the client/server approach may be best, even if not meeting the paradigm above.

Professional and Analytical Work

Executive information systems are generally based on client/server technology. Although some older systems are mainframe-based, these can be rehosted now onto a UNIX-based system. Decision support systems, which add a more analytical component, are also good candidates.

Any system that has a substantial component involving information access and presentation is, in general, appropriate, since the technology provides a good user interface. Most systems can use intelligent front ends. This includes data entry and editing, as well as reporting systems. Some very high volume data entry systems can be built using client/server systems as a front end to a transaction processing engine.

Financial, mathematical, and statistical analysis work (for example, many uses of Lotus 1-2-3, Mathematica, SAS, and similar packages) are clearly workstation candidates. Even the largest analytical jobs are often being downsized today off Crays and IBM mainframes. IBM has documented many cases where an RS/6000 can perform work previously done on a supercomputer. Not only are the cost advantages compelling, but the opportunity to schedule work on a system dedicated to the analyst is too good to refuse.

Support for professionals, for instance CAD, trader workstations, medical, engineering, and software development itself, is a clear candidate. Professional work is often characterized by a need for a wide range of information sources, switching between activities, and a high value on currency of information. These were areas that were once supported with time-sharing. In recent years, the UNIX workstation vendors, led by Apollo and then Sun, have made inroads. Now, the commodity PC is powerful enough for most purposes.

Marketing information systems are a particular case of opportunity for the "circumscribe" strategy. Many companies now wish to understand their customers in more depth, so that they can target them with specific products. Some companies already have the information they need but cannot use it. A book club company, for instance, may have information on separate clubs but not be able to bring it together. Many banks have trouble integrating the information on their many accounts for a single customer. A client/server system based on a relational database will often enable new ways of organizing and looking at the customer data.

End-user directed systems can be created now by giving users tools, such as Quest and Excel, and access to a relational database. This is a way to get through some of the backlog in the MIS department.

Training systems are well suited to the intelligent workstation, particularly now that multimedia systems are available.

Interdepartmental work-flow systems are one of the most exciting opportunities at the moment. These tools, which are now becoming available, should allow us to automate the flow of work in many professional and white-collar functions, without expensive custom programming. These are functions that were not succesfully approached by earlier mainframe automation, which was too rigid, or by PCs, which missed the workgroup aspect.

More interestingly, some high-volume systems today might lose their economies of scale and be better broken up. Some systems may centralize processing because they were built around a mainframe. If the database can be partitioned reasonably into regions, companies, or some other entities, what seems to be a monolithic high-volume database might become a group of smaller databases communicating infrequently. Figure 3.3 summarizes the rules for downsizing candidates.

Special Situations

Despite the word "downsizing," many systems that are appropriate for client/server have come up from the PC. A lot of creative development is

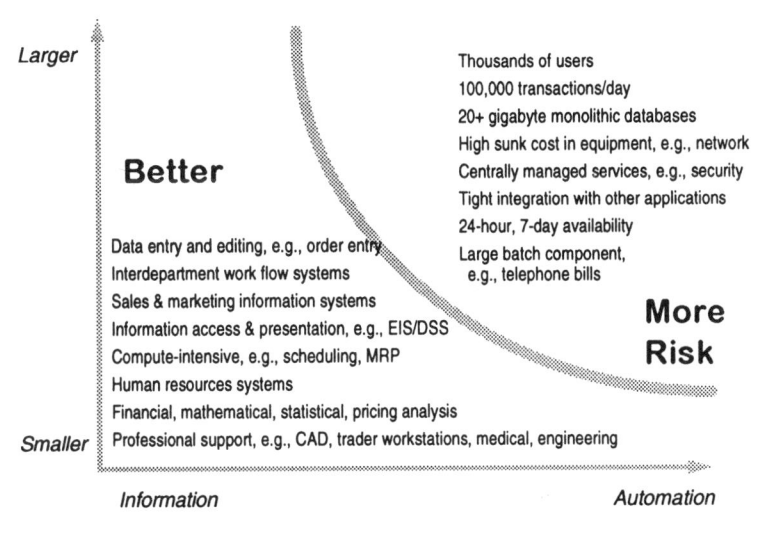

Figure 3.3 Downsizing candidates

performed on small departmental systems using languages such as FoxPro and Paradox. By using a gateway product to store these databases on servers, the data can be made more widely accessible. Ultimately, this could produce an explosion in the availability of application solutions from third-party suppliers or those developed by local custom programmers, who are familiar with these tools.

Unfortunately, these systems generally have all of the characteristics of mainframe "legacy systems." They are written in third-generation procedural languages, one application at a time. Data files are created by application without regard for the overall data model. System documentation is either nonexistent or extensive but unusable. The same type of decision must be made as for any legacy system—whether to migrate the code, redevelop, or retain and circumscribe.

A number of minicomputers have become obsolete in recent years. Companies such as Wang, Concurrent, and Prime are no longer serving the same markets as they used to and have left orphan machines behind. This problem is not confined to systems purchased from small or financially weak companies. The IBM Series/1 is a clear case, as was the DEC System 10 in its day. It is not a problem peculiar to an older generation of companies; Sun and Apple have left orphans too. A user company using one of these systems faces an expensive move to a new system. One option is to use a conversion package to migrate the system essentially unchanged, and this is often exercised by small firms. For many companies, however, the business has changed sufficiently, and it is time for a new design. In this size category, a system based on accounting and/or manufacturing packages and a relational database on a midsized UNIX processor will have the horsepower to automate all their operations. It is attractive to such a firm to invest in an open system, which offers a migration path—once bitten, twice shy.

Another special case is the system that is undergoing massive change anyway, perhaps owing to a merger, acquisition, breakup, or substantial change in business operations. While we are saying that the "gain" from reengineering transactional systems is not worth the "pain," if you are in for the pain anyway you may as well.

Some systems are a maintenance nightmare. They were possibly written poorly to begin with, or they have a poor maintenance staff, or there is a volatility to their business rules (which was too much for mainframe technology), or the force of entropy has simply worked its way over time. In this case, too, the pain is already upon you. It may be worth going for the rewrite, simply because there is no choice.

Sometimes, modern tools can give a respite from some of these problems. In particular, there is a type of system that may benefit from an object-oriented approach. For example, the products of financial services companies are defined entirely by their business rules. A CD differs from a money-market account or a municipal bond fund in terms of rules on withdrawal, transfer of funds, interest paid, allocation, and so on. These companies compete on the basis of products, attempting to be first to market offerings exploiting new investment possibilities, responding to legislation offering tax advantages, etc. A company that can define a new product in terms of inheritance from existing products with a few added rules is going to be more competitive than one which must copy or rewrite the system each time.

Which Systems to Build First

The special situations covered above are not the systems to develop first. The project to replace a system that is complex, difficult to maintain, and/or obsolete will attract great visibility. It will test the limits of some tools and of the development team. It will almost certainly be late and over budget (most projects are). It would be better to start with a system that is going to be a success.

A good pilot system (see Figure 3.4) will have a smaller number of end users and demonstrate a good payback in either function (benefiting from

- Necessary
    - has to be paid for
- Good functional payback
    - exploits GUI
    - performs poorly on mainframe
- Not too technically complex
    - database
    - connectivity
- Not time-critical
    - allow time for training, migration, mistakes
- Smaller number of end users

Figure 3.4 A good pilot system

the GUI, for instance, or performing poorly on the mainframe) or cost. It should avoid severe technical complexity in the database or connectivity areas. Should it be mission-critical? In some sense, it must be essential—how else will you justify it? Try to find a project that, while important, avoids undue risk.

At the other end of the scale, some practiced organizations are planning to move the most demanding systems to client/server in 1993. For the systems identified as inappropriate for client/server, the problem is that the paradigm is not well developed in terms of the volume of data, the number of users, and the sophistication of the tools available to address them. Client/server applications can be built to address these problems today, but the risk and time of development are higher than for the other application domains. Experience and careful project planning, management, and estimation can reduce these risks to an appropriate level.

Strengths of the Old Environment

The typical environment in the data center of a large enterprise includes an IBM ES/9000 and a large body of installed software (Figure 3.5). Non-IBM large-system environments contain similar products with different names.

This combination has many strengths. It has pursued a stable, evolutionary path since the late 1960s. It is a rich environment, with many well-financed vendors offering products and solutions available for the problems faced by managers of these systems. It is a familiar environment; although it has changed greatly over 25 years, the evolution has allowed all of the customers to keep up. There are large investments in this technology—in hardware and system software but overwhelmingly in application software.

The mainframe is more secure in its nature, since the data to be protected are centralized and kept behind walls and since practices and tools have evolved to defend that security. It is also in its nature a cheaper way to get limited, fixed computing needs to many users. If many users have low processing and interface needs, it is cheaper for them to use a shared-logic system because terminals are cheaper than workstations. A terminal-based system is thus appropriate for situations where a dedicated application is made available. Also, mainframes offer easy enterprise-wide communications (such as IBM PROFS electronic mail), since no intercomputer communication may be involved at all.

There are a million staff members with skills in the current systems, and many COBOL programmers cannot be retrained. C programmers are scarce

- Stable 25-year evolution
- Mature, well-understood products:
  - IBM System/370
  - MVS/ESA
  - SNA
  - COBOL
  - IMS
  - CICS
  - DB2
- Large investments in computers, networks, staff, system software
- Massive investment in application software

Figure 3.5 The mainframe advantage

in many parts of the country, and they generally have no commercial experience. There are so many of the new 4GLs that it is very hard to predict which ones will eventually become standard, if any.

The management tools that evolved over the past 25 years on the mainframe are much less mature in the distributed system environment. An organization moving to client/server systems faces risk of severe disruption in data quality, personnel, and systems management. This is why most large enterprises today retain mainframes.

BUSINESS ASSESSMENT

The preceding text identified the types of applications that can benefit from client/server and that other organizations are addressing in this way. This can help in identifying specific opportunities for the application of the architecture, but, as for all system development opportunities, the key to the decision is to solve a business problem. The most common failure we see is companies applying the "right" technology to the "wrong" problem. Once the business problems are identified and prioritized, the appropriate technology for implementation can be selected.

In looking for opportunities, we generally assess the current business organization and installed technology and then consider that in relation to the customers and competitors of the organization, new ideas in business organization, and available technology. This effort can be conducted in a complete and formal way, leading to an information strategy plan. Alternatively, the formal activities can be short-circuited, and a rapid opportunity analysis can be performed. The choice depends on the nature of the organization. Many managers must justify strategic decisions with formal documents; other organizations may have an entrepreneurial approach.

One way to present the analysis of this information is a SWOT analysis. SWOT is an acronym for Strengths, Weaknesses, Opportunities, Threats. Strengths and weaknesses are internal characteristics, while opportunities and threats are external.

Typical strengths of businesses with older systems include:

- good data quality
- system reliability and availability
- data security
- low cost of basic terminal and network
- basic operating efficiency

Typical weaknesses include:

- poor response to changes in the business
- low data quality
- inability to access data in different systems
- multiyear backlog of enhancement requests
- inability to see data in new ways
- problems with system availability, scheduled or unscheduled
- difficulty in use, such as high training costs or data entry error rates
- high cost of maintenance and enhancement
- poor development productivity

Typical opportunities include:

- access marketing information and target customers with new products
- compress time to bring new products to market
- compress time to satisfy a customer order
- price orders or access inventory immediately
- improve customer service
- sell information as a product
- measure and improve operating efficiency
- move to other markets

Typical threats include:

- changing sales channels need new support processes
- benchmarking our processes reveals a performance gap
- losing market share to competition
- competitors routinely beat us on price
- competitors routinely beat us on speed of response or product introduction
- margins are reduced
- sales volume is down
- global competitors moving in
- expectations of customer service are increasing
- demographic changes are altering our market or workforce
- change in size through mergers and acquisitions

TECHNOLOGY ASSESSMENT

The project team assessing existing systems should have considerable experience. There are many pitfalls in assessing a system; one common danger is to end up writing the same system over again. The team must look on code as a liability, not an asset, and be alert to the possibility of throwing it away.

The team must understand the old technology. The maintainers of the existing system always have an exaggerated idea of the system's complexity and value. They may have written their own file access method at some time in the past, because a good indexed retrieval scheme was not available or was too expensive. They may have implemented a clever buffering scheme or in-memory database, because disk access was too slow. They may have implemented complex rules in support of obsolete business processes. They may have done near-impossible technical tricks in COBOL, which are easy to do in a newer rule-based tool. They may have written a large reporting subsystem, which is never used. They will not realize and will actively deny that much of the code they maintain is unnecessary, but this will be the case. If you ask the owners of the old system to document it, size it, triage it, or cost it, they cannot help but mislead you. If you are the owner of an old system, you need to get outside help to assess it.

The team must also understand the potential role of new technology. It is, after all, the possibilities offered by the new technology that make the migration worth doing.

You will not be able to create an assessment team where everyone has experience in assessments, the old technology, and the new. The point is to create a team where the whole is greater than the parts.

1. Assess Existing Applications

For each application, assess:

- size
    - —scope
    - —count of on-line transactions and modules
    - —count of batch processes and modules
    - —size of largest batch procedure, largest program, and largest subroutine
    - —count of database tables and views
    - —count of files and record types
- performance
    - —transaction throughput
    - —transaction response time
    - —scheduled and required uptime
    - —batch window and volumes
    - —data volatility
- complexity
    - —essential complexity (innate complication and volatility of business functions addressed, multiple locations, and user bodies)
    - —accidental complexity (multiple processors, languages, databases, etc.)
    - —interfaces to other applications
    - —interfaces to other systems or special equipment
- condition
    - —age
    - —code modularity, structure, and consistency
    - —quality of the system documentation

Identify any major subsystems that have significantly different characteristics or support requirements. Distinguish between operational and information systems, breaking out reporting and decision support components. Look for opportunities to chip off pieces of the system and attack them with a different tool.

Chapter 3 • Planning the Downsizing

For each module in an application, assess:

- lines of code
- language used
- file or database system
- environment (on-line or batch)
- code quality (structured, modular)
- complexity
- function points

This should be done at a high level, taking less than five minutes per application. It is not to be considered a detailed analysis of applications. Consider the characteristics of the application using the function point rules as a guide (complex, on-line, etc).

Module	Lines	Language	Environment	Files	Quality	Complexity
AMX2745	2350	COBOL	CICS	VSAM	High	Medium
AMX31005	1890	COBOL	Batch	VSAM	Medium	Medium
BRC7490	4100	PL/I	Batch	IMS	Low	High

For each database table or file in an application, assess:

- number of fields
- number of records
- associated views or logical records
- volatility of data
- technology

Table	#Field	#Record	#View	Volatility	Type	Comments
Employee	100	5000	1	Low	IMS	Disorganized
Line Item	24	75000	1	High	VSAM	
Customer	50	700	3	Medium	DB2	

A similar analysis should be performed for each screen and report.

2. Assess Infrastructure

List all processor and network hardware, by major component and in round numbers. For each processor, there should be an estimate of attached disks and controller units. If multiple sites are involved, this should be broken out by site. List system software, including the operating system, database, TP monitor, security, and management packages.

All of this data are normally available from the systems administration staff. The objective here is to get a two- or three-page summary of the situation, not an inventory list with the serial number of every terminal.

If there are special requirements of uptime or security, they may be discovered during this process.

Of particular interest are considerations relevant to the timing of the migration—for instance, if upgrades to the CPU or disk storage are due, software licensing conditions are changing, or the operating system or hardware has become obsolete.

3. Assess Current Work and Staffing

Review the service history of the applications. This can be done by examining the service requests. The results need careful interpretation. Applications with unusually low service levels are often not being used. Applications with high levels may be poorly structured or servicing volatile business areas. It can be helpful to analyze the work with a Pareto analysis to see if there are particular components that need attention. Application components with high maintenance activity due to poor design may be candidates for rewriting, whereas components that are naturally volatile might require a rule-based system or end-user involvement.

Examine the current workload and maintenance requests. Interview the users of the system about their satisfaction. In our consulting practice, we employ a set of questionnaires to drive this assessment. The goal is to calculate the number of staff required to do basic maintenance and also to identify applications or components of applications that might be candidates for termination or redesign.

4. Assess the Current Costs and Problems

The current costs include the staffing baseline and the costs to maintain the technology (license and maintenance charges, etc.).

Current problems will be seen differently by different observers. The IT department may see problems in terms of maintenance or development productivity, upgrading to new releases, performance issues, and so on. These may or may not correspond well with the problems reported by the users.

5. Analyze the Results

It is useful to cross-reference the collected data. This serves as a consistency check and may highlight problems in the analysis or problems in the system. For example:

- application programs versus databases accessed
- databases versus DASD
- application characteristics versus maintenance logs

It is possible to derive approximate numbers for the total cost of an application. Generally, when the costs of all applications are plotted against the needs of the business, the correlation is poor, and for applications under development, it is worse.

6. Prepare Migration and Nonmigration Costs for Each Application

From the data gathered so far, we can tell which applications are candidates to be migrated, based on which software is supported in downsized environments and the given capacity needs of the applications. Other things being equal, applications that can be rehosted relatively easily will be less expensive than those that need to be rewritten or replaced.

We can also tell the cost of not migrating, based on the cost of upgrades, the differential cost of software licensing, and the differential cost of service and support over the period considered.

7. Determine a Basis for Migration

On the basis of this assessment, a business case for the downsizing activity can now be created. The goals of the project can be stated (for instance, cut costs or improve service) and quantified, and the scope can be defined. Scope of a downsizing project can include:

- application development and maintenance
- end-user support and help-desk
- operations
- training
- documentation

The first application migrated is much more likely than subsequent ones to meet problems in these areas.

The following example of a business case, based on Rob Thomsett's excellent book *Third Wave Project Management*, shows an overview of the information to include.

Project Business Case

Overview	Brief description of project and background
Scope	Statement of boundaries and areas of impact
Objectives	Precise description of strategic, business, and technical objectives
Benefits	Expected returns from project
Costs	Costs (people, equipment, etc.) associated with development, introduction, and continued running of the system
Strategy	Work breakdown structure: sequence and parallelism
Risk	Assessment of risk and exposure
Plan	Project development schedule
Externals	Legislation, key external groups, issues outside project control
Staffing	Assumptions, skills, critical needs
Quality	Measures of quality
Constraints	Time deadlines, technology choices, etc.
Related jobs	Other projects whose dependencies interlock with this

Thomsett (1993)

RISK ASSESSMENT

The risks of the project should be considered. There are risks in the transition; for instance, the project may overrun in time and/or cost, and it may fail (totally or partially) against objectives. There may also be risks in not doing the project; for instance, a competitor could become faster in responding to orders.

The first and greatest set of risk factors is external to the development team. The following questions should be asked:

Is there sufficient commitment from senior management and the user team?

Chapter 3 • Planning the Downsizing

What is the business impact on the users, and how much change must they undergo?

Do the users understand the technology, its effects, and its limitations?

A single user expert or advocate is a danger sign. He or she may retire, leave, or get promoted. The new vice-president implementing an agenda from his or her last company is not unusual; if he or she moves on, the system has no customer. Some users have unreasonable expectations, expecting the computer to make decisions or know information that it cannot do; others have no faith at all. If a new interface technology is being introduced, it may be resisted.

How many outside bodies, such as regulatory boards, unions, or external partners are involved?

Are there multiple user branches or sites?

A single determined party can often prevent change. Every external body will introduce delays and changes in the specifications. Some may have no interest in the success of the system.

Can we expect the requirements to be stable?

Are the deadlines fixed or movable?

Of course, requirements are never stable, but some are more so than others. Some systems are clearly subject to change from external sources. Hard deadlines can be a good thing, because they will focus a committed user on making progress, but they bring a risk of total failure.

The next set of risk factors pertains to the development team.

Was the team size and development schedule calculated from the project requirements?

Has the project manager done this sort of thing before?

Do the team members have sufficient knowledge?

The experience of the project manager is a major risk, which can cause an otherwise adequate project to fail. This is difficult to determine, because the critical factor on a project may be one of several things, including political skill, team building, or technical judgment.

The team needs to have adequate knowledge of the functional area and the development tools and platform. All members do not need to know all things, but someone should be able to answer key questions and solve problems on each important aspect of the application. The team also needs to develop cohesion, so that all members are free to access the informed individuals without fear of seeming ignorant. In a migration project, there must be specific knowledge available on:

- source platform language, database, operating system, and tools
- target platform language, database, operating system, and tools
- analysis, migration, and testing tools

There are risks in system complexity. The measures used by the function point calculation can be used to assess risk.

An Example

Consumer products manufacturing company

Large, good revenues, margins under pressure, wishes to cut costs
Consolidating some acquired operations, reengineering order-to-deliver function

Technical environment:

IBM 3081 MVS, CICS, VSAM, DB2 installed but not used much

SNA network, PC LANs in extensive use

Application environment:

Manufacturing	Old COBOL package, heavily customized
Customer orders	Old custom COBOL
Distribution	Old COBOL package, heavily customized; FoxPro/PC system in some warehouses
Forecasting	Not much, new system needed
HR/benefits	Old custom COBOL code
Accounting	10-year-old package, IDMS/COBOL
E-mail/office	Variety of ad hoc systems

A migration plan might be: Move gradually to open systems, using the ORACLE database and HP 9000 servers with Windows tools to develop new applications.

| Manufacturing | Refurbish/rehost | DB2, COBOL, CICS/9000, ORACLE |

Customer orders/inventory	Circumscribe	PowerBuilder, ORACLE, DB2
Distribution	Rehost/circumscribe	COBOL/ORACLE, FoxPro, PowerBuilder
Forecasting	Rewrite	PowerBuilder, ORACLE
HR/benefits	Replace	PeopleSoft
Accounting	Replace	ORACLE Financials
E-mail/office	Replace	Lotus Notes, Lotus SmartSuite

COST/BENEFIT ANALYSIS

Given a business problem and a technology assessment, we must now proceed to a financial justification of the proposed project. We need to develop an understanding of the cost and benefits of operating both the current system and the proposed system.

Is a cost or performance benefit sought? If a cost payback, what time frame is used? Five years used to be traditional, but in these cost-conscious times, you may want to use two or three years for larger projects and one year for small projects without significant development.

Costs will include initial costs and ongoing operating costs. All of these costs should be treated conservatively—that is, on the high side. There are many more hidden costs than hidden benefits.

Initial costs:

- workstations
    - —hardware
    - —standard software
- servers
    - —hardware
    - —systems software
- application software
    - —database management system and associated tools
    - —middleware, gateways
    - —application packages
    - —management tools

- LAN/WAN communications
    - adapter cards
    - hubs
    - wiring
    - installation cost
- application development
    - development staff
    - development tools, including CASE, methodologies, project and source code management
- transitional costs
    - IT staff redeployment and training
    - consulting and temporary help
    - end-user training
    - parallel running during transition
- intangible costs
    - loss of service quality during transition and training
    - loss of user time during development, testing, training, and conversion

Ongoing operating costs:

- maintenance of hardware
- maintenance of software
- software maintenance staff
- operations staff
- remote system management
- support at remote sites
- hidden support and training time spent by users
- software package upgrades and replacements
- upgrades to hardware to meet changing performance expectations
- ongoing training costs

Benefits are much harder to calculate than costs and tend to be "motherhood and apple pie," such as "better communications" or "improved productivity." Some benefits should be tangible, delivering more revenue, improving quality or service, or lowering cost in measurable ways. If the benefits of a project are entirely intangible, that is a bad sign. One rule of thumb is that if we take a real objective away, the project must differ in scope.

Revenue generation is the preferred justification for a system. The new system might, for instance, respond better to changes in the business. In some operations, this can generate revenue, because it enables new products or customers. For example, ADP gets a competitive advantage from the speed with which it can get a new payroll on-line. A company might downsize to push an application out to the field. Better sales or marketing information may win business. Faster order-to-delivery time will improve the competitive situation.

Reduced costs could be achieved in hard computer costs or in manpower, or both. Today, hardware and database vendors often stress the cost savings of new open systems-based computers over mainframes. Most consulting firms look for manpower savings in operations, as these can be quantifiable and large enough to justify custom development efforts.

Improved customer service or the quality of the product should be measurable, though not necessarily financially. In some circumstances, the new system may improve availability, data integrity, or administrative costs. The variety of available software or the improved interface might improve user productivity and may enhance core competencies.

CLIENT/SERVER COST ANALYSIS

The question as to whether a client/server system is more expensive than a monolithic system is often debated. Published answers have varied from much more expensive to somewhat less, with widely differing numbers. A big reason for this swing is that there are different approaches to the cost. An approach that looks at the cost of a single application on either configuration will tend to benefit the monolithic system, because the cost of the terminals dominates the decision and that system has less expensive terminals. An approach that looks at the cost to make a variety of applications available is fairer, because the cost of infrastructure investments is spread over several applications. One corollary is that the first client/server application will be expensive unless the infrastructure investment is treated this way. Another is that if the users in a business area only want access to one system that does not require workstations, it will not be cost justifiable to buy workstations.

Table 3.1 Purchase Costs of Workstations and Terminals

	Monolithic (M)	Client/Server (C)	Caveats
Workstation	500	1,500+	C much better quality
MIPS	30,000	3,000	M used 3 times
1 Mb disk	4,000	2,000	M used better, safer

Moving One Application

The following elementary financial model shows a view of the basic cost of moving one application to client/server. In the typical on-line transaction processing (OLTP) situation, where a great number of terminals are supported by an application that does little processing, the costs are much higher for client/server. Of course, the systems are not exactly equivalent. The client/server system has a much better user interface. Subsequent client/server systems benefit from reuse of the LAN and support infrastructure and are much cheaper. The model assumes the present existence of a mainframe and support environment, so it is strongly biased towards that type of system.

Table 3.1 shows relative purchase costs of workstations and terminals. Mainframe MIPS are rated fully because of 24-hour usage, whereas client/server MIPS are discounted, because they are used over 8 hours and are not used efficiently.

To use the table, we simply calculate the desired processor power, disk, and number of workstations for the application and sum them for total cost.

Total = MIPS + DASD + Terminals (network)

Example 1:

An application uses 20 MIPS, 40 GB, and 1000 terminals:

(30000 * 20) + (40 * 4000) + (1000 * 500) = 1,260,000 (M)
(3000 * 20) + (40 * 2000) + (1000 * 1500) = 1,640,000 (C)

The application should remain on the mainframe.

Example 2:

An application uses 30 MIPS, 70 GB, and 400 terminals:

(30000 * 30) + (70 * 4000) + (400 * 500) = 1,380,000 (M)
(3000 * 30) + (70 * 2000) + (400 * 1500) = 830,000 (C)

This application is much cheaper on client/server.

This does not take into account the cost of software, which can tilt the balance in either direction, or support, which tends to cost more on the newer systems. Many companies downsize to flee from high mainframe licensing fees. Others have discovered the high cost of personal computing packages purchased for every workstation.

The Cost of the Second Application

Table 3.2 shows the cost of the first and second client/server applications delivered to a group of 200 users. The infrastructure developed for the first system includes development tools (ObjectView and Sybase, for example), PCs, Novell NetWare servers and LAN wiring, and training of the personnel who will develop and maintain the system. All of this is there for the second system.

The first system has an annualized cost per seat of $3,250; the second costs $1,375.

Table 3.2 Cost of New System (in thousands of dollars)

Item	First	Second	Details
Development tools	100	25	Tools, database
Application development	500	500	8 man-years
Infrastructure	700	25	200 PCs, 5 NetWare, installed
Application server	100	100	RS/6000 or similar, installed
IT training	50	0	5 developers, 1 database administrator, 2 systems analysts
User training	50	50	200 users
Infrastructure support/ maintenance	700	0	4-year cost
Application server support	400	400	4-year cost
Total	**2600**	**1100**	

ESTABLISHING MEASUREMENTS OF PAYBACK

To establish the financial payback of a project, we need the costs and financial benefits of the alternatives, including the status quo, for the period under consideration. We can then produce a justification in terms of internal rate of return (IRR), payback time (the point at which we break even from the investment), or return on investment (ROI). The preferred form is generally an enterprise standard. All of these results can be derived from a single spreadsheet containing the costs and benefits by time using a standard net present value formula.

The costs of people can be calculated as the sum of their salary, benefits, direct administrative support, space, and corporate overhead. A good rule of thumb is two times salary.

A full set of measurements for a project should be prepared as part of the project plan. It will include all of the following:

- **technical performance**
    - —transaction volumes
    - —database size
    - —system response time
    - —network capabilities
    - —system uptime
- **cost/benefit performance**
    - —costs of service
    - —salaries
    - —equipment maintenance
    - —delivered benefits
- **quality performance**
    - —customer service
    - —empowerment
    - —defect levels
- **operating performance**
    - —utilization
    - —actual transaction volumes
    - —user acceptance

Chapter 3 • Planning the Downsizing

The new implementation should be reviewed about six months after its introduction or earlier if there are other systems depending on this one as a pilot. The review could include all of the system or just chosen subsystems. If the system is used at multiple locations, it may not be necessary to review operations at all locations, but enough should be considered to allow for differences.

The review should analyze both the manual and automated aspects of the system. Collect measurements on inputs (transactions, tables), stores and processing, and outputs (reports, logs, screens, transmitted data). Collect data on facts and opinions of users, operations, and systems development through interviews, surveys, and questionnaires.

The review should also consider the organization in which the system is embedded. This includes staffing, job functions, support, and training at the various locations of the new system. Actual operating costs for the system should be calculated.

Compare the actual results to the proposed system performance and benefits. The following should be generated:

- system effectiveness
- system cost/benefit
- system improvement opportunities

CALCULATING WORKSTATION COST

The loaded monthly cost of a workstation, including all of the costs cited above, averages around $5,000 for Fortune 500 companies. It is more for client/server systems than for proprietary minicomputers, such as AS/400 or VAX/VMS, or for mainframes, because the workstation hardware and software cost more and dominate the numbers.

System Type	*Lowest*	*Median*	*Highest*
Open client/server	$3,500	$5,000	$7,000
Proprietary minis	$3,000	$4,000	$5,000
Mainframes	$2,000	$3,000	$4,000

The Cost of Moving to Windows

The controversial part of client/server is the graphical workstation. The server choice can be made on its financial merits, with open system solutions costing less than proprietary. The network choice is justified, because the network is a shared resource offering general benefits in reduced operation and management costs over individual connections. Common word processing, calendar, forms, and e-mail also speak for an integrated network, although this could be monolithic (like Profs and All-in-One). Some enterprises will be reluctant to spend the extra cost of supporting a graphical workstation over a character-based one, and some users will be reluctant to switch, regardless of cost.

As mentioned before, the big question in calculating the cost of a GUI is whether to factor in expected general productivity improvements or to focus on one key application with specific benefit. The general benefits include ease of training and support because of the common Windows interface and improved built-in help, the benefit of switching between tasks, and the improved quality of documents and other deliverables.

The costs of moving to Windows in a DOS environment consist of both physical upgrades and enhanced training and support. Hardware and software upgrades include disk, RAM, a graphics adapter, a processor upgrade, a mouse, and a larger monitor. Windows requires a 386 processor, 80 Mb disk, and 4 Mb RAM and runs best with 8 Mb RAM and a super VGA monitor with a graphics accelerator. It is reasonable to budget $500 per user for training in Windows and the Windows versions of their applications, including word processing, e-mail, and so on.

These costs can be lowered if the current PC inventory is already Windows-capable, and training and support costs are kept the same as before. Within two years, the relative cost of Windows over DOS will be zero, because the entire PC inventory in an enterprise will be Windows-capable, and most users will be Windows-literate.

Some surveys have been published attributing very high costs to training and support for distributed systems. These findings should be treated very cautiously. There are many activities in an automated company which were formerly done manually, and which always had training and support costs. These activities occurred previously, but are now possibly being reclassified as computer-related expenses. For example, training employees where the file cabinet and mailroom are is not easily distinguished from teaching them Microsoft Word and Mail.

The costs associated with electronic office functions, particularly mail, are also likely to be higher in a transition period when many organizations are learning how to best exploit them.

Transition Costs

Figure 3.6 shows various costs associated with migrating a system. In addition to the ongoing costs of the new and old systems, we must consider these transitional costs:

- development of the new system
- parallel operation of the two systems
- training and other transition costs (e.g. turnover)

This leads to the "hump" depicted in Figure 3.7. For large systems, this can be two or more years long; for small systems, six months. For many manag-

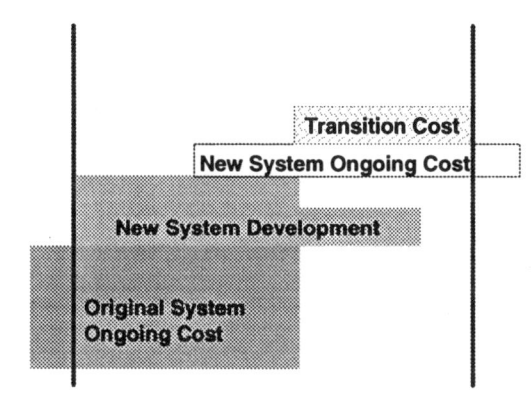

Figure 3.6 Managing transition cost 1

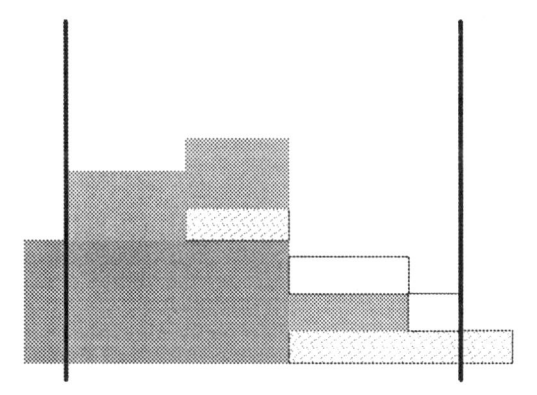

Figure 3.7 Managing transition cost 2

ers, it is difficult to get the funding to cope with this. The resources needed to plan and develop the new system are locked up maintaining the old.

Summary

In consulting, we are often asked for easy answers to these issues. There are none; any migration must be undertaken for good business reasons, and grounded in good detailed models of the cost, risk, and technology involved.

4

Reengineering the Business Process

THE PRINCIPLES OF REENGINEERING

The fundamental design of many of today's jobs, including the work flow and the organizational structure, dates from the 1950s. It predates the introduction not only of the computer, but of the television. Jobs were designed for a population quite different from that of today—in education, age, and expectations. Many jobs were not designed at all. When they were, the focus was on efficiency and control.

The world of the 1990s is very different from that of the 1950s. For Americans, it is an era of much more significant competition. Customer choices are much richer and expectations higher. It is necessary to move beyond efficiency and control (without losing them) to issues of speed, service, and quality.

In 1991, MIT published the results of an extensive study of the introduction of automation to a variety of large enterprises. A major conclusion was that automation without redesign of the fundamental business process is not justified. This automation without rethinking is a significant cause of the poor productivity in service jobs over the last two decades.

Much work in the 1970s was structured around the computer as a centralized machine that had to be used in an efficient and controlled manner. Older disciplines of manual systems and work flow fell into disuse, as we designed work around the structured job control and reporting of the batch mainframe computer. As on-line terminals became more common, we began to move back to a more ad hoc, user-driven approach. We have now moved all the way to the point where computer technology is so ubiquitous that it can almost be ignored. The big, expensive, difficult to manage monster in the middle of the business isn't the computer now; it is people. The disciplines of industrial engineering, cost accounting, and work-flow analysis return to prominence to help us manage the changes in human organization and behavior we need.

It may be necessary to make a system available at many more locations and have it share data with or be cooperable with other systems. This requires easier to operate systems with standard interfaces and access to data across traditional functional boundaries.

Mike Hammer's influential 1990 *Harvard Business Review* article on this subject contained several summary points. These principles exploit the technology that has become available since our present thinking on job design was formed. It is augmented with three ideas from the quality movement.

1. Reduce the cycle time of product development and delivery.
2. Anticipate, ensure, and measure your product's success on the key dimensions of customer satisfaction.
3. Be capable of continuously improving the quality and efficiency of service.

Organize around Outcomes, Not Tasks

Many companies put a case manager or customer service manager in charge of customer issues. This individual or small team is empowered to solve the customer problem, using whatever resources are needed. Such a design may require systems to put information in these people's hands and/or job design to allow them to make decisions quickly. The empowerment is reinforced by education and technology to produce the result: flexibility and customer satisfaction.

This approach requires a workforce that is flexible, since it performs a variety of tasks and often makes important decisions. This may require a better education or may be achieved through computer and communications assistance. Some industries face less-educated people than in the past; all must deal with more diversity. They may need to manage large quantities of information and deliver it where and when needed.

A computer system that brings all customer orders and maintenance equipment to the service representative, or an automated help-desk, where the head operator can take responsibility for and track the query to completion, is an example. The Volvo plants, where workers build entire cars in work cells instead of a production line, are an extreme example.

This approach leads to multifunction teams, not a hierarchy of specialists and a pool of unskilled labor. It integrates the functions of planning, hiring, evaluating, and quality into teams. These people are often trained and informed as needed, just-in-time. Process design, improvement, and performance are concentrated around these teams.

Have Those Who Use the Output of the Process Perform the Process

This principle compresses steps in a process, removing the overhead of additional staff (which costs money) and interfaces (which costs time in delays and often leads to rework).

A process was often split into tasks because expensive equipment or special training was needed to perform a step. As steps are merged together, the equipment may need to be more flexible or available at more places. Fortunately, this is just the type of change facilitated by today's computers.

In modern automobile factories, the line worker performs maintenance and the setup of the machine as the product being produced changes. By training the employee to perform functions once done by specialists, the changeover time is reduced, and an increasing number of operators are made available for the value-added work on the line.

Some companies are choosing to organize around processes and to put senior leaders in charge of processes, so that processes are seen as the fundamental organizing principle, rather than functions. Many companies are building a matrix structure, which is less radical.

Subsume Information-Processing Work into the Real Work That Produces the Information

In the mass production model, one group of workers performs the work while another group measures them or collects information on the quality and use of the product. These activities can often be combined. In the Japanese car factory, for example, workers produce control charts for their own machines.

If a team is empowered, trained, and supported to plan, hire, and measure quality and performance, it can supervise the collection of information on these activities, or even make it unnecessary.

Treat Geographically Dispersed Resources As Though They Were Centralized

Of course, the lower cost and widespread use of a variety of communications advances have made this possible. This includes the telephone, voice mail, electronic mail, one-day package delivery, television and videotape, fax, telephone conferencing, and videoconferencing. Middle management is not needed as a relay any more.

We can use computer systems to get the scale and flexibility we once had to centralize for. By using electronic mail and an electronic bulletin board, we can create exchanges of technical information (the "electronic village"). Image processing can be used to capture information that is not on the computer and make it available wherever and whenever it is needed.

Rethinking an organizational chart to reduce the once all-important role of geography and allow division on functional, technical, or customer-driven lines is a radical change to many organizations. If it can be achieved, it can lead to tremendous competitive advantage. Resources can be concentrated where and when needed.

Link Parallel Activities Instead of Integrating Their Results

Just as serial activities can be pressed together, parallel efforts can be coordinated as they occur. Again, we can use computers and communication to ensure that the results will operate as needed.

Improved communication within and between workgroups is enabled by products such as Lotus Notes and the various types of tools that improve teamwork between groups at remote sites.

This type of change is one of the hardest to introduce, because it requires sophisticated project management over large scales of space and time and because errors are very costly. But it has become the norm in large corporate information system development, because the requirement to reduce development cycle time is just too much to resist.

Put the Decision Point Where the Work Is Performed, and Build Control into the Process

We make the performers of work self-managing by putting information in their hands and prescribing the limits within which they are empowered. When this is done, we can remove unnecessary steps of authorization. This reduces time to deliver and leads to a flattening of the organizational hierarchy.

It is often necessary to make a vigorous, prolonged effort to document and manage processes better, using automated systems to make this possible. In some cases, an assessment of risk has to be made.

Smaller, more powerful workstations can support this principle, accessing data for decisions from a corporate "information warehouse." The "Executive Information System" is used to support the everyday professional.

There are additional benefits to this approach. The user department is often closely involved in the design and support of the system. The costs of system development and maintenance are incurred close to their business justification, where cost/benefit trade-off decisions can be more accurately made. For these reasons, system alterations can often be made very rapidly in response to changes in external conditions.

Capture Information Once and at the Source

It is easier to store and transmit information than to reenter it. This reduces opportunities for error, lowers cost, and allows new uses of the collected information. It also generally requires cooperation between functions in an organization, such as when the point of sale collects data for a marketing database. Technology supporting this principle includes integrated databases ("information warehouse"). It also includes electronic data interchange (EDI) and barcoding, since there is no reason to reenter information that a supplier organization has captured. In this way, information flows across intra- and interenterprise boundaries.

The technical problem here is the issue of standards. Data from different systems in different organizations must be able to travel to where it is needed in a cost-effective manner, so that we are not forced to reenter it. This requires communications and database standards, plus the higher-level vertical market specific architecture efforts that support EDI.

Recognize and Manage Processes

A process is a sequence of activities that produces something of value for the customer. Most processes in the contemporary organization are cross-functional by nature. Many of the ideas above can lead to organizing around a process and reducing the steps and interfaces that cause delays and errors. However, these will not remove the need to manage the "white space" on the organizational chart. Many important processes still cross boundaries in the organization and beyond it, and some have no natural owners. It is necessary to recognize the processes that are important to an organization and ensure that they are managed correctly. Examples of processes include:

- customer billing
- software development
- handling customer complaints
- developing new products
- managing distribution of retail product from order to delivery

Triage the Process Based on Customer Need

Often, a process is found to go through many steps because of the level of risk or complexity of a few of the products or services that are being performed. It may be appropriate to break these products out and produce two processes—only one of which will have the elaborate protections. Sometimes, this type of analysis is supported by activity-based costing and will lead to the realization that some services should be abandoned.

Alternatively, there may be one service that is performed in more volume. It can be broken out and performed with less resources or time. For example, oil and fluid changes do not require the skills and resources of true automotive repair and have become a separate industry. Best-selling paperback books are sold through supermarkets, not bookstores. Many IT shops will give their users a read-only subset of the production database, for example, allowing satisfaction of a simpler service with user-generated reports.

Reduce the Cycle Time of Product Development and Delivery

The phrase "time-based competition" refers to the tremendous advantages a company with shorter development cycle time has. In 1987, for instance, the Acura Legend and Sterling 825SL were introduced to the American market.

These two cars, introduced with new brand names through new dealer networks, were essentially equivalent, the product of joint design by Honda and Austin-Rover. Early reviews indicated that these rather good cars had a number of acceptance problems; one was that the engine was insufficiently powerful for this type of car. Within 18 months, the Japanese company had a more powerful engine installed. It took the British firm three years, by which time the Japanese had a complete new model, with a new engine and body style, on sale. The British are still making their car, but since 1991 it is only sold in their protected home market.

IBM's struggles with PCs, particularly portables, have presented us with years of anecdotes on uncompetitive development cycle time. Invariably, they produce a product that is eclipsed within weeks by a new generation of lighter, more capable systems; yet the IBM product persists on sale, at increasing discount, well past the point of embarrassment. Perhaps this story has a happy ending; in 1992–1993, they seem to have found the answer with their ValuePoint and Thinkpad lines, by reorganizing to reduce cycle time, removing unnecessary review steps, and staying close to customer needs.

Delivery cycle time is equally important. Customers' obsessions with time have created numerous new markets. Examples in the last few years include:

- fast food
- one-hour glasses
- one-hour photo processing and instant cameras
- Federal Express and fax
- Pizza Hut's "5-minute lunch"

Compression of cycle time is of particular importance in information delivery. Information is the most perishable commodity in the world. Much of the information technology industry is clearly founded on this, from the telegraph to the supercomputer.

Another time-based competitive requirement is constant availability of service. There are a number of ways to meet this need: with simple labor practices, such as the 24-hour supermarket; with automation (the ATM); with globalization (linked electronic exchanges or telephone help-desks following the sun from Ireland to the United States to Australia); or with transfer of the labor to the customer (Pizza Hut and Benihana selling frozen foods). Most involve complete reengineering of the business of the "don't automate, obliterate" type. In the above examples, we obliterated the "mom-and-pop" grocery store, the retail bank branch, the local support worker, and the restaurant, respectively.

By reducing the steps in a process, we bring more of the process closer to the customer and reduce opportunities for error—improving quality and operating efficiency.

Anticipate, Measure, and Continuously Improve Your Product's Success on the Key Dimensions of Customer Satisfaction

This emphasis on customer service can be used to drive decisions on the choice of process or the order to make the various decisions implied above. For many companies, the answer is to put customer satisfaction first and to link the measurement of this to unit and personal performance goals and compensation. Measures of throughput and quality should be instituted with any new system, to measure both its payback and that of the business systems it supports.

The requirement for continuous improvement is an important balancing need. Sometimes, it is possible to come up with a breakthrough that is dangerous in its commitment to a narrow base. As an example, Edward Luttwak, in his book *Strategy*, cites the antitank missile. This achieved strategic parity with tanks for a period in the 1970s and at much lower cost. However, this was achieved by a very narrow technological breakthrough (the hollow charge), which temporarily negated the tank's superior mobility and safety. Within a few years, an armor had been developed (reactive armor), and the threat was negated. A similar case might occur in a food company that abolished its kitchens to serve food based on a narrow technology. The consumer taste might shift, leaving the company high and dry. A system that is broad-based enough to respond flexibly to change might be worth the extra cost.

This trade-off is very difficult. It simply suggests that there may be no substitute for continuous vigilance and response to changing market needs.

BUSINESS TRANSFORMATION

Business transformation must be viewed in two perspectives.

1. Business components (i.e., organizations, policies, procedures, technologies, facilities, and systems) needed to provide the products/services in support of the mission and objectives of the enterprise.

Chapter 4 • Reengineering the Business Process

2. Information Resource Management including those components (i.e., policies, organizations, technologies, facilities, and internal systems) needed to develop, maintain, support, and operate the systems required by the business.

To do this requires the wider scope of effort. The widest scope appears to be offered by business transformation, which is based upon the premise that radical or dramatic changes can be made in the business architecture—not simply incremental changes for improvements in efficiency and effectiveness.

To accomplish business transformation, a "vision" must be developed for each of these perspectives (i.e., business and information resources). These visions must be aligned, with the IS vision firmly based on the business vision. What is complex is that the distinction between these two visions is blurring because many of the activities of an enterprise are now being automated. Other factors, such as the business and regulatory environment, shareholders, funding, and time, all further constrain the development of the vision.

Another complicating issue is the breadth of most organizations that may be addressed. To solve this, a "peel the onion" approach must be taken to first make strategic decisions that will affect the architecture and then make tactical decisions that will serve to structure the operational procedures. This implies a multiphased approach.

Information engineering concepts and techniques provide a means of developing the vision in a rigorous and disciplined manner. By using techniques such as functional decomposition and data modeling, the activities of the business can be analyzed on a logical basis, resulting in a set of abstract models of the high-level function processes and data, which must be performed by the business and supported by information resources.

At a strategic level, two assessments must be made. First, how well the existing business operates in light of the objectives. Second, the information systems must also be assessed from both a technical and functional basis to determine how well the business is supported. Decisions of a strategic nature regarding what should be altered or remain the same can also be made using these models from a strategic basis. Additionally, the dimensions (e.g., quality, reduced time, reduced cost) upon which change must be made can be defined. This allows for a clear definition of the criteria for success, which must constantly be referenced as decisions are made.

These models serve as the basis for the development of formal structured deliverables, which portray the two visions. For the IS visions, it is the IS architecture, which is composed of system, application, and data architectures, as well as a definition of the overall IS strategy. These govern the construction of the envisioned architecture. Similarly, a business architecture, which is an abstract of what and how the enterprise will function, must be prepared. Depending upon the business strategy, it may provide direction on significant strategic business decisions, which will impact the enterprise. Examples are: outsourcing, use of strategic alliances, relationships with external agents, and even use of concepts such as just-in-time. Once these architectures are agreed to by management, then an implementation plan can be constructed.

In order to be able to develop and analyze to keep these models synchronized, CASE tools must be used. There is too much information to be organized and summarized to accomplish this without automated tools.

The tactical levels require analysis of work flows, material flows, and information flows, both within a functional area and across interface boundaries, to ensure that the overall objectives (e.g., order to delivery within five days) are accomplished. This results in a more detailed definition of how the major processes will be conducted.

Once this is accomplished, business management can then begin the detailed operational design of its organization, procedures, facilities, etc., and IS management can design the application systems.

Since this IS effort is more time consuming than the business management's efforts (i.e., it takes longer to develop, test, and implement a system than hire a person), some compromise may be required. There are many alternatives possible to address this issue—one is the use of package software; others are to use existing systems or develop only core functionality. Since these decisions are structural in nature, they can be addressed strategically, but they must be reviewed and assessed as the operational design progresses.

BUSINESS PROCESS SELECTION

Potential Benefits of Business Reengineering

The potential benefits of a business process improvement effort can generally be classified in the categories of cost, quality, and time:

Costs:

Reduce costs
Improve use of resources

Quality:

Reduce defect levels
Improve customer service

Time:

Reduce development cycle time
Reduce delivery cycle time

Because we often approach these issues as consumers, we expect tradeoffs between these values. The consumer often approaches the market at a single point in time. The market establishes the value of items for sale to create trade-offs. A more expensive car has more features or is better made; a meal is served more rapidly but is lower quality; a means of transportation gets you there quicker and costs more money. However, a producer may be in the market over a long period. Over time, cars, computers and other products have developed more features and less defects, but are faster and cheaper. By exploiting the right enabling technology, a business may drive steps out of a process, reducing the time it takes and reducing opportunities for error. Quality is improved at lower time and cost.

While a look at the business processes at some level never hurts, a serious attempt to reengineer the business is expensive and will not bring short-term results. Industry leaders will do it to maintain and improve their competitive advantage; new entrants or failing competitors will do it to change the ground on which a battle is fought, moving it to their own core competencies, for instance. The following are indicators of a need:

- user dissatisfaction with information systems—systems may not be aligned with needs of business
- poor competitive position, evidenced by loss of market share or by loss of business to lower-priced or faster-responding competitors
- response to change at competitors
- poor communication between different functions (e.g., departments)
- after rapid growth or entry into new market area, systems may be outgrown or inappropriate
- after acquisition or merger, systems will probably contain large-scale redundancies

Any large TQM effort or large MIS development or replacement project should be examined to see if it is a reengineering opportunity in disguise.

Transformation or Improvement

The effort involved to create a new business process based on new technology and ways of thinking can be very substantial. For this reason, there is much emphasis on dramatic benefits. Many reengineering efforts aim for transformation to achieve quantum leaps in performance, not incremental improvement.

> Reengineering: "The fundamental rethinking and radical redesign of an entire business system to achieve dramatic improvements in critical measures of performance."
>
> — Michael Hammer

However, it is often possible to achieve valuable, less dramatic gains through a more incremental approach. This is an issue of available resources and of judgment. (See Figure 4.1.)

Overview of the Approach

In this section, we focus on the business process redesign phase. This is often preceded by conceptual reengineering and is always followed by implementation.

Before the project, management must prioritize and select the processes for analysis and design in the following phases. This is often driven by recognition of areas critical to the business. Examples are:

- losing market share
- changing product mix
- customer complaints
- competition is faster to market
- product or service costs too much
- processes take too long

Typically, we prefer to focus the improvement on processes most critical to future business success and on the one critical issue. One important issue is much more effective than a laundry list of vague "apple pie" objectives. Figure 4.2 summarizes the redesign objectives.

Chapter 4 • Reengineering the Business Process

Process Capability ↑

Transformation
- more expensive
- radical change
- quantum leaps in performance
- break everything
- benchmark and brainstorm
- exploit change enablers

Improvement
- less expensive
- incremental change
- 10 to 25% improvement
- fix what's broken
- analyze current process, staff
- keep culture, org, technology

Time →

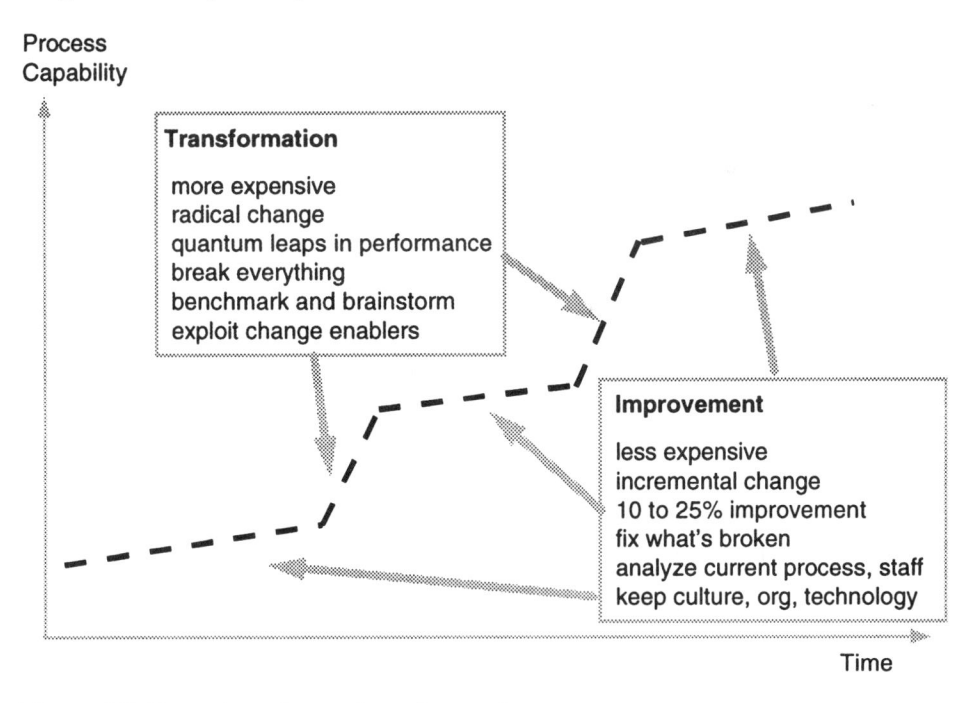

Figure 4.1 Reengineering and continuous improvement

- Transform an area of the business using information technology as an enabler
- Process generally crosses organization boundaries inside and outside the enterprise
- Radically reduce
  - cycle time
  - costs
  - defect levels

Figure 4.2 Redesign objectives and scope

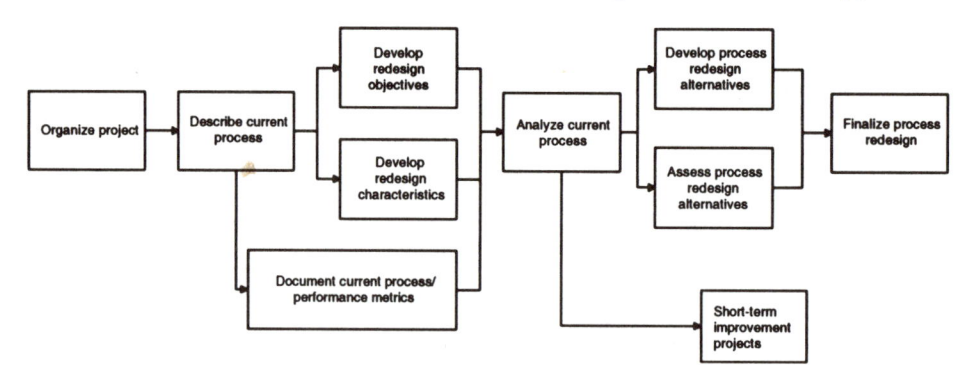

Figure 4.3 Process redesign roadmap

It is important to review the prioritized processes against the risk factors and payback possibilities. In particular:

1. What is the business need?
2. What tangible payback will be achieved?
3. How difficult is the system to build?
4. Can the organization accept the change?

It is not the case that every organization and process are ready for radical change. (See Figure 4.3.)

The deliverables from a process redesign project include the following.

- Project scope (redesigned process boundaries)
- Current process flow
- Redesign objectives
- Redesign characteristics
- Current process performance metrics
- Problems with current process
- Redesign alternatives with strengths and weaknesses
- Redesigned process:
    —objectives

    —characteristics

    —process flow, with activities and cycle times

    —policies, with assumptions, practices, and documented changes

    —process model

    —high-level data model

Organize the Project

At this stage, the objectives are to:

- establish the process boundaries
- develop the detailed project work plan
- finalize the project team
- determine workshop participants
- conduct the kickoff

The team may begin with a roundtable discussion with the sponsoring management on the business scope and goals and a workshop on the techniques being followed, or they may meet with each member of the management team one on one.

For the kickoff, background material should be assembled and reviewed. This should include:

- organizational chart
- financial information, such as budgets
- recent management reports, particularly of problems or changes
- system documentation
- strategic plan (business goals, CSFs)

Describe the Current Process

After examining the background material and meeting with the project sponsor, a preliminary business process model is developed. The objective of this step is to document the processes within the project scope, document the staff required by each process, and prioritize and select the processes for following phases.

We generally use generic business process models, if available; if not, we will develop a "straw man" model. Existing process specifications and procedures documentation should be available and reviewed by the team.

We conduct a series of facilitated sessions to develop the business process model. We typically begin departmentally, for example, by asking an individual from each department represented to list the 10 or less "major things done by their department." After every department has done this, we begin to ask the group to link these "things" together, forming 10 or less processes. Everyone in the room should agree on the processes identified. While facilitating the session, we refer to the generic business process models ("straw men") to ask the "right" questions to ensure that no processes are missed.

A top-down approach is used to develop the model. It is particularly important that all of the client individuals involved in the development of the model agree to and understand the model, because the time estimates and the rest of the project will be based on it. It is critical for the project team to review the model before the time estimates are applied to it. This will allow them to make minor modifications to eliminate "problem" processes and/or individuals from the scope of the remaining portion of the project.

Develop Redesign Objectives

In this activity, we review the operating vision and determine the objectives. This phase starts from a "blank sheet" with regard to existing processes. The object is to develop an understanding of:

- the goals and objectives of the business area
- management concerns and ideas on opportunities for improvement
- the context, including other business areas and projects
- customer requirements and perceptions, particularly what constitutes value to the customer
- the goals of this process
- change targets (i.e., cost reduction, quality improvement, cycle time reduction)

Develop Redesign Characteristics

This activity also starts from a "blank sheet" inspired by the operating vision. We review industry and competitive benchmarks. We identify relevant enablers, which include technology and organizational design. We then design at a high level the characteristics and principles of operation. (See Figure 4.4.)

Document the Current Process and Performance Metrics

This activity prepares the baseline against which redesign alternatives are assessed. It is the basis for future introduction of change and ensures in detail that all of the current activities are accounted for. This review should not be too extensive, but it must extend across boundaries to customers and suppliers and should include an understanding of the current policies and culture.

> - ◆ Distributed systems
>   - Department, portable, at customers, groupware
> - ◆ Better interfaces
>   - image, video output, speech/writing recognition
> - ◆ Computerized support of performance
>   - pricing, catalogs, call distribution, help-desk, knowledge-based systems
> - ◆ Electronic commerce (EDI/ EFT)
>   - eliminating data entry, making markets
> - ◆ New forms of publishing
>   - desktop publishing/video, interactive video services, on-line databases, CD-ROM publishing

Figure 4.4 Sample enablers for reengineering

Analyze the Current Business Process

Analysis is entered after the redesign objectives and approaches have been identified and completed before the actual redesign begins. This activity completes and demonstrates the understanding of the current process. This ensures that current problems will not be repeated in the new design. A byproduct of this activity is a list of improvements that can be implemented in the short term.

In this phase, after training the team and scheduling the work, we chart the activities for each chosen process, document cycle time and costs, and identify gaps and root causes. For each process, we identify and classify each activity/task. We determine the time spent on each activity/task by individuals and document the average cycle time of each process. The process is assessed against the objectives and characteristics of the redesign that has been prepared. Current policies, organization, and information technology are reviewed with a view to change.

Analysis includes a review and identification of current problems, including the following.

Organizational Level

Goals of different functions may be in conflict
Business policy may prevent a process from meeting the customer requirement

Sufficient resources may not be allocated to a function
No one may be responsible for a process

Process Level

Process steps may not be clearly defined
Steps in the process may add no value
No performance feedback may be available
Unnecessary steps may cause delay time
Unnecessary approvals may cause a bottleneck
A process may wait on necessary inputs
Outputs of a process may not be what are needed

Individual Level

Individual goals may conflict with process goals (e.g., compensation, quotas)
The individual may not have necessary resources
The individual may not have necessary knowledge or skill

Some of these problems may be resolvable without waiting for process redesign. These short-term improvements are identified at this time.

In some organizations, there will be pressure to rush past this step to the redesign. Why document it when it is going away? It is a mistake to short-circuit this step. The current activities and their problems must be well understood.

Develop Process Redesign Alternatives

Simply stated, the goal of this activity is to develop and document the design possibilities that can achieve the redesign objectives. This is the heart of the effort, requiring experience, knowledge, and creativity. The team must brainstorm, constantly asking, "Why do we?" and "What if we?"

The direction of the design is driven by benchmarking in some cases, by the operating vision in others, or it may come out of a technology. The most important quality initially is an open attitude; later, design rigor becomes more important as the activities and process flow are mapped and modeled with cycle times.

An obsession with the needs of the customer is essential to this process. Participants must be able to think with the viewpoint of the customer; including customers is often a way to achieve this. A key role of the consultant or facilitator at this point is the "fresh view," secure from internal pressures. As an objective third party, the facilitator can propose new solutions where appropriate, even if such solutions differ dramatically from the current approach.

Assess Redesign Alternatives

The redesign alternatives are assessed, with strengths and weaknesses. This is often an economic decision; it may also be one of timing, since some changes are very disruptive and expensive, and there are limits to organizational change.

Finalize Redesign

In this activity, the redesign is selected, then reviewed and finalized. During this step, changes to the current organization and work flows are identified and validated. Current processes are reengineered to reduce functional redundancies and fragmentation. Deficiencies and limitations in the current environment are identified and resolved. Then the overall plan for implementation is sketched out. The design is presented, and the organization moves on to implementation.

The Selection Process

At this stage, the objective is to discover the best opportunities for improvement for the company. The team may begin with a roundtable discussion with the sponsoring management on the business goals and a workshop on the techniques being followed, or they may meet with each member of the management team one on one. The object in selection is to develop an understanding of:

- the goals and objectives of the business area
- existing staffing, costs, and performance measures
- management concerns and ideas on opportunities for improvement
- purpose of the project (i.e., cost reduction, quality improvement, cycle time reduction)
- context, including other business areas and projects

and to develop an approved work plan for subsequent phases.

In this phase, the team will document the processes within the project scope, the work flow through those processes, and the people and resources required by each process. They will prioritize and select the processes for analysis and design in the following phases.

For the kickoff, background material should be assembled and reviewed. This should include:

- organizational chart
- financial information, such as budgets
- recent management reports, particularly of problems or changes
- system documentation
- strategic plan (business goals, CSFs)

Examples of critical issues include:

- losing market share
- changing product mix
- customer complaints
- competition is faster to market
- product or service costs too much
- processes have a long cycle time

Focus the improvement on processes most critical to future business success. Which is the one critical issue? One important issue is much more effective than a laundry list of vague "apple pie" objectives.

If the expectation for the project is to reduce head count, the positioning of the project should be discussed very carefully. This type of expectation makes acceptance of the project by other client personnel particularly difficult.

BUSINESS MODELING

After examining the background material and meeting with the project sponsor, a preliminary business process model should be developed. The objective of this step is to document the processes within the project scope, document the staff required by each process, and prioritize and select the processes for the following phases.

Generic business process models should be used, if available; if not, attempt to develop a "straw man" model. Existing process specifications and procedures documentation should be available and reviewed by the team.

Conduct one or more facilitated sessions to develop the business process model. Begin departmentally, by asking an individual from each department

Chapter 4 • Reengineering the Business Process

represented to list the 10 or less "major things done by their department." After every department has done this, begin to ask the group to link these "things" together, forming 10 or less processes. Everyone in the room should agree on the processes identified. While facilitating the session, refer to the generic business process models ("straw men") to ask the "right" questions to ensure that no processes are missed.

A top-down approach should be used to develop the business process model. It is particularly important that all of the client individuals involved in the development of the model agree to and understand the model, because the time estimates and the rest of the project will be based on it. It is critical for the project team to review the model before the time estimates are applied to it. This will allow them to make minor modifications to eliminate "problem" processes and/or individuals from the scope of the remaining portion of the project.

After the development of the model, meet briefly with a "systems" person to:

- gain a systems perspective on the model
- identify any areas "missed" during the development of the model
- obtain an "outsider's" perspective on the processes

Conduct one or more additional facilitated sessions to obtain final agreement on the model. Whenever possible, limit the number of participants in a facilitated session to less than 10. These sessions may also be used to estimate the staff by process and by department, completing a process/resource matrix.

After the session(s), finalize the process/resource matrix and create a preliminary list of prioritized processes based on the items discussed with the project sponsor and the management team. Conduct a final session with the management team to prioritize and select the processes, facilitating the discussion with the preliminary list.

After the meeting, review the prioritized processes and score them, considering the risk factors and payback possibilities. In particular:

- What is the business need?
- What tangible payback will be achieved?
- How difficult is the system to build?
- Can the organization accept the change?

Review and finalize the model and the prioritized processes.

If other opportunities for improvement are uncovered, they should be addressed. Not everything needs a system, or even a design.

This type of work is generally best performed by two people; at least one should have done it before several times. It can take two to four weeks.

BUSINESS PROCESS ANALYSIS

In this phase, after training the team and scheduling the work, we chart the activities for each chosen process, document cycle time and costs, and identify gaps and root causes. For each process, we identify the activity/task flow. We classify each activity/task into activity classifications. We determine time spent on each activity/task by individuals and document the average cycle time of each process. We identify process and activity drivers and performance measures for each process.

Education and Scheduling

The objective of this step is to identify the key individuals for participation in this phase, kick off the involved portion of the organization, provide basic education on process improvement, schedule the walkthroughs and facilitated sessions, and continue to identify performance measures currently in place.

The team meets with the project sponsor and, optionally, with his/her management team to clarify these objectives. Then, they conduct the kick-off/education meeting to provide the involved client personnel with a better understanding of the process.

1. The client individuals involved in this phase should be the people who actually perform the work in the processes and, perhaps, their direct supervisors. However, the facilitated sessions should be limited to 10 or less people whenever possible. Therefore, consider including different people in the walkthroughs and facilitated sessions.
2. Finalize the schedule for all facilitated sessions at this point. The schedule should correspond to the project budget. As the project progresses, if the client cannot meet the schedule, this will allow for schedule and budget adjustments.

Activity/Task Identification

The objectives of this step are to document the activity/task flow for each process; classify each activity/task into activity classifications; identify the departments and individuals responsible for each activity/task; document

Chapter 4 • Reengineering the Business Process

the average cycle time of each process; document process drivers, activity drivers, and action plans as they are discussed; and understand the inputs, outputs, and customers of each process.

First, review the organizational chart, process specifications, procedures documentation, and job descriptions, if provided, to gain a better understanding of each process.

Conduct process walkthroughs to:

- gain a basic understanding of each process
- meet some of the participants of the facilitated sessions
- "set the stage" for the facilitated sessions
- develop initial ideas for action plans, process drivers, activity drivers, and performance measures

Conduct one or more facilitated sessions for each process. During each session, document the process flow and activities/tasks into process flow charts. When each process flow is completed, review the flow with the group, documenting:

- activity/task classifications
- department responsible by activity/task
- individual responsible by activity/task
- average process cycle time

At the end of each session, explain that one of the purposes of the next session will be to gather the amount of time spent on each activity by individual by the cycle time of the process. Indicate that a "cleaned-up" version of the process flow charts will be distributed to the individuals who are involved in the process. The purpose of distributing the flow charts is to have people think through and document the amount of time they spend on each activity and to have them bring the information to the next session in order to facilitate the discussions.

After each facilitated session, finalize the process flow charts in deliverable format. When they are distributed, clear instructions should be included detailing how the time should be documented (i.e., by activity or by average cycle time). Also, prepare slides at the appropriate level of detail for the final presentation.

1. It is particularly important to capture all action plans that are/will be implemented during the duration of the project. The final presentation will be more powerful if these action plans can be captured and quantified.

2. Remember, time estimates should include all client personnel involved in the processes, not just the individuals involved in the facilitated sessions.

Detailed Analysis

The objectives of this step are to determine the time spent on each activity/task by individual, identify the process and activity drivers, and identify performance measures for each process.

Gather the background material: relevant process cycle times, departmental goals and objectives, and current performance measures.

Conduct one or more facilitated sessions for each process. During each session, review the process flow chart, documenting the time spent on each activity by classification. Capture the activity drivers by asking the group for the reasons and/or problems preventing the process from working as it would in the "perfect world," only performing the activities that the "customer" finds valuable.

Document the activity drivers by category, and capture the time associated with each.

As the group identifies the drivers, begin to identify potential performance measures. Explain the importance of performance measures and their relationship to the drivers. Performance measures should be identified activity by activity, documenting measures of all inputs, outputs, and activities. The performance measure list should reference related activity driver detail whenever possible.

Use the list of current performance measures to "prompt" the group. Also use the conceptual model of inputs, processes, and outputs. Remember, performance measures should measure quality, timeliness, and productivity.

After each facilitated session, update the process flow charts adding the dimension of time categorized as value added and nonvalue added. Remember to verify the time estimates against the process time estimates from Phase I, and check the estimates by individual for reasonableness.

1. The departmental goals and objectives may be useful in developing performance measures.
2. Process cost charts are important client deliverables because they graphically depict the processes as the client will remember them from the sales "pitch."

Process Flow Chart Guidelines

1. Use the following "rules" to define activities when drawing a flow chart:
   - a new activity should be created whenever responsibility crosses departmental lines or job titles (individuals)
   - an activity should have only one significant output
   - an activity should fall under only one activity classification
   - an activity should require no more than five tasks as detail explanation

2. The flow chart mainline should depict the process if "all input was right and on time" and "everything was done right the first time." In other words, include activities classified as "conversion," "quality," "reporting," and "rework" on the mainline, and show "rework" activities branching off the mainline.

   Ultimately, the action plans will be developed to minimize/optimize the mainline activities and to eliminate the "rework" activities.

3. Whenever possible, try to limit the number of activities to 12 on one process flow chart. If the chart becomes too complicated, consider drawing separate charts by subprocess.

4. For complicated activities, consider conducting a separate facilitated session to further model the activities using Information Engineering techniques.

BUSINESS PROCESS DESIGN

In process design, we ask the questions "why do we?" and "what if we?". We collect ideas for improvement by benchmarking and brainstorming. The intention is to develop a shared vision of the goals of the process, then use that to drive through change. The participants should feel secure from internal pressures, which is easier said than done. Some external participants may be needed to support this. Moving quickly and spending time off-site can help.

At the end of process design, action plans are identified and prioritized. These plans specifically reduce or eliminate activities which are not adding value, optimize the value-added activities, develop a performance measurement portfolio, and plan for monitoring the processes after implementation.

Design Alternatives Direction

The objectives of this step are to identify design alternative participants, develop a "direction" for action plans, and establish the extent of use of benchmark and enabling technology information.

First, meet with the client project sponsor to identify the design alternatives participants and the overall goals of the sessions.

Then, meet with functional experts to:

- review the detailed work products from the previous phase
- identify and document the "direction" for the action plans
- establish profiles of benchmarking candidates

Benchmarking

The objectives of this step are to establish benchmarking partners, collect information from them, analyze this information, and publish it to the design team.

First, meet with functional experts to agree on selected candidates.

Determine required information and collection approach.

Design data collection materials and tactics, e.g., questionnaire and interview.

Identify benchmarking partner contacts, schedule data-gathering activities.

Collect benchmarking data.

Collate and analyze benchmarking results to produce the report.

Benchmarking should be confined to carefully-prepared research into narrowly defined processes. It should not be confused with "fishing expeditions." It should look for enabling ideas; technology, organization, training. There are costs and risks to benchmarking. The most likely problem is failure to find anything of value; benchmarking trips take a great deal of money and time. Also, in businesses where new processes take a long time to be introduced, simply catching up to the state of the art may not be an adequate goal. The most expensive problem is the adoption of inappropriate ideas, or partial adoption of concepts in the wrong context.

Alternatives to benchmarking include the use of experienced consultants in the process or industry, and hiring permanent staff with the expertise.

Brainstorming

All participants should understand the company, its customers, and its operating vision. The work products from the prior phase are reviewed, and the benchmarking information available is organized. Brainstorming candidates are selected. The right balance is important. Creative thinkers are preferred, plus those with knowledge of enabling technologies and processes. Breakthroughs generally come from technology, so technology experts should be there throughout the endeavor, not just at the end. All of the following are technologies that can enable fundamental change:

- client/server systems
- object-oriented design
- EDI/EFT
- Portable computers
- Imaging and document management
- Mail-enabled applications
- digital multimedia
- high-speed wide-area networks
- information publishing.

Direction should be based on the established goals of the project, particularly performance gaps. Typical measurement targets are ROI, cost of production, cycle time, customer expectations, resource usage.

The objective of this step is to brainstorm action plans to address the process and activity drivers.

Distribute the business analysis and benchmarking materials for them to review and develop preliminary actions prior to the brainstorming sessions.

Conduct the high-level brainstorming session and document identified action plans. During this session, the Process Driver Detail should be used and mapped to the action plans. The functional expert and key client decision makers should participate in this session.

Conduct the brainstorming session(s) with the client management team and individuals in the selected processes.

There should be a separate brainstorming session for each process. In addition, there should be a higher-level brainstorming session to address primary drivers.

Rules for Brainstorming

1. One idea per person
2. Pass if no idea
3. "Piggybacking" ideas is OK
4. No criticism or comments
5. Judging after
6. Freewheeling
7. Laughter OK/No ridicule

Action Prioritization and Scheduling

In this step, the objectives are to finalize the action portfolio, quantify savings by action plan, and develop an implementation plan.

Review action plans from the brainstorming sessions and put them into a format that will be easy for the client to review. Also, develop preliminary savings for each action plan, and document the assumptions used to estimate the savings.

Distribute this preliminary action portfolio to the client project sponsor and management team to:

- delete actions that will not be considered
- consolidate action plans where appropriate
- review estimated savings for each action plan

Meet with the client project sponsor and management team to review their input and categorize the preliminary action portfolio. Examples of action plan categories include:

- action plans in progress
- action plans to be scheduled and implemented
- action plans outside of the client's control
- action plans affecting current organization
- action plans to be considered in the future

Chapter 4 • Reengineering the Business Process

Most importantly in this meeting, work with the client to obtain agreement and buy in on action plan savings.

Based on the results from this meeting, finalize the portfolio in deliverable format and distribute it to the client project sponsor and management team to begin developing the implementation plan by:

- estimating implementation time frame and benefit recognition
- identifying cost and resources to implement
- identifying performance measures by action plan

Meet with the client sponsor and management team to complete the Implementation Plan. Start and completion dates, required resources, and timing of estimated savings should be documented.

Complete the action portfolio, target process cost charts, and benefit chart in deliverable format.

Summary

Get and sustain commitment from senior management.

Set specific objectives, not vague ones like "improving quality". Know and address the critical success factors for the business area. Select specific processes which impact the customer and set specific stretch goals.

Never select the technology first and force-fit it, even if it's what you know. Also, many problems are not solved with technology.

Don't design systems to avoid conflicts between business functions.

Don't assume that users can tell you exactly what they need.

Don't try to do everything at once. Fix some real problems quickly. Build support as you go. Structure big projects to deliver visible payoffs along the way.

Start from customer needs and work backwards. Don't simply automate the existing procedures, and don't accept incremental improvement where real change is possible. Do test radical ideas or approaches with prototypes.

5

Selecting the New Architecture

DEFINITION OF CLIENT/SERVER ARCHITECTURE

The term client/server is used broadly in our industry by many different people to refer to a number of different system implementations or models. In the first chapter, we discussed how a loose definition of client/server relates to various other terms, such as open systems, distributed databases, networked systems, Windows systems, downsizing, and rapid development. Let's review our working definition from Chapter 1: *A client/server application is an application developed so that parts of it can be run on different computers.*

Note the following points, which expand on this definition.

- An application is client/server, not a hardware configuration.
- An application has to be developed specifically to be client/server, i.e., to run on different systems.
- The application does not have to run on different computers in any specific instance; it has to be able to do so in general.
- An open client/server application is a client/server application that easily can be made to run on a variety of computers from different manufacturers; the more the variety, the more open the application.
- An open client/server architecture is an architecture that supports the development of open client/server applications.

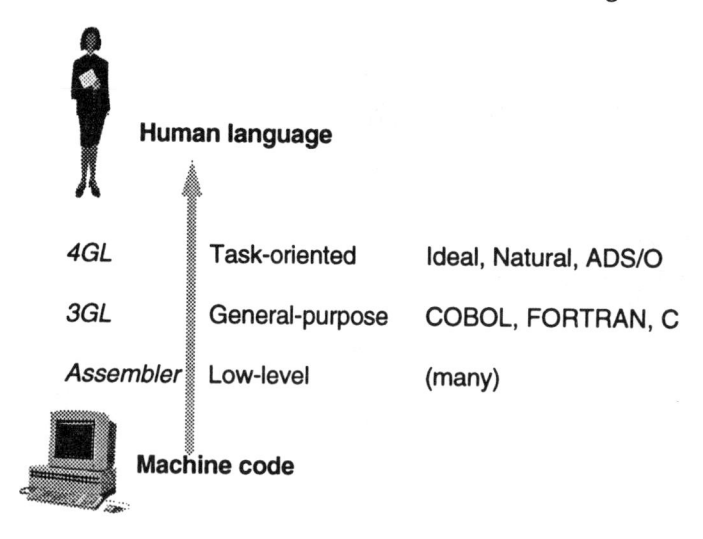

4GL	Task-oriented	Ideal, Natural, ADS/O
3GL	General-purpose	COBOL, FORTRAN, C
Assembler	Low-level	(many)

Human language ↑ Machine code

Figure 5.1 Language evolution

Development of Languages and Interfaces

Figure 5.1 shows development of languages from the earliest (machine code) to progressively higher levels of abstraction. Our systems are getting very large and complex. Progress in this direction now seems to rely on object-oriented approaches to reduce the complexity that must be dealt with and graphical interfaces to improve navigation through what remains.

Figure 5.2 shows the communication possibilities in a client/server system. The application and its logic, expressed in a programming language, communicate with databases, other computer systems over networks, other applications, and the user, all through interfaces. In addition, users can communicate with each other using the same technology, using computer-mediated forms such as voicemail, e-mail, and teleconferencing. All of these areas are becoming standardized, which is enabling a component model of systems.

In enterprise business systems, there have been three waves of systems, broadly corresponding with the 1970s, 80s, and 90s. They are batch, online, and client/server. The batch system is pictured in Figure 5.3. Data is processed in a serial manner, using serial files. The user interface is stacked punched cards and reports. The languages of the day had built-in support for this model. The online system (see Figure 5.4) offers direct access. The user accesses the system with forms on the screen, and data is accesses through indexed file systems and early databases. The languages of the

Chapter 5 • Selecting the New Architecture

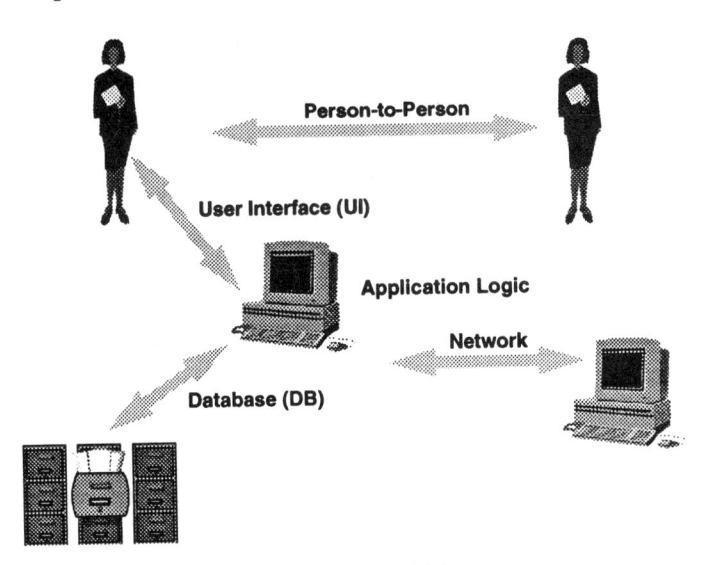

Figure 5.2 Communication possibilities

batch model were extended with extra syntax for these functions (CICS-VSAM or DL/I, IMS DB/DC, DEC FMS/RMS). Later, new fourth-generation languages (4gls) were introduced to simplify business applications, such as Focus, Ideal, and Natural. The client/server system (see Figure 5.5) ex-

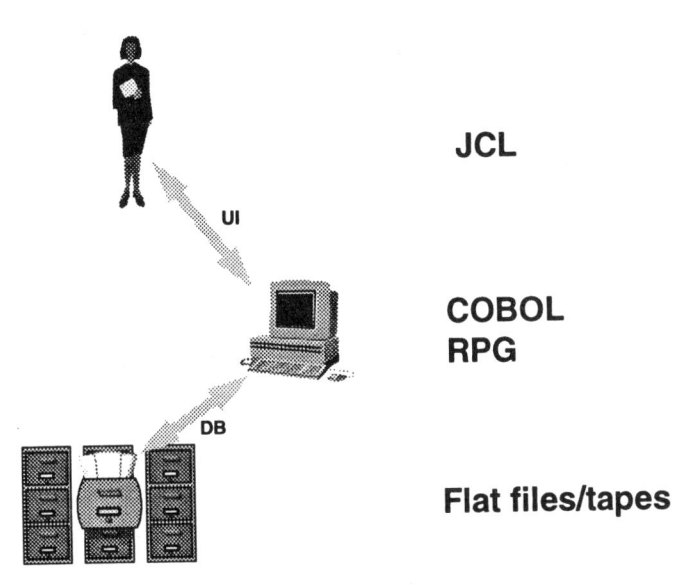

Figure 5.3 Batch layers

CICS

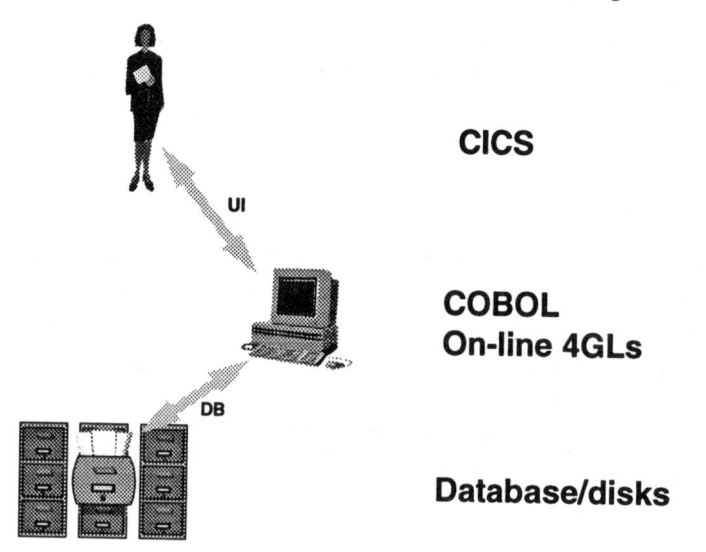

**COBOL
On-line 4GLs**

Database/disks

Figure 5.4 Online layers

tends the system to allow access to data and functions from different application areas, at the user's discretion. A new user interface using multiple windows, pointing, and graphics and new databases allowing access to data independently of the application have been introduced. It has not proved practical to extend Cobol, Fortran, or the 4gls to accomodate these exten-

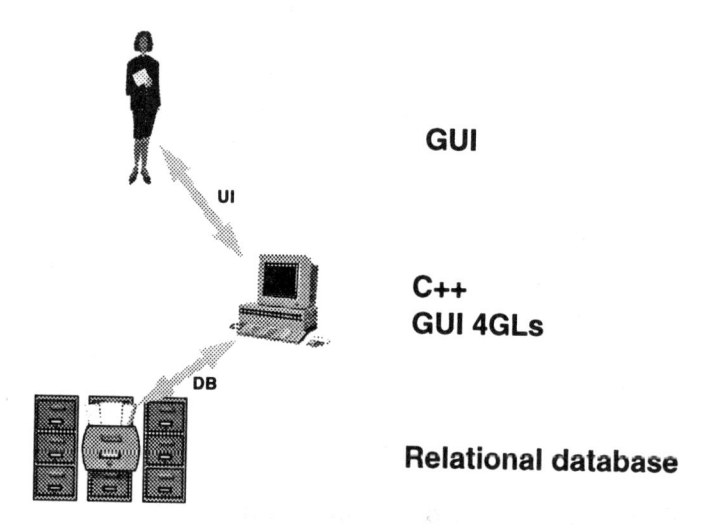

GUI

**C++
GUI 4GLs**

Relational database

Figure 5.5 Client/server layers

Chapter 5 • Selecting the New Architecture

sions, and new languages have been introduced. Experience with the last of these transitions leads us to believe that the process of absorbing this change will take many years.

Decomposing an Application

The key point of a client/server architecture is to decide on how the application is to be broken into parts and on the manner in which the parts will be assigned to different computers. A good architecture will allow the different components to exploit the characteristics of the platforms they run on—for example, fast color display workstations or fault-tolerant servers.

What the parts of an application are is very dependent on the specific nature of the application. There are, however, three common parts of business systems that almost always occur, so that the majority of business systems can be considered as having three layers.

User Interface Layer: Accepts input from and presents information to the user on the user interface device, usually a screen.

Application Logic Layer: Performs the core business processing of the application, including performing calculations, applying rules, producing graphics, and other functions.

Data Management Layer: Manages the database(s) used by the application, including consistency checking, storing data, checking database query syntax, accessing database records, and retrieving database records that meet the user's selection criteria.

In a monolithic system, such as the typical mainframe systems developed in most commercial environments, these layers generally all run on the same computer. In a CICS application, for example, a program module may contain user interface code, database management code, and application logic all intertwined together.

Some application architectures will separate the functions, even for a monolithic system. For example, the Tandem architecture includes client and server software modules generally running on the same host; this facilitates reconfiguration of the software for a distributed environment. You can use an application architecture that divides database access, user interface, and the application processing logic rigidly into separate modules, even when building a single mainframe system.

In a client/server application, these components will be distributed between different processors. A popular way to differentiate client/server systems, published by the Gartner Group in 1991, distinguishes five separate models based on how these three layers of an application are partitioned between the client and the server. This is a good place to begin, recognizing that there is much more to the architectural decision than this partitioning.

Distributed Presentation

In this approach, the presentation layer is distributed between client and server, or duplicated between them (see Figure 5.6). A common situation is where existing applications on the host are enhanced with micro-based front ends. This is often called a "facelift" or "wallpaper" solution. Products such as Easel, Knowledgeware Flashpoint, and Mozart employ this model, which, in a mainframe environment, is generally based on the IBM Extended High-Level Language Application Programming Interface (EHLLAPI). The mainframe contains all of the code to display an application at a 3270 terminal, and the front-end system contains code to pick apart the terminal stream and display it on a graphical workstation with radio buttons, pop-up menus, and so on.

While useful, this does not offer the benefits of a true client/server approach. The application is not partitioned; instead, the host presentation

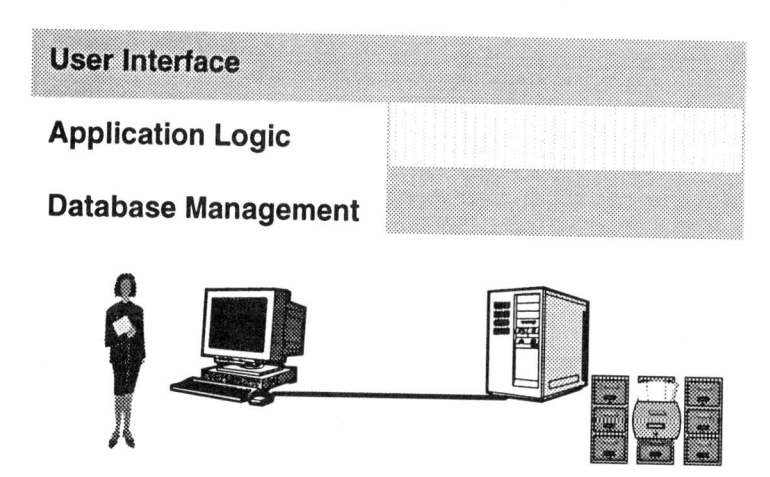

Figure 5.6 Distributed presentation

services are replicated at the workstation. It can be a useful means of introducing the ease of use and standardization of a GUI to a user area. Such an approach can be used as a LAN is introduced to support access to a range of legacy systems, for example. In the long run, this approach is generally supplemented, then replaced, with a tool that allows more application logic at the front end. This is why Easel also offers Enfin, and Knowledgeware offers ObjectView.

Remote Presentation

In this approach, the client machine performs all of the presentation services (see Figure 5.7). The X Windows System on UNIX lies somewhere between the remote and distributed presentation models, since not all presentation logic actually runs on the client, but it can be considered an example. For new applications, Easel and Mozart can be used to develop applications using this model, because the host system can be developed without a significant presentation layer.

The advantage of this approach is that it can exploit a certain amount of the power of the workstation, off-loading cycles from the central system, without leading to the issues raised by distributed application logic, such as version control and security. On the other hand, it leaves most of the application processing on the host. This is another intermediate step towards the benefits of client/server.

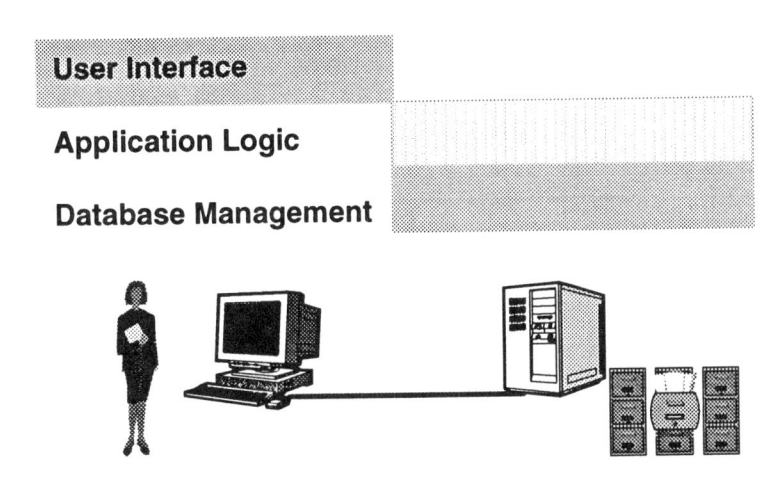

Figure 5.7 Remote presentation

Distributed Processing

This is the purest, most desirable client/server model. It is also the most flexible; if you can control the distribution of application logic, you can design a Remote Presentation or Remote Data Management system within this model. This meets the definition above, because it gives the freedom to distribute the parts of the application in what is usually the most appropriate manner. (See Figure 5.8.)

Ideally, you should be able to develop the code for an application with a single model and language, then select the implementation environment and distribute the logic between different platforms to suit your needs. Today, there are very few commercial 4GL application development products that implement this model. The Cooperative Solutions Ellipse product was one example, although this is not on the market now. Over the next two years, we can expect great advances in this area.

It is possible to build products using, for instance, C, which follow this model. This can be done using a network-specific API, such as TCP/IP sockets, or a set of distributed services based around a remote procedure call. The choices today are the ONC and OSF/DCE frameworks or tools such as UCS and Galaxy.

It is possible to distribute some application logic to the server using stored procedures or triggers. This is the approach pioneered by Sybase and now available on many database products. This is a hybrid between distributed

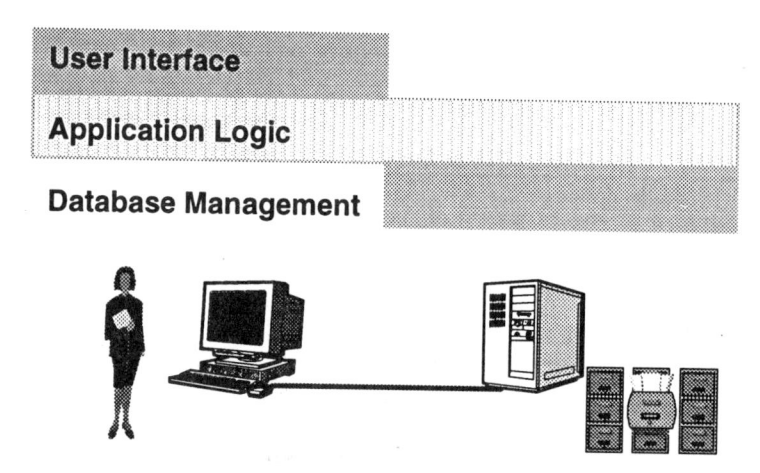

Figure 5.8 Distributed logic

Chapter 5 • Selecting the New Architecture

logic and remote data management; the problem is that the application logic is written in two languages with two models.

Remote Data Access

In this model, the workstation runs the application, calling on the server for data (see Figure 5.9). This is the most well-understood client/server model today and the most common. Gartner Group estimates that this model is 80 percent of the client/server market. This model dominates because of the success of the relational databases (e.g., ORACLE, Informix, Sybase SQL Server), development tools (especially Windows development tools, such as PowerBuilder, SQLWindows, etc.), and middleware (e.g., ORACLE SQL*NET, Informix I-Star, Sybase Open Client) that are used to develop such applications.

The dividing line between remote data access and *distributed processing*, where the application logic is divided between the client and the server, is thin. For example, an SQL query statement may actually perform processing (e.g., the sum of two columns, the sum of a column for rows that can be grouped together, etc.) that could also be performed by the client application. The amount of processing that the RDBMS performs increases with the use of stored procedures and triggers to perform various functions, such as maintaining referential integrity of the database tables. Some applications

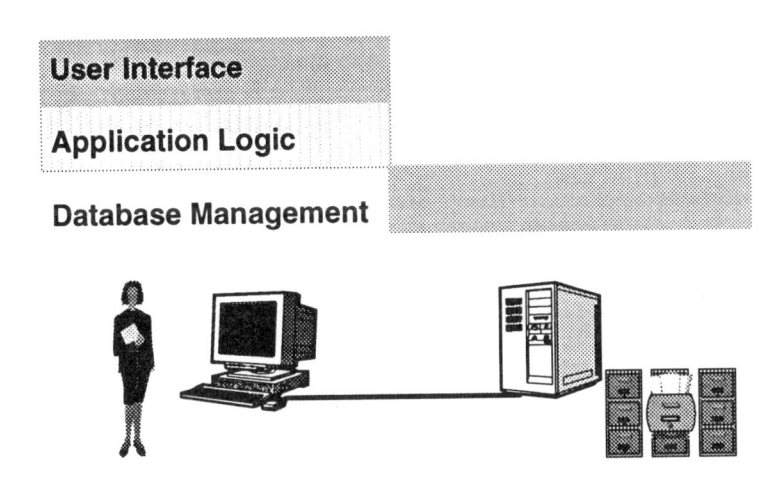

Figure 5.9 Remote data management

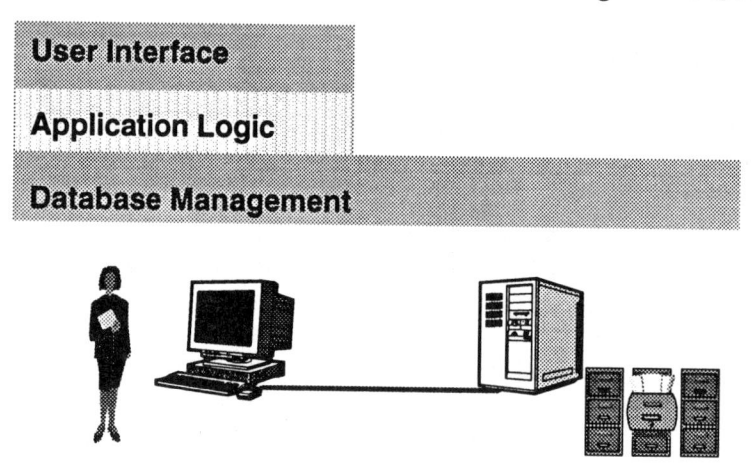

Figure 5.10 Distributed database

that use the database in this way may be considered to be distributed processing applications.

Distributed Database

Although this, the fifth of the Gartner categories (see Figure 5.10), is included for completeness, the distribution of database management across the network is the province of database companies. Their work is used by the commercial applications developer.

A Practical Approach to Architecture

This book focuses primarily on the remote data access model, because that is a well-proven way to build systems useful to everyone today. The first client/server applications that a company attempts should usually be remote data access, because the databases and 4GLs are stable and readily available. Remote data access is an ideal model for decision support and information display systems.

The distributed processing model, which is preferable for core business systems, is covered in less detail in this book. The tools and methodologies for fully exploiting this model are available today for sophisticated developers working in C or C++, although the standards are not established yet. The object models, 4GLs and CASE tools that will enable high productivity in commercial environments are still not commercially available.

A pragmatic approach for an organization developing an architecture is to define two intersecting architectures—one using the remote data access (RDA) model, to be employed today for empowerment systems, and one using the distributed processing (DP) model, to be updated and reviewed as standards and products are introduced and evolve. The RDA architecture will be based around a relational database management system and enterprise data model, with various tools and middleware interacting by channeling access through that core. The DP architecture will extend that center with an object-oriented set of reusable procedures and frameworks, allowing application components and tools to interact in a richer variety of ways.

ISSUES IN SELECTING CLIENT/SERVER TOOLS

In selecting the tools for client/server applications, we should consider the application systems they will be employed to produce, the environment where they will operate, and the intended technological direction of the business. Different tools are employed in different circumstances, for example:

- transactional versus decision support
- on-line versus batch
- end-user developed versus experienced developers

If the enterprise has a strategic plan for information technology, the overall direction, standards, and any planned new infrastructure should be considered. The current technical infrastructure of the enterprise includes:

- host computers and operating systems
- data communication networks
- databases and file formats
- client workstations
- development languages and tools
- skills of available developers and support staff

This affects the tools in two ways. First, not all tools can access all existing systems, so there may be constraints from a technical point of view. Second, the current developers may have a set of skills that indicates a particular type of tool. For example, a department that is currently using the Cincom tool Mantis and has developers skilled in it is more likely to consider a Cincom client/server toolset based on Mantis. A company that has several AS/400 systems is going to restrict its front-end tools to those which work well with the AS/400. An enterprise that has installed a great number of OS/2 workstations is going to select OS/2-based development tools. A company that is skilled at building transactional systems in COBOL is going to consider developing at least some of its client/server systems with a product such as Micro Focus COBOL.

There is a type of project that deliberately "pushes the envelope" of current technology. It is typically the product of a large enterprise working with one or more technology partners. These R&D projects may create new tools and methods as they go. They involve a great deal of risk and cost a great deal of money. The architecture selection for this type of project may be ground-breaking, involving untested or nonexistent tools. Often, the tools are selected on business grounds. An internal IBM project using an IBM-developed beta-test development tool would be an example; the project pays a penalty in excess risk for a good business reason. The relationship with the vendor makes a difference. A company with a close relationship with Microsoft might be a beta tester for their Exchange servers, for instance. The prerelease code may fail on occasion, but the vendor support will recover the situation. This type of project breaks all of the rules for tool selection. Most commercial projects, however, need to select a stable, well-tested set of tools. The following section discusses the procedures to do this.

Evaluating Tools

While tools should certainly be evaluated on technical grounds, particularly performance and the constraints of existing infrastructure, the most important considerations are not technical. The tool vendor should be regarded as a vital partner in the business of development over the long term. The true cost of a tool is the investment that your company makes in it, training your staff and implementing your business systems in it. If a tool acquisition is a success, it will be part of your environment for years, outliving the hardware it runs on and the staff who first adopted it.

When a technical evaluation of a tool is performed, two scenarios should be avoided. One is the gold-plated research project. At first, two or three tools are known, either from the current vendor or from reading the trade press. It seems that any of them could do the job, based on the initial criteria. Then, as the evaluators do their research, they learn of more tools. They spend several months reading materials and visiting shows. They develop a matrix of 46 tools against 63 technical criteria. And they uncover a surprise winner: a little-known foreign tool, perhaps, which has all the features of the market leader for half the price, or a new type of tool, which has an amazing demo and will go into beta test soon. This discovery justifies the long, expensive search. Two years later, the tool is obsolete and the search begins again.

A second scenario is "the devil you know." Again, at first, two or three tools are known, one of which is from the current vendor. The evaluation group is composed of developers familiar with that vendor, who go to the users' groups and read the newsletters. They compare the rosy glow of inside information on future plans from their known vendor with current or obsolete information on the competitors. As a consulting company, we often meet this scenario. To use an analogy, a client will be selecting between Acura, Lexus, Infiniti, and Hyundai. We politely point out that the Hyundai is outclassed in this competition; the answer is, "You obviously haven't signed the nondisclosure. Their new product, due in 1994, is going to turn the industry on its head."

In order to avoid these biases, which are very common, the following approach is recommended. Select up to four "best of breed" vendors in a category. They should be among the leaders in market share, defining the category broadly. Add no more than one "dark horse," based on published or local information, only if appropriate for some special reason. This should be a company that has the potential to develop into a market share leader soon, not an also-ran. Good "dark horse" selections in the past were ORACLE in 1983, Sybase in 1988, SQLWindows in 1991, and PowerBuilder in early 1992.

Consider the viability of the vendors and their products as separate equal critical factors in product selection. Examine the age, size, and prospects of the company and the age and sales of the product. Although a good product sometimes survives a shaky vendor, and a mediocre product is sometimes improved by a healthy vendor, the most common situation is market consolidation to two or three healthy vendors with the weaker going to the wall.

The strategic direction of the vendor and product may be important, although such directions can change.

Every vendor has a unique selling proposition, and for a financially weak or new company it will usually be a technology feature. The vendors always stress their new features as differentiators. It is no surprise that this can bias selection towards these glitzy features rather than the "meat and potatoes" issues; that is why they are there. The key points about new technology features are shown in the following list.

New Ideas

They don't generally work well when first released.

People don't know how to use them effectively for years.

Once they work well, the competition gets them too.

And, finally . . .

Better is the enemy of good enough.

In the database market, for example, we have had a series of technology features introduced, which, in sum, have made tremendous progress over the last 10 years. They include:

- relational technology
- SQL language
- query optimization
- declarative referential integrity
- stored procedures
- improving performance
- distributed databases

All of these improvements took more than one release to get right and took a long time for developers to exploit. All have been replicated widely after their introduction.

The leading vendors leapfrog each other, so that over time they stay in the same race. The leading five database vendors are the same now as five years ago, although their share has changed. In 1992, Sybase was regarded as the technical leader. In 1993, that position was held by ORACLE Version 7. If you are selecting an architecture for the long term, a temporary advantage in the leapfrogging race is much less important than other business factors. The evaluation should avoid scoring "nice to have" features introduced in the last few months, or about to be introduced, unless they are truly critical to the success of the project, but focus on the core requirements of the product.

One question to ask is, "How would we have done this project one year ago?" If the project relies on technology introduced to the market in the last year, it may be unacceptably risky.

While there is a value to standards, you should avoid a set of rules that forces all applications to employ the same database or tools. This can lose the advantage of open systems. In particular, you want to be free to buy the best components. The goal should be an architecture that allows you to buy or build using the "best of breed" choices. This may mean the best database management software, middleware, servers, workstations, and development tools. Or it may mean that your database standard is preventing you from getting the best of breed MRP or order-entry system. It may be of more use to make sure that the tools chosen can communicate in standard ways with others and that all products support a common desktop environment.

Portability

The architecture should support the development of applications whose components can be run on a variety of different types of computers from different manufacturers, exploiting the unique features of those systems.

Application components should be portable to the greatest possible extent. Experience has shown that nobody can predict which hardware and operating system platforms will survive in even the near future. Most applications that are successful outlive their original platform. While portability is difficult, these rules help.

1. Applications strictly separated into components are more portable than monolithic systems.
2. SQL databases are much easier to access than any other database format.
3. TCP/IP is the most portable communication standard.
4. The most portable development tools at any one time are the well-established 4GLs, but over long time periods they become obsolete.
5. The tools which are most reliably portable over long periods of time are standard languages, such as COBOL, C, C++, and FORTRAN, particularly if the application is structured into components, isolating user interface and database management.
6. UNIX is the single most likely operating system to survive, but it will change beyond recognition. The architecture should consider:
    - server hardware and operating systems
    - client hardware and operating systems
    - database management systems
    - networking standards
    - development languages and tools

- systems management tools
- interoperability and portability standards
- reliability, availability, and security standards.

These subjects will be covered in detail in the rest of this and the following chapters.

STANDARDS

Standards enable us to achieve connectivity and portability. Of course, *connectivity provides far less function and requires far more expertise than expected.*

Standards Offer Choices

There is general agreement that open systems are good, but little agreement on what they are. Many people have seen the word as synonymous with UNIX. UNIX users, in fact, tend to see adoption of a standard operating system, UNIX, as the way to achieve standards. Non-UNIX users are more likely to see a standard database or communications system as leading to open systems.

In practice, a system is open to the degree that it offers its owner choices. The set of de facto standards based on the IBM PC defines an open system today. In the PC market, components are standard commodities. You can purchase every component part from a multitude of vendors: disk drive, processor, operating system, applications software, case, power supply. This is almost equally true of DOS, OS/2, Windows NT, and SCO UNIX with regard to hardware. In software, DOS offers more choices than the other systems.

The standard can be set in one of three ways:

- by monopoly
- by distribution
- by agreement

Standards through Monopoly

Ironically, the choices that are enabled by open systems seem to have come from the near-monopoly positions that the developers of the IBM PC have established, particularly the Intel 80x86 series and Microsoft DOS and Windows. Because all the systems are assembled from key components provided by Intel and Microsoft, many vendors compete to perform the commodity service of assembly. They add value through various dimensions: the original

Compaq with portability, Texas Instruments with reduction in cost and size, Dell with a focus on direct marketing and customer service. On that commodity platform, the widest choice of application software ever is offered.

PostScript is another example of a standard based on a near-monopoly position. Because PostScript was, for a long time, the only good imaging language, all software and printers came to support it and it became a standard for desktop publishing.

Standards through Distribution

The UNIX operating system has long been open in another sense. Operating systems are very expensive to develop. Because UNIX was, for many years, distributed freely, it was the operating system of choice for a number of startup companies. These companies possibly could not have afforded to develop an operating system alone; worse, they would have had trouble persuading users to adopt one if they developed it. As history showed, even IBM and Microsoft together had trouble introducing a new operating system. UNIX thus became available on a variety of systems. Because the source code to the system was distributed widely, a number of individuals volunteered to improve it. This led to UNIX developing from a fairly simple, if elegant, system to a rich one with an unrivaled range of software tools.

The TCP/IP suite of networking software was developed through DoD funding in the 1970s. It became a standard after it was adopted in Berkeley UNIX and distributed in 4.1 and 4.2 BSD. It worked well and cost nothing, so it was quickly adopted on a widespread basis.

Sun Microsystems was formed by a group of bright young people from Stanford University. By using Berkeley UNIX and other standard components, they were able to build a powerful workstation on a shoestring budget. Sun then became a champion of a type of open system. They adopted technology where they could and invented it where they had to, and, in several cases, instead of using the technology to gain a proprietary advantage, they made it freely available, then made money by being the best or the first in the market. In this way, Sun capitalized on and introduced first UNIX, then TCP/IP, then NFS, and then the SPARC architecture.

NFS was the last time Sun was able to invent a software technology and succeed in defining a standard without competition. The Sun network-extensible windowing system, NeWS, was ahead of its time, but rather than allowing a competitor to set the standard, the other companies banded together to support the MIT-developed X Windows System. X is also a system that has become a standard, because it is freely distributed.

Standards by Agreement

Initially, most computer companies were not in favor of open standards. However, if standards were to be set, the companies preferred a level playing field to one where the rules were set by Sun. Many people say that the Open Software Foundation (OSF) was motivated by a desire to replace unilateral innovation from companies such as Sun with a level playing field process managed by the vendors together. And it is a fact that the OSF choices have tended not to include the Sun technology, by and large.

OSF has introduced a number of proposed standards, to date:

- OSF/Motif
- OSF/1
- OSF/DCE
- OSF/DME
- ANDF

The OSF offerings have met with limited success to date. Motif is the standard in the UNIX workstation field now that Sun is finally adopting it, but during the long battle between Motif and Open Look for a dominant share of the UNIX market, Windows and OS/2 ran away with the desktop. OSF/1 is really only supported by DEC among the major players. DCE and DME are eagerly awaited, but we still do not know if they will be established as real de facto standards.

Standards that are adopted by agreement typically have a hard time reaching commercial success. They are often sponsored by bureaucrats and developed by academics. It is unusual for everyone to agree; there is generally a competing, often proprietary, standard that can out-maneuver the public one. An example of this would be OSI versus TCP/IP. The more practical TCP/IP has stayed ahead of OSI, adopting OSI choices when they are superior and inventing other approaches where the OSI standard is slow-moving or inadequate.

Further, there may not be much advantage to vendors to put the work into building systems that may have no advantage over those from the competition. As a result, although the open systems standards such as DCE, DME, and Motif are available, it is not clear how well they are being embraced. Many software and hardware vendors accommodate open standards but still provide their own proprietary approaches. IBM, for example, may accommodate DCE but offers LU6.2/APPC as the approved IBM solution.

What to Do about Standards

1. *Adopt real working standards whenever possible:* Where a standard exists and is proven, it is normally desirable to adopt it if it is technically adequate. It is usually worth paying a small performance or cost penalty to do this. Where the standard is being eclipsed by proprietary advances, it may be necessary to rethink it, but this is unusual. Emerging standards should be evaluated very carefully, as most never emerge.

2. *A standard is just as good however it came about:* Novell is a standard through monopoly—it has 60 percent of the LAN market and is supported on most systems. TCP/IP is a standard through distribution—it is available on almost every system, always works the same way, and is well understood. OSI is a standard through agreement—it is less well known in the United States, but it may be the best choice in some international environments. All of these are good networking choices.

3. *If a system supports your communication standards, it is open enough to use:* An AS/400 is a single-vendor computer with an unusual operating system, development language, and database. It is one of the clearest examples of a proprietary system on the market. But if you run SQL/400 and TCP/IP on it, your data are as accessible to you as any Intel-based UNIX "open system." You can develop PowerBuilder systems and access it like any other system.

SELECTING THE NETWORK

Networks are best understood in layers (see Figure 5.11). The OSI model, which is widely accepted, delineates seven layers—from hardware to applications. To keep this practical, we will group those into three: the hardware, the protocol stacks, and the application program interface. The great merit of the layered approach is that we do not need to be concerned with the details of lower levels from the higher.

The local area network has become a business standard in the last few years. Today, we can expect to network all of the PCs in a company, using either Ethernet or Token Ring. Functioning LANs are one of the precondi-

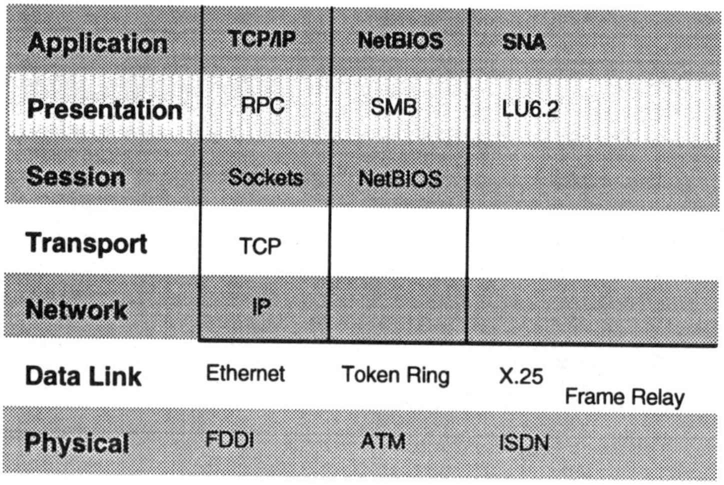

Application	TCP/IP	NetBIOS	SNA
Presentation	RPC	SMB	LU6.2
Session	Sockets	NetBIOS	
Transport	TCP		
Network	IP		
Data Link	Ethernet	Token Ring	X.25 / Frame Relay
Physical	FDDI	ATM	ISDN

Figure 5.11 Network layers

tions for client/server computing. The key moves for the next five years are twofold:

- upgrading of local area network speed
- connection of LANs into enterprise networks

First, let's understand the hardware of the local area network.

NETWORK HARDWARE

A local area network provides a logical connection between all of a group of computers, so that each can talk to any other. This is done over shared facilities (wire), where only one communication can be traveling at any instant. Different systems use different protocols to coordinate use of the shared facility.

Ethernet was invented by Robert Metcalf. Early adoption was driven by DEC, Intel, and Xerox (DIX). Ethernet became the standard LAN for UNIX workstations and also for DEC systems (DECnet). In the early days, its primary competitor was ARCnet. Then IBM introduced the token-ring LAN. Token Ring has advantages in terms of reliability but has always been more costly than Ethernet. It was slow to be introduced for this reason, except in dedicated IBM sites. In 1989, the leading network choices were:

Ethernet	10 Mb/sec
Token Ring	4 Mb/sec
ARCnet	1 Mb/sec

At this time, there were a variety of cabling schemes for each of these systems. The cable was thick, difficult to run, and difficult to tap. Over the last two to three years, both Ethernet and Token Ring have been run over twisted-pair (telephone) wire, and the faster form of Token Ring has been introduced. At the same time, faster options have become available, led by FDDI. The leading network choices in 1993 were:

Ethernet	10 Mb/sec	cheapest
Token Ring	16 Mb/sec	more expensive
FDDI, etc.	100 Mb/sec	much more expensive

Ethernet

Ethernet is a tested, popular, inexpensive solution. More than half of the installed LAN workstations are on Ethernet, which has a cost advantage over Token Ring. Ethernet has been available with three different cabling schemes:

10Base5	thick coaxial cable
10Base2	thin cable with BNC connectors
10BaseT	twisted-pair wire with active hub

Ethernet runs at 10 Mb/sec using a collision-detection protocol called CSMA/CD. In this protocol, any host can transmit at any time. If, at the time of transmission, another host is also transmitting, a "collision" occurs and both hosts try again after a short interval. This performs well except where many hosts must transmit continuously, when performance can fall off owing to too many collisions. This does restrict the effective bandwidth of an Ethernet to 70 to 80 percent of its 10 Mb rate in many situations.

There are two flavors of Ethernet: the original Digital-Intel-Xerox (DIX) specification and IEEE 802.3. The differences are minor but lead to an incompatibility, so that two stations on the same network cannot receive each other's messages.

Token Ring

Token Ring is a tested, reliable solution. Compared to Ethernet, you could say it is twice the performance at twice the price. It also has a little better reliability. Token Ring has less market share because:

- it was introduced later
- many people have not hit the capacity limit of Ethernet yet
- some people who need more capacity have gone to higher-speed solutions

It is available with shielded twisted-pair wiring, which looks rather like thin Ethernet, and unshielded twisted-pair wiring. Token-ring LANs use a hub, which makes them appear like a star for practical purposes.

Token Ring runs at 16 or 4 Mb/sec, generally 16 today. The protocol is more complex than Ethernet, using a special bit-pattern (the token), which circulates on the network. Only a station holding the token can transmit. There is no delay caused by collisions; instead, there is a delay caused by waiting for the token. This makes the system more deterministic than Ethernet. Token Ring will perform less well in the broadcast situation, where one or two systems do all the transmission. In most other cases, it will perform better than Ethernet.

One advantage of Token Ring is in failure recovery. An individual wire or card failure can bring down all or a segment of an Ethernet but will simply take one station off-line on Token Ring.

High-Speed LANs

Currently, a high-speed LAN delivers 10 times Ethernet performance at 10 times the price. The price will drop as sales volume increases. Today, high-speed LANS are employed as backbones where cost is less of an issue (see Table 5.1). As more applications move to client/server, and particularly as images are transferred on networks, this type of LAN will become the corporate standard to the desktop. There are several choices today in high-speed LANs: FDDI, CDDI, Fast Ethernet, and ATM.

Table 5.1 Approximate Networking Costs

	Card	Hub
Ethernet	$150	$250
Token Ring	$350	$600
Fast Ethernet	$600	$700
Switched Ethernet	$150	$4000
Twisted-pair FDDI	$800	$1000
CDDI	$1000	$1000
FDDI	$2000	$1000
ATM	$1500	$3000

FDDI

Fiber Distributed Data Interface is a 100 Mb/sec fiber-optic LAN. Despite the name, FDDI can also run on two shielded twisted-pair media, known as Green Book and SDDI (Shielded twisted-pair Distributed Data Interface). FDDI (over fiber) is an ANSI standard. There are more than 10 vendors selling FDDI equipment. It is tested at the Advanced Networking Testing Center for compatibility. Reliability is high. FDDI offers fault tolerance due to its double-ring architecture. FDDI Dual Access Stations can use the secondary ring if the primary fails. This feature is optional but commonly adopted. Most hub and concentrator devices allow hot swapping of cards. Many offer redundant power supplies.

CDDI

Copper Distributed Data Interface is a version of FDDI that runs on unshielded twisted-pair cabling. The goal is to support FDDI over the STP (Token Ring) and UTP (10BaseT) installed base. Hubs and adapters would be replaced, using existing wiring to the desktop. Backbone networks would be fiber. Crescendo, for instance, sells a Workgroup Hub, which allows FDDI and CDDI networks to be connected.

Fast Ethernet

Fast Ethernet plans to bring 100 Mb/sec performance to the most poular network standard. Unfortunately, at the time of writing, the standards for

Fast Ethernet were not agreed upon yet between two competing proposals, each with vendors lined up. One uses the IEEE 802.3 CSMA/CD media access layer, so is more like Ethernet. This is supported by Grand Junction Networks, Cabletron, Intel, 3Com, SynOptics, etc. The other proposal is 100BaseVG, supported by H-P, Banyan, Wellfleet, Ungermann-Bass, and AT&T. This replaces CSMA/CD wth a new Demand Priority Access Method (DPAM), allowing a central hub to control the transmission priority. The protocol uses the four pairs of wires in 10BaseT twisted-pair wiring to transmit or receive.

Switched Ethernet

Switched Ethernet provides the full bandwidth of Ethernet to each workstation. The Kalpana Full Duplex EtherSwitch, for example, offers 20 Mbps to a workstation. This doubles the speed of Ethernet, and the five-port switch dedicates traffic to one station-pair at a time. The system costs about $1,000 per user. With switched Ethernet, you don't need to buy new adapters.

Asynchronous Transfer Mode (ATM)

ATM is a high-bandwidth, low-delay, packet-based switching and multiplexing technique. It is an outgrowth from broadband ISDN standards, specified for use over fast optical fiber networks. In 1991, a consortium called the ATM Forum was founded to promote the technology. This is now international and has over 200 members, including local exchange and interexchange carriers, equipment manufacturers, and large user organizations. It appears that there is a broad consensus on ATM as the next major networking standard. ATM offers a common standard for faster local and wide area networks, although it is particularly suited today to inter-LAN connectivity and enterprise-wide networking, where its performance is demanded and its higher cost is justified.

In an ATM network, information is broken into "cells," each fixed at 53 bytes in length, and transmitted at any speed up to 2.5 Gbps that the network can handle. ATM is protocol independent and performs no error-checking. It is simply very fast; ATM switches can provide data rates up to 140 Mb/sec, or SONET speeds. It can operate at 25 Mbps or 51 Mbps standards over existing wire. ATM also handles "bursts" of data very well, because the entire bandwidth of a connection can be made available for one point-to-point transmission. Applications involving the transfer of multimedia information are much "burstier" than OLTP applications.

ATM supports voice, data, and other high-bandwidth services, such as multimedia, and may lower the barriers between local and wide area networking. ATM is switched through a central hub, as opposed to shared bandwidth, such as a conventional LAN.

ATM is expensive for the LAN compared to the other fast options: FDDI, CDDI, and Fast Ethernet. Current equipment cannot interoperate.

Early adopters of ATM include Bear Stearns, Hughes Aircraft, Time Warner, and Texas Instruments. AT&T, Sprint, and the RBOCSs are all announcing support for ATM. The ATM Forum can be contacted at Interop, Inc., Mountain View, California (415) 941-2570.

Wireless LANs

Most LAN installations employ copper wire to the desktop, mostly unshielded twisted-pair wire (UTP), which looks like telephone wire. Since the cost of running cable is high in some environments, and many users relocate frequently, some installations will pay a premium for wireless LANs. These can be based on infrared or UHF radio. Wireless LAN is particularly suitable for notebook computers.

Wide Area Network Choices

Wide area network media include:

- Fast serial modems
- X.25
- T1/T3
- ISDN
- SONET
- Frame relay
- Cell Relay (SMDS)
- ATM

Modems with a capacity of 14,400 bps are now only about $200. Using these speeds, it is possible to bridge LANS with dial-up phone lines. A product such as the DCA Remote LAN option supports this using multiple protocols (i.e., TCP/IP and Novell SPX/IPX).

If you are willing to consider leased lines, you can employ 56K lines, T1 (1.5 Mb/sec), fractional T1, or T3 (45 Mb/sec). Fractional T1 means you can lease some number of 56K pieces of the bandwidth of a T1 line. T3 is generally used on backbone nets, such as the NSFnet, rather than individual hookups.

The various high-speed wide area networking schemes have different advantages, and it is not the place of this book to go into them. They offer, for a price, the ability to connect local networks at speeds from 10 Kbps to 10 Mbps.

COMMUNICATIONS PROTOCOLS

Fortunately for application developers, it is not necessary to become involved with the details of network hardware. Software is available that can support all of the available network configurations. We simply program to that. There are several networking transports that are in reasonably common use today:

- Novell
- TCP/IP
- DECnet
- NetBIOS
- SNA
- OSI
- XNS
- AppleTalk

The commonest in most corporations are Novell (which has about 60 percent of the market), TCP/IP, NetBIOS, and DECnet. There are 19 million workstations running IPX/SPX and 4 million running TCP/IP. Recent Novell announcements indicate that all NetWare versions will have native support for TCP/IP and all UNIX licensed from USL will have native support for IPX/SPX.

While these are different, they can all run over the same hardware at the same time. In designing a client/server application, our networking choice will normally be one of these. Using the tools in this book, the choice of network protocol is simply installation of libraries and has no effect on the application. When writing in C, we would attempt to use a programming method such as OSF/DCE remote procedure call to isolate ourselves from the network choice. Otherwise, we will code to a different API for each network.

By confining a design to one of these, we ensure that it can run over the widest variety of hardware options. In some IBM environments, we might encounter SNA APPC or even native token-ring protocols, and in many DEC environments, we might find DECnet. Advocates will claim better performance, but these proprietary choices risk confining us later.

Multiple stacks include Microsoft Network Driver Interface Specification (NDIS) and Novell Open Data-Link Interface (ODI).

NETWORK OPERATING SYSTEMS

Network Operating System Features

The basic functions offered by a network operating system are file and printer sharing, with associated security. Most installed networks today are used primarily for this purpose. Often, the network is justified because it allows shared access to resources, reducing expenditure on printers and software licenses.

The advanced functions offered by a network operating system include global directory services, fault-tolerant file storage, and network management. These functions are unusual today, but are all essential for effective delivery of client/server applications. The net effect of these services is that "the network is the computer"; resources can be managed on the network with the same abilities as on a monolithic system.

The concept of a network operating system evolved to respond to the limitations of DOS, which offered no support for resource sharing and is not a suitable platform on which to build a server. Other systems, such as the Apple Macintosh, UNIX, OS/2, or Windows NT, do not require a separate network operating system for basic functions, although they offer additional services on the base operating system to support more advanced needs.

The leading network operating systems are Novell, TCP/IP, LAN Manager, and Banyan VINES.

Novell NetWare

Novell NetWare offers client support for almost everything you could want and server support on IBM PC systems (as a self-contained operating system) and UNIX, OS/2, Macintosh, VAX/VMS, Windows NT, AS/400, MVS, etc.

NetWare has transitioned from its original role as a "fix" for DOS problems to become the integration platform for the corporation. It has a 60 percent share of the network operating system market. The majority of

NetWare customers are using it mostly as a file server, with many still on the old first-generation, 16-bit version, 2.x.

NetWare was always a high performer. The early versions can run effectively on a 286 PC. Version 3.11 is 32-bit and requires a 386, and this also performs well. Databases often run twice as fast on Novell as on OS/2 on the same hardware. The main functions of NetWare are file and print management, with security on the server.

NetWare has its own protocols, IPX/SPX, which are, of course, widely supported. The recent merger of NetWare and UNIX will lead to integrated support for TCP/IP on all NetWare platforms.

Applications written to run on the Novell server are called Novell Loadable Modules (NLMs). There have not been many NLMs to purchase, although most major databases are available. This problem is being addressed with Novell's introduction of AppWare, which is a set of tools for development of applications portable to Novell and other platforms.

The server-centric naming approach of Novell has been a big problem. A user has to log on to different Novell servers, so that it is difficult to navigate an enterprise network based on Novell 3.11. The new NetWare 4.0 includes NDS, which is a network directory system that competes with Banyan StreetTalk and TCP/IP Domain Naming System.

TCP/IP

TCP/IP client support is available for every system imaginable; if not, the source code is freely available, so it could be ported to a system that had a C compiler and some communications capability. Other than DOS, any system that is a TCP/IP client can also be a server. TCP/IP does not require a separate server and is not a network operating system, but a suite of peer-to-peer communications programs and APIs using a common protocol suite.

TCP/IP was originally developed with DoD funding for the ARPANET, and from the beginning it was an internetworking standard. It has a rich set of available applications and several alternate APIs. Originally, TCP/IP supported a set of programs (Telnet, FTP), which allowed users to log on to remote computers, copy files, run jobs, and send mail.

The major protocols of TCP/IP are IP and the higher-level TCP and UDP.

The Network File System implements file sharing across the network, and other programs support printer sharing, so that the basic NOS functions are available. Further programs support directory services (Domain Naming System, NIS) and network management (SNMP). Fault-tolerant file storage is available where a host operating system suppports it.

LAN Manager and LAN Server

Microsoft LAN Manager and IBM LAN Server are similar programs descended from the same source. Client support is for DOS, Windows, OS/2, and Macintosh; server support is for UNIX, OS/2, and Windows NT.

The basic protocols of these systems are NetBIOS and Named Pipes, but TCP/IP is also supported. The vendor emphasis with these products is on LAN Manager going to Windows NT and the IBM LAN Server to OS/2. AT&T is now the support vendor for LAN Manager/X, which runs on UNIX.

The latest release, IBM LAN Server 4.0, incorporates the OSF/DCE directory, security, and time functions.

Banyan VINES

Banyan VINES has historically been the high-end PC network operating system, leading the way in its support for features such as multiprocessing and enterprise-wide directories. As Novell 4.0 and Windows NT Advanced Server add more strength, VINES will probably become a technology for inclusion in other operating systems, supporting directory services, rather than an operating system with a significant share of the market.

Peer-to-Peer LANs

There are also some peer-to-peer LANs available for DOS. A peer-to-peer LAN has no dedicated server. Because of the DOS limitations, these systems are best for a light load, such as resource sharing in small offices. This category was pioneered by Artisoft with LANtastic. Novell followed with NetWare Lite, but the big seller is now Microsoft Windows for Workgroups. These are not generally networks suitable for client/server applications, but entry-level systems, which can grow up later. AppleTalk for the Macintosh is similar in some respects.

Summary

The last few years have seen a rise in the importance of standards, which has contributed to lowering costs and improving application portability. The combination of standards and networks enables us to construct client/server applications that work on this infrastructure.

6
Server Hardware Selection

The servers are the systems where we store data and perform essential shared operations—the heart of the system. While they have become much less expensive, and in some cases not distinguishable physically from a desktop system, the responsibilities on these machines are greater. Accordingly, we may specify additional reliability features and overspecify some components critical to performance or continuous availability.

These days, a server can be literally any kind of computer, from a PC to a minicomputer to a mainframe. That is not to say that this is simply a matter of naming. Traditional minicomputers and mainframes do not all perform cost effectively in the server role. Many of these were designed to efficiently process batch operations or many "dumb" terminals. The features and components that support these activities can be expensive but are unnecessary for a LAN-based server supporting intelligent workstations. A computer such as the IBM AS/400 or DEC VAX was originally designed to perform all of the functions for a computer center, including database management, processing, and the management of user terminals. An AS/400 can handle far more user terminals than a RISC system of similar price, even though the RISC system has more processing power, because the AS/400 is designed to handle terminals very efficiently. This powerful feature of the AS/400 is not required when using it solely as a back-end server.

The server, then, is more specialized than a general-purpose system. This trend is increasing. The Auspex system, for example, which functions solely as an NFS file server, is unable to perform most of the functions of a minicomputer. It is far superior as an NFS machine, offering high performance at a lower price than a generalized system.

The software packages for many of these systems are not written for the client/server model. Many packages treat a PC as a dumb terminal rather than exploiting its potential to offer a better interface or faster processing.

We are at an early stage in the introduction of client/server systems, when most of the hardware and software we use comes from a previous era. Our systems today generally use servers that are based on general-purpose systems. Eventually, there may be many types of dedicated servers available to attach to a network.

Servers in use can be classified into several types. These include:

- file servers
- resource servers
- database servers
- application servers

These roles can be combined into one system or divided among several. A very small installation will often have one server performing all functions; most installations will have several servers, spreading the load to ensure reasonable performance of all functions. Database servers and application servers are typical of true client/server systems.

FILE SERVERS

Most servers in use in corporations today are functioning as file and print servers. They make files available to client systems, so that users can share their data and software, rely on scheduled maintenance such as upgrades and backups, and achieve economies of scale in purchase of resources, such as disk drives and printers. File servers run appropriate software such as Novell NetWare, LAN Manager, or NFS. Most file servers are PC or uniprocessor UNIX systems, so the processor of the system is not the performance bottleneck. Heavily used file servers should have multiple disk drives and network adapter cards.

RESOURCE SERVERS

There can be a range of resource servers, depending on the resource being managed. At any time, there are typically devices that are too expensive to dedicate to one client. One example is printers. The print server, often combined with the file server, will manage the various printers on the network, such as high-volume or color printers, routing print as requested. Communications servers are usually dedicated systems, because of the performance requirement, with modems attached or running gateway software to connect to remote systems. Multimedia resources, such as a CD-ROM jukebox, might also be attached to a resource server.

The resource server is sometimes an old model computer, such as a Sun-3 or slow 386 PC, which would not be adequate in any other role.

DATABASE SERVERS

In a client/server application, the server runs a database management system and possibly other components of the application and needs more power than a file server. Relational DBMS software uses processor power for indexing and searching. The database server should normally be a very fast system based on a fast chip, such as the 486DX2, Pentium, or RISC. The servers we discuss here will primarily be used in this role. Chapter 7 includes a review of the DBMS systems.

APPLICATION SERVERS

An application server runs application software. Clearly, the performance level and class of system depend on the application. At present, the application and database server are generally the same thing. In some advanced uses, we employ dedicated application servers to run floating point calculations or graphically intensive work, such as visualization.

We can run one or more systems as batch process servers. This is a good way to allow interactive packages, such as PowerBuilder, for instance, to offer some batch processes to their users. The workstation schedules operation on a dedicated batch machine and retrieves the work later.

Alternatively, we might buy a package that runs on SCO UNIX, or inherit a system that runs on a Wang mini, where these are not our usual standards, and leave the application on a dedicated server rather than go to the trouble of porting it to another system.

It is likely that we will see much more use of application servers in the future. This will be enabled by the adoption of application development tools that allow applications to be hosted on arbitrary systems on the network. The application could then be upgraded by replacing a single server with a more powerful one. At present, most client/server systems employ tools that put most processing on the individual workstation.

CLASSES OF SERVER

Servers vary in capability from PC-class machines to supercomputers. Table 6.1 puts them in seven classes based on throughput and general configuration.

Mainframes are superior as enterprise-level systems, serving as the systems management focal point and corporate repository. We have discussed the current trend toward lower mainframe sales; however, very few large corporations are planning to replace their mainframe data centers entirely in the near future.

The large symmetric multiprocessor (SMP) UNIX systems rival the mainframe in benchmarks for processing power and relational database performance but still fall short on systems management and other data center issues. These systems are catching up as the established software vendors move their products onto these platforms, but the activity has been disappointing. Hardware companies, such as Sequent, Sequoia, and Pyramid, together with software firms, such as Integris and VISystems, that attempted to cater to customers moving wholesale off mainframes, have not done as well as they hoped. The technical issues are discussed in Chapter 11. In addition, this is a risk-averse and slow-moving group of customers, for good reason.

The midrange group of servers is the most interesting category. The UNIX/RISC system, the proprietary mini, and the PC-technology superserver have very different heritages but are becoming increasingly alike. The Hewlett-Packard 3000 and 9000 are actually now mechanically identical. The IBM AS/400 and RS/6000 share parts, including disk subsystems and the large system chassis. DEC offers their proprietary OpenVMS or the UNIX variant OSF/1 on otherwise identical Alpha systems.

The choice can be made based on the operating system preferred from a technology point of view, or on available applications. The vendors of proprietary systems generally argue that the best application should be selected,

Chapter 6 • Server Hardware Selection

Table 6.1 Classes of Server

Server Class	Examples	MIPS	TPS
PC-class	Compaq, Dell, AST	5–20	5–30
PC-class superserver	Tricord IBM 195/295 Sequent WinServer Compaq ProLiant	20–100	10–50
Proprietary mini	IBM AS/400 DEC VAX 6000 HP 3000	10–50	10–100
Uniprocessor RISC/UNIX	HP 9000 800 IBM RS/6000 DEC Alpha	30–100	20–100
Large SMP UNIX	Pyramid, Sequent Sun, HP 9000-890 NCR, SGI Challenge	50–1000	100–500
Mainframe	IBM ES/9000, HDS NEC, VAX 9000 Unisys, Amdahl	60–600	400–1000
Specialized	Netframe Auspex/IBM 7051		

and they often have the best choice of applications today. This is a strong argument, since these systems are accessible enough to serve as application servers in a mixed environment. It is countered somewhat by their often poorer price/performance and the tendency of application developers to move to PC and RISC systems.

The PC-technology systems run Windows NT, OS/2, and Novell and are more familiar to many operations. The common technology presents particular advantages the further their use extends from a traditional data center environment. If servers need to be supported at 50 remote locations, for example, commonality with the workstations could reduce costs for parts inventory by half and require only one support person instead of two. If the system must run in Argentina or Malaysia, there may be limited support except for the largest-volume systems, and that may be expensive. In some countries or business areas or in very small business units, only PC technology may be affordable.

PC technology was formerly unattractive for those who needed the ability to scale their system upward in the future, which includes most companies and all software vendors. Several developments in the last year or so have made this an attractive choice now:

- new, fast Intel processors and an announced upgrade path to even faster systems
- PC operating systems that can run on RISC processors, including Windows NT, SCO UNIX, and eventually OS/2
- PC systems from established suppliers that support multiple processors
- database systems that support all of the above

Of course, a system can be developed that supports several or all of these platforms as a database server. The ability to do this was one of the most compelling arguments for the vendor-independent database companies. ORACLE, for one, has always made this point effectively in their advertising.

HARDWARE CHOICES IN PC-CLASS SERVERS

While a server is not a "personal computer," the servers based on PC technology have evolved into powerful systems. That technology includes processors, operating systems, buses, and storage devices developed originally for personal computers. We will class servers somewhat arbitrarily into three categories by price:

Deskside	$3,000–$10,000
Server	$15,000–$25,000
Superserver	$25,000–$300,000

Deskside

The cheapest class of machine to use as a server can be purchased for well under $5,000. This is a machine that is identical to a client workstation—for example, a 66 MHz 486DX or Pentium. Such a machine could be configured with plenty of disk and memory, optionally stood on its side, and used as a database server. Most smaller development environments will do this routinely, since they will not need the large data storage supported by larger machines. The market for this type of system is the most aggressive, leading to a more rapid product introduction cycle and lower margins, which makes these machines very attractive.

Chapter 6 • Server Hardware Selection   131

This is more problematic in the production environment. When we cover the advantages of the more expensive machines, it becomes clear that the extra money is buying a significant degree of additional security against system failure. This varies from ease of maintenance and management to better service and support. This class of machine is reviewed in the Client Workstation section.

Server

Desktop computers are usually engineered for a small footprint on the desk at the expense of access and expandability. Server machines are used by a group of people and are more likely to need expansion and maintenance. It makes sense to build a different line of systems as servers to capitalize on this difference, and almost all manufacturers do this. A typical server is based today on a fast 486 processor in a tower (deskside) box. These are specifically engineered to be server systems, with large accessible interiors, fast buses, and plenty of disk and RAM expansion space. Good vendors include Compaq, Dell, AST, NEC, IBM, Apple, and H-P.

A good configuration for such a machine might include:

- 66 to 100 MHz CPU (IntelDX4, Pentium, or PowerPC)
- 32 Mb RAM (should support up to 128 Mb RAM)
- 2 GB disk (two or more drives)
- multiple network adapters
- six bus slots (EISA or PCI)
- five to eight drive bays

These machines cost approximately $10,000 to $15,000 and make very good small servers. The number of users supported per server depends heavily on the applications. One such machine could support 50 to 100 users as a file server, assuming that they are not accessing concurrently—perhaps 25 to 30 concurrent users.

Superserver

The next class of system is higher-end, intended to serve 75 or more concurrent clients or to act as an application server. These systems cost from $25,000 to $75,000 for reasonable systems and are also expandable to very large and very expensive configurations.

This class of system offers features typical of the minicomputer class of systems, such as:

- multiprocessing
- error-checking and correcting (ECC) memory
- bus parity checking
- reliability and systems management features

These systems are still not in widespread use, because the promised power requires both Pentium processors and operating systems that support symmetric multiprocessing. Two examples are the IBM PS/2 195/295 systems, built by Parallan, and the Tricord.

The IBM PS/2 195 is sold in a large cabinet similar to the RS/6000. The base system has a single 486DX processor with a 256K cache and 32M ECC memory expandable to 128M. It has dual micro channel buses offering eight slots on the Model 195, 12 on the Model 295. The 64-bit interprocessor bus transfers data at 200 Mbps. The system is upgradeable to the 295 Model 2, with two processors. Up to 28 GB of disk is available. Disk options include MASS/2, which offers local or remote server monitoring, and a RAID array supporting RAID-5. The system, which costs upwards of $20,000, supports Novell NetWare, OS/2, LAN Server, and LAN Manager.

The Tricord PowerFrame ES5000 was introduced early in 1993. It is a large server, running up to six 486DX or Pentium CPUs. The ES5000 supports up to 1 GB memory (4 GB in 1994) and up to 290 GB of disk using fast wide SCSI-2, which has a 20 Mb/sec transfer rate. Data striping and disk mirroring are standard. A separate subsystem with multiple Intel processors handles I/O. The system has a very fast 64-bit bus, transferring at 267 Mb/sec. The system supports NetWare, SCO UNIX, UNIXware, LAN Manager, and VINES; it is mostly used for NetWare, which represents 70 percent of sales. Sequent is marketing a version of this machine specialized for Windows NT as the Sequent WinServer.

For the right application, these systems can offer a painless growth path using the identical system, database, and application software from the smallest $3,000 server to a million-dollar system capable of supporting hundreds of users.

ISSUES IN SELECTING PC-CLASS SERVERS

When selecting PC-class systems, there are many more issues with servers than with workstations for individual users. This class of system can experience near-constant use for 60 or more hours per week in a conventional corporate business environment and may be up almost the entire time in other uses, such as retail. The problems and solutions are akin to those of the minicomputer technology with which these systems compete.

Most inexperienced people configuring server systems underestimate their need. They find that they need to upgrade shortly after their first installation because the processor is not fast enough, there is not enough disk, or the network interface is too slow.

Considerations for hardware selection in this class are:

- processor type and speed
- number of processors
- cache and memory
- disk storage
- removable storage
- communication
- fault tolerance
- scalability
- support

Processors

Although processor speed is generally not the worst server bottleneck, there is little sense in economizing on the CPU. This is a small part of the total cost today and will have a considerable effect on the performance of at least some of the workload. Also, faster processors have a longer economic life. When reviewing a two-year-old inventory of systems, I will usually find that only systems with the fastest processors of the original purchase can be saved for further use.

The number of processors to get depends first on the operating system and application software. Some operating systems, such as Novell 3.11 or OS/2 2.1, can only support one processor. Others, such as Windows NT, can support two or more. Similarly, some database management systems can support multiple processors (MP) and some cannot. Some applications may be unable to support MP or to exploit it effectively. Only if all these factors are in favor can a multiprocessor system be considered at all. It still needs early benchmarking for two reasons. First, the performance gains from an MP configuration are not linear and need to be measured. Second, the application may be designed in a way that prevents the MP configuration from helping, and, if discovered early, this can be corrected.

While particularly important for MP systems, benchmarking should be attempted in all cases. For some applications, the published figures from the computer press may be appropriate. This is most likely if the application approximates the standard benchmarks. These vary but are often either simple tasks on standard products, such as word processors and spreadsheets, or transactional benchmarks similar to the TPC series. These tests are very good at finding systems that may have an inadequate cache, a slow bus, slow video performance, or slow disk access.

If an application is in any sense unusual, it must be benchmarked individually, with its specific performance simulated as closely as possible. Processor benchmarks reveal little about database performance in the real world.

Disk Storage

Disk storage, rather than processor speed, is the usual performance constraint for servers. It is also commonly underestimated ahead of time. It is, therefore, appropriate to throw hardware at the problem. Buy three times the disk you think you'll need. Several small disks are generally better than one large one from a performance and reliability point of view. Striping, which is storing a file across several disks, improves performance because it shares the work of storage or retrieval. Even without considering RAID (see the following paragraph) or striping, several disks willl perform better, since this removes the bottleneck on the disk and allows several users to access data concurrently. There are more reliability options with several disks, including mirroring and RAID.

Systems with a Redundant Array of Inexpensive Disks (RAID) use several disks and allow one (or more) disk to fail. This is less expensive than full redundancy, because you are not paying for twice as many disks, but it is not free, because small drives cost more per megabyte than large drives. A RAID system generally costs up to twice as much as a single large disk of the same size. The single large disk is sometimes called a SLED (single large expensive disk).

In addition to improved reliability, a RAID system can reduce the time to retrieve data, since it is retrieving across several disks that can seek and transfer data concurrently. Inevitably, this will increase the time to store, which can slow up the system by 25 percent on writing.

There are several different categories of RAID, of which three are important in this type of small server. RAID 0 is simply disk striping, or writing data across several drives. RAID 1 is 100 percent redundant storage, essentially mirroring. RAID 5, which is what people usually mean by RAID, spreads data and parity information across several drives with enough redundancy to achieve fault tolerance. This also allows performance-enhancing striping and seeking algorithms to operate.

There are many examples of small RAID systems, such as those from Micropolis and Mylex. A small system will provide 2 to 4 GB of data storage for ten to twenty thousand dollars.

Fault Tolerance

Backups are an important procedure for any server. In the past, backup was a time-consuming weekend or late-night chore, because the backup medium (tape) had a much smaller capacity than the disk drives to be off-loaded. New advances have assisted greatly with that problem. Every server that has data of any value (and what does not?) should have a backup device, which allows unattended, automated backup of modified data. That means an 8 mm video or 4 mm digital audio tape drive, not the QIC-format cartridges, which do not hold enough data. For smaller systems, a single 8 mm video or 4 mm DAT tape can hold an incremental backup. Larger systems may require a tape loading device, which can change the tapes.

Different levels of fault tolerance can be achieved. The popular method these days is RAID, which offers several different levels of performance and fault tolerance, as discussed above. A good adjunct to RAID is hot drive replacement, allowing the system to be kept up in the face of multiple drive failures.

For the most important data, the use of mirrored hard disks or redundant servers can be considered. Some systems offer a redundant disk controller option. Novell, for instance, offers disk mirroring, which is two drives off one controller card writing the same image; disk duplexing, which is two storage systems (drive or drive array), each with their own controller; and a wholly redundant server. Novell NetWare SFT III supports redundant servers, automatically switching clients to the backup on failure of the primary. It will cost about $50,000 to install a 250-user version on two Pentium servers with 100 Mbps Mirrored Server Link cards. It may be worth pricing such a system against a more expensive superserver class system for the file server role. An appropriate combination of these features offers reasonable high availability in relatively inexpensive servers.

An Uninterruptible Power Supply (UPS) is a commonly neglected essential item for a server. Many server systems now offer problem notification, including remote notification through a modem. This is indispensable if the system is to run remotely. Some servers have locks on the front panel and keyboard, and/or password security. If the machine will be kept in an insecure area, it is advisable to get such a system or to house it within a protective casing.

Scalability

A scalable system is one that can be field-upgraded to improve its performance and capacity. Processor upgrades can be achieved with modular CPU cards upgrading the processor or by adding a second processor on some systems. Of course, the other components are as important as the CPU. This includes RAM and cache size limits, bus speed, adapter cards, and disk. This feature may be a lifesaver in the first few months, if initial estimates of performance were inaccurate.

Disk expansion is a function of the number of drive bays and bus slots, although there are also options for adding an external chassis or external drives. Some systems may have a power supply that cannot support disk expansion. Something to watch for is early obsolescence. Some companies may be changing their product line so fast that you will not be able to order the spare parts when you need them. This is particularly critical with RAID or disk array installations, where every drive may have to be the same model. Some users stock spares to cover for this problem; this also improves the time to repair. Another option is to require a guarantee of parts availability from the vendor in the contract.

In practice, small systems are not upgraded often after initial installation. Within a year or two, the overall package is usually obsolete and the upgrades may no longer be available. For smaller servers, it may be simpler to replace than to upgrade. This is particularly true when an enterprise has a number of server systems or is experiencing growth. New systems can be better balanced overall and generally have superior price/performance.

Support

The only thing more expensive than good support and maintenance for systems is inadequate support. The cost of system downtime or lost data is lost confidence in the entire system. The cost of replacing parts is less today, now that components are modular and reasonably inexpensive. However, on-site support and training for distributed systems is a cost that is going out of control.

You may wish to consider the quality of the system construction in this category. Some systems are manufactured to enable simple maintenance in the field. The original IBM PS/2 was a landmark example; disk drives on the desktop systems could be swapped by the end user in seconds.

PROCESSOR CHOICES

The buyer of a small system over the next year or so has a wealth of choice in processor technology available. Some very powerful processors have been introduced, and others have been announced for release soon.

Whatever happens, Intel will have the bulk of the market share for these chips in the near future. Forecasts show Intel shipping about 12 million processors a year in 1994 and 1995. The number two chip, the PowerPC, will not pass the million mark until 1996.

Although there were once several competing incompatible types of processors for small systems, the choice now comes down to a small group of RISC processors on the one hand and the Intel varieties and clones on the other. RISC processors have always been significantly faster than the Intel chips in general performance, and this seems to continue to hold when looking at the various companies' plans for the next few years. However, in the past, there was a massive gap in floating point performance between Intel processors and RISC workstation systems. The Pentium has closed that gap considerably.

Given the pace at which Intel processors improve, it is not likely that many workstation users will abandon the Intel architecture for performance reasons. The RISC systems do improve at a similar rate, so they maintain a performance advantage and will presumably keep their position as the performance leader. This makes RISC systems likely to do well as servers, since servers typically run a restricted range of software that will likely be available on RISC or Intel systems.

RISC systems are also good candidates for powerful professional workstations. This includes the graphic design professionals who currently use the Macintosh, the various engineering and other professionals who use UNIX systems today, and it may spread to other areas if suitable software is developed.

The RISC systems continue to improve. They are moving from 32-bit to 64-bit registers and data paths. The MIPS R4000 and DEC Alpha are 64-bit, and IBM and SPARC have announced plans for 64-bit systems in the future. The memory and I/O buses are also getting commensurately wider. These processors also have far more transistors than previous generations, run at higher clock speeds, and perform more operations in a clock cycle. This will allow support of more powerful software. The needs of video in particular seem to call for this class of system.

Processor Benchmarks

We used to measure performance by million instructions per second (MIPS). This was a somewhat meaningless number, since what is meant by an instruction is not defined and is subject to widespread abuse. MIPS were replaced after the introduction of the SPECmark around 1991. The SPECmark had a better measurement basis and was policed by the System Performance Evaluation Cooperative (hence the name SPECmark). However, there are very wide differences between floating point performance on machines with similar integer performance, so the SPECmark has now been replaced by the SPECint92 and SPECfp92 measures. SPECint92 is derived by running six integer C programs. SPECfp92 is calculated from a suite of nine double-precision FORTRAN, three single-precision FORTRAN, and two single-precision C programs. These measures have effectively replaced the Dhrystone and Linpack benchmarks.

Two capacity metrics (SPECrate_int92 and SPECrate_fp92) measure how many tasks a system can complete in a time interval, or the throughput. This is a good test to compare uniprocessor and multiprocessor systems.

These benchmarks measure the processor and compiler combination of the system, not overall performance. Table 6.2 will probably be obsolete by publication date, but it does indicate the following, which seems to hold true over time.

- These systems match the processor performance of the large four-way and six-way 3090 generation of IBM mainframes.
- Even the slowest beats the performance of the fastest uniprocessor mainframe shipping in early 1994.
- The fastest Intel 486 is slower than any current RISC chip and much slower on floating point.
- The Intel Pentium competes with the slower RISC chips but has slower floating point.

- The Sun SPARC is the slowest of the RISC chips.
- H-P, DEC, SGI, and IBM compete for the fastest chip in a leapfrog manner.

Performance Trends

The price/performance of these systems improves constantly, approximately doubling every 18 months. This is expressed in the performance of the various processor lines and goes up considerably every year. The prices of higher-end systems sometimes fall substantially. At the lower end, the price is fairly stable or drops slightly.

Table 6.2 shows the standard processors for commercial systems from 1993 to 1994. These are tenfold performance increases over five years ago. Announced chip plans for these vendors demonstrate further dramatic performance increases lying ahead. Sun has plans for a 90 MHz SuperSPARC in 1995, delivering 160 SPECint, and a 500 MHz 64-bit UltraSPARC III in 1997, delivering 800 SPECint. IBM and Motorola have announced plans for a 300 SPECmark PowerPC in 1994/95.

At the high end of these systems, available performance doubles twice, with the uniprocessor power increase plus advances in symmetric multiprocessing. For example, the HP 890 business servers supported 4-way processing in late 1992, 8-way in late 1993, and plan 16-way by late 1994, while also increasing clock speeds. At the same time, the smaller HP 800 series went from uniprocessor to dual, with four-way expected.

Table 6.2 Benchmarks

Vendor	Chip	SPECint92	SPECfp92	Clock MHz
DEC	Alpha	109	163	200
DEC	Alpha	65	112	133
H-P	PA 7100	80	142	99
IBM/Motorola	PowerPC 601	50	80	66
IBM	RS6000/580	59	125	62.5
Intel	Pentium	64	57	66
Intel	486DX4	48	24	99
SGI	MIPS R4400	93	95	100
Sun	SuperSPARC	53	63	40

OPERATING SYSTEM CHOICES IN SERVERS

The Intel PC-class type of server we are considering here can run a variety of operating systems. The available choices for database servers, all of which are good choices in appropriate circumstances, are listed in Figure 6.1.

UNIX, OS/2, and Windows NT are database or application server platforms, but it is unusual to use Novell NetWare as an application server, because there the applications would have to be written as Novell Loadable Modules (NLMs), and there are no applications written this way.

The same three systems are available, or will be soon, for RISC systems. RISC-based systems have generally run a variant of UNIX, such as Solaris from Sun, HP-UX from Hewlett-Packard, AIX from IBM, OSF/1 from DEC, or Irix from Silicon Graphics. These systems may now also run Windows NT.

The other reasonable midrange server choices are the proprietary platforms, particularly the IBM AS/400 with OS/400, DEC VAX/VMS with DEC OpenVMS, and the HP 3000 running HP MPE/ix. Each of these systems has a large installed base, a high reputation for quality and service, a high-performance relational database, and a choice of proven applications in many fields.

Novell NLM

The NetWare Loadable Module (NLM) version of a database is often preferable in an existing small Novell NetWare environment, because it will be a combination that performs well, is cheaper, and is easier to manage. NLMs

- UNIX
  - Solaris, HP-UX, AIX, OSF/1, Irix
  - SCO, UNIXware
- OS/2
- Windows NT
- Novell NetWare
- VMS, OS/400, MVS, MPE
- ...

Figure 6.1 Server O/S choices

run in 32-bit native mode under NetWare 3.11 and offer surprising performance, because they function as extensions to the NetWare operating system, and the NetWare system has very good file I/O. Some systems have produced very reasonable performance benchmarks. Only one server is needed, and the expertise to manage the operating system probably already exists. However, using the same computer for network operating system and database manager is a practice that does not scale well. Larger databases must use a different system. The economic advantage then disappears. And the NLM databases only run on uniprocessor Intel machines.

Novell systems cannot function as application servers. Porting code to an NLM is fairly difficult, which is why it took a while for the database systems to become available. NLM programs are linked into the Novell operating system and must release control periodically, since Novell does not have a preemptive scheduler—although this changes in Novell 4.0.

Application vendors are not writing to Novell NLM in any numbers in 1994.

OS/2

OS/2 is well supported by all the major relational databases, including the new DB2/2. It is one of the safest choice for a small system and was, until recently, the most economic. Many databases, including SQL Server and ORACLE, have run as server systems on OS/2 for years and have a large installed base. OS/2 can be installed and administered with less special expertise than UNIX, and it has been around long enough to have a body of experienced staff available. The lack of application software, which hurts OS/2 on the desktop, does not matter in this role. Recent versions have offered improvements in performance and operation.

OS/2 still does not support multiple processors or non-Intel processors yet, and this limits the performance of OS/2 for servers at the high end. Of course, that limitation will be addressed soon with PowerPC and then other platform support. There are some additional limitations of file length that can restrict large databases. There is a concern that porting schedules for databases may not place OS/2 first, so that some databases, SQL Server in particular, are not available in the most current version on OS/2. This can be countered by selecting DB2/2, of course. DB2/2 on OS/2 is a very inexpensive and powerful small database server, scalable by moving up to other members of the DB2 family. The DB2/6000 product is available on several UNIX systems and shares the same code base as DB2/2.

Windows NT

Windows NT is the newest of the server operating systems by a considerable margin, and that is a sizable problem to overcome. For those who like to avoid early versions of operating systems, Windows NT has now been around long enough to be in its second release. Windows NT 3.5 (Daytona) is stable and performs well. It is available on RISC platforms; those based on the MIPS R4400 and DEC Alpha processors initially, then PowerPC. NT is being offered at very reasonable prices in an attempt to build share. The bargain price of Microsoft SQL Server on Windows NT compared to Sybase SQL Server on UNIX seems to have caused the rift between those two companies.

The availability of the Sequent WinServer, DEC Alpha, and NEC R4400 machines is evidence that NT has succeeded in gathering support from a variety of vendors and architectures. Of all the server database platforms that can service the low-end market (under $5,000), SQL Server with Windows NT scales up to a greater range of performance than any other platform.

UNIX

The top five UNIX suppliers by sales volume are shown in Table 6.3.

This order changes little over time. These rankings were true for 1991, 1992, and 1993. Sun and IBM have been increasing share, DEC losing a little. The largest volumes are made up in UNIX workstation shipments, often for CASE and CAD/CAM work; in commercial UNIX servers, it appears that H-P is the market leader, followed by IBM and Sun. Santa Cruz Operation (SCO) should actually be included in this table because, if the hardware on which their system runs is included in the count, as it is for the other companies here, their sales are significant.

Table 6.3 Top UNIX Suppliers

Vendor	*OS Name*	*Processor*
Sun	Solaris	SPARC
H-P	HP-UX	HP-PA
IBM	AIX	PowerPC
DEC	OSF/1	Alpha
Silicon Graphics	Irix	MIPS R4400

Table 6.4 Vendor System Names

Vendor	Desktop	Server	Rack-mount
Sun	SPARCstation	SPARCserver	SPARCcenter
H-P	700	800	890
IBM	2xx/3xx	5xx	9xx
DEC	300	500	
SGI	Indy/Irix	Challenge	Power Challenge

The standard range of choices for a UNIX product line generally includes three categories. First, there are desktop workstations with PC form factors and large screens, priced from just below $5,000, and aimed at individual professionals. The prices can be misleading, often having insufficient disk or memory to even run the operating system; UNIX vendors point out that PCs come without network adapters, multitasking operating systems, and so on. Second, there is the midsized server, usually packaged as a large deskside box with a range of power combinations, aimed at departments as application servers. Third, there are the rack-mount servers, which are data center-class machines in standard racks, available with multiprocessing options.

Table 6.4 shows the names each vendor was giving to each class of system at the time of writing.

H-P SERVER LINE

In the H-P line, the 700 series are desktop workstations built by the former Apollo organization in Massachusetts, the 800 series are midsized servers, and the 890 series are rack-mounted data center servers. Up to now, H-P has also offered the Series 1200, which are fault-tolerant servers built by Sequoia running different hardware and a different operating system.

The HP Series 800 uses a letter (F, G, H, I) to indicate the form factor. There are more slots, memory, and disk in the higher models. A two-digit number (10, 20, 30, 40, 50, 60) indicates processor power, which varies from 30 to 150 transactions per second for uniprocessors.

The data center class 890 models can have up to eight processors, giving well over 1,000 transactions per second. They can be configured with over 100 I/O slots, 2 GB of memory, and over a terabyte of disk to support thousands of users.

IBM SERVER LINE

In the IBM line, the first digit generally represents form factor, the second and third processor power, although the numbering scheme is not quite this simple; some models have a letter, which confuses the issue. The 2xx series is a pizza box-sized desktop; the 3xx series a desktop or small deskside system; the 5xx series a standard server; and the 9xx series a data center-class, rack-mounted system. Suffixes (20, 30, 50, 60, 70, 75, 80) indicate faster systems. The 220, then, is a small, slow machine; the 980 is a large, fast one.

IBM sells three classes of specialized server. They recently introduced their 9076SPI Power Parallel Series, which is a symmetric multiprocessing system having from 8 to 64 processors and performing at up to 8 gigaflops, which is in the supercomputer class. This system starts at over a quarter-million dollars. The Power Visualization Server has a specialized use as a server supporting powerful graphics. IBM also offers the 7051 Power Network Dataserver; this is the machine built by Auspex as a dedicated NFS server. Recent small systems use the PowerPC processor. The possibility of buying a system that can run AIX, Macintosh System 7.5, and Windows NT is attractive.

SUN SERVER LINE

In the Sun line, the SPARCclassic and SPARCstation 2 are the desktop systems. The SPARCclassic is an entry-level system, which competes with high-end PCs. The SPARCserver 10, which replaced the older 6xx, is a standard server, and the SPARCCenter 2000 is a data center rack-mount machine offering SMP.

The SPARCserver 1000 is unusual; it is a small desktop machine, which supports SMP—a completely new packaging idea. This is not the first time Sun led the way in reducing the size of UNIX workstation packaging; they invented the "pizza box," for instance.

The SPARCcenter 2000 contains up to eight 40 MHz SuperSPARC processors, rated at up to 864 MIPS, and 130 GB of storage. By the beginning of 1994, a 20-processor system supporting up to a terabyte will be available.

DEC SERVER LINE

The DEC 3000 AXP Alpha systems come in three configurations ranging from $5,000 to $70,000. The 300L and 300 are desktop systems. The 500 is a standard-sized server.

SMALL UNIX SERVERS

There are many choices for UNIX servers. For smaller Intel-based systems, the market leader has long been Santa Cruz Operation (SCO). This is often employed in the terminal market rather than client/server but is also one of the popular choices as the operating system for small database servers. While reliable and probably the leading choice in smaller businesses, it has been our experience that many corporate operations are reluctant to add this system, because of the need for UNIX expertise to support it, preferring to use OS/2 and going to RISC systems when they adopt UNIX.

Other options include Novell UNIXware, Sun Solaris, formerly from Interactive, and NeXTStep. These systems are covered in Chapter 8.

LARGE UNIX SERVERS

When examining large UNIX systems, there are several other strong players. Some of these will be discussed later under systems management, since they are essentially mainframe replacements, and the full range of data center issues may need to be considered.

Table 6.5 shows symmetric multiprocessor systems based on large numbers of standard processors.

The number of processors tails off because the diminishing returns of multiprocessor overhead get worse until adding another processor produces no performance gain at all.

This is not a commodity market; these systems vary greatly in architecture, in performance on different mixes of tasks, in application and system software available, and in support options and long-term viability.

Other systems have different architectures. The large H-P systems have fewer but more powerful processors. There are several "mainframe UNIX"

Table 6.5 Symmetric Multiprocessor Systems

Vendor	Name	Processor	Max processors
Sequent	Symmetry 2000	Intel 486	30-way
Pyramid	MIServer	MIPS	24-way
Silicon Graphics	Challenge	MIPS	36-way
DG	Aviion	88000	
NCR	3600, etc.	Intel	30-way
Sun	SPARCcenter	SPARC	30-way

systems, which have more traditional combinations of one to eight proprietary CPUs; Amdahl is the leader here, having had considerable success offering its UNIX variant UTS on its mainframe line. Massively parallel systems are becoming a commercial proposition. Worldwide, ICL, and Siemens should also be considered as large UNIX suppliers.

Rather than examine this specialized market in great detail, I would like to point out that there is no general reason to be concerned about the performance limitations of a general business database system based on a UNIX operating system variant. The benchmarks published by various vendors demonstrate extremely high throughput for this class of system. In fact, plans are in place to put the largest databases, most secure systems, and highest throughput systems on this type of technology in the next three to five years. There are legitimate concerns in other areas than raw performance, and these are discussed later in the book. The key point is that a medium-sized system can be built with this technology in the confidence that it can be scaled up as necessary.

GENERAL ISSUES WITH UNIX SYSTEMS

In the UNIX category, there is a greater variety of strong vendors than almost any other area. Every significant computer company in the world offers a UNIX variant as a key part of its product line, and several companies offer nothing else. Many major governments have standards in place mandating the purchase of systems conforming to the UNIX interfaces. Astonishingly, despite all this, there are doubts about UNIX viability!

Although UNIX has led the move to standards-based computing from a theoretical standpoint, UNIX has suffered from its lack of a single standard when compared to PCs. Each version of the system has a different name, partly to emphasize particular advantages of the particular version but also to avoid the AT&T trademark attribution (now Novell/USL). There is no practical software distribution or user interface standard. While this is certainly no worse than the pre-UNIX system of proprietary systems, it is clearly inferior to the world of DOS, OS/2, Novell, and Windows. If, as it appears, Windows NT applications will be distributed on CD-ROM with all binary versions on a single disk, that will be an advantage over UNIX.

Summary

There is tremendous power available today in microprocessor-based servers. Available processor power is increasing very quickly, roughly doubling in power every 18 months. Disk storage and other components are improving at lesser speeds but still rapidly. The choice in operating systems has grown to include several powerful, well-supported options.

In response to all this progress, manufacturers of traditional servers, including mainframes, are also bringing out faster, cheaper lines, which also offer open access in many cases.

This offers many opportunities for migrating systems from older platforms to new choices that offer substantially better price/performance. It also opens up many new possibilities for systems that might not have been affordable previously.

7

Selecting the Database

The commonest scenario for mainframe replacement is to install LANs and PCs, then replace the mainframe with a smaller computer running a relational database. The database management system is the heart of the rightsizing effort, providing the central facilities and transaction management that allow production systems to be built with workstation-based tools. In other words, we rely on the database software to provide the mainframe-like features of reliability, integrity, and generalized access to data. Such a combination offers tremendous cost savings (Figure 7.1).

While the major databases have been the same few players for several years, the platforms on which to run them are undergoing a wave of change. Fortunately, the platform makes little difference to the application code, so it is possible to grow into a new one as necessary. The platforms were discussed in Chapter 6. Here, we will take a look at the database choices.

There are a great many specialized textbooks on relational databases and a number of documents focusing on each one. The objective here is to put the choices in context and compare the products to the mainframe environment that may have preceded them.

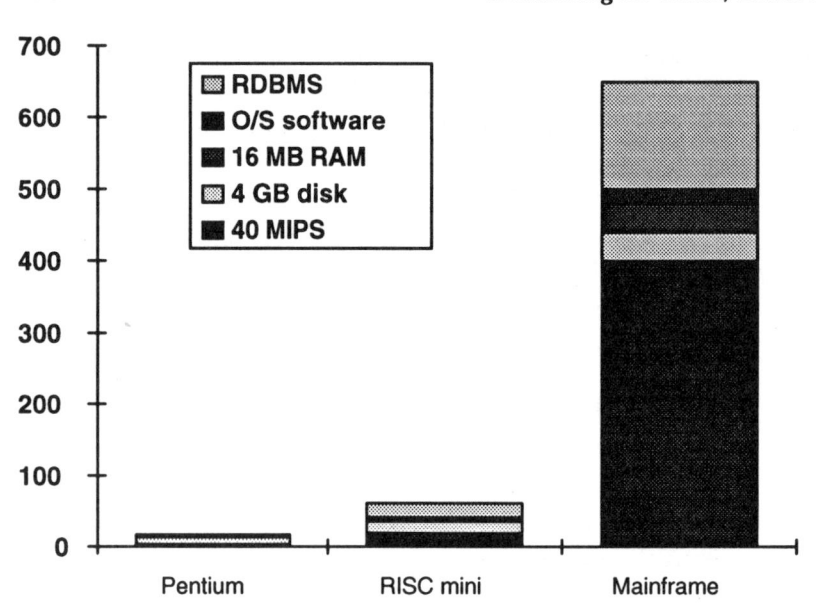

Figure 7.1 Relative costs

THE ADVANTAGE OF RELATIONAL DATABASES

The advantages of a database management system over a collection of files are well understood today. In a file-based system, each application has a series of files. These vary according to the algorithmic processes through which they pass. Each data element is repeated in many places. These systems were most prevalent in the days of tape-based processing but continued on because they optimize computer use and application development time for an individual application. Actually, the information of an organization is a precious asset, which should be reused, not lost and reentered between different applications. In order to achieve this, the programs must be designed independent of the data storage design. Once a database has been designed for an enterprise based on a data model, new applications and reports can be rapidly generated using this information. User access to data is easier and more flexible, since tools can be designed to navigate the database without extensive help from professional programmers. The development of new features is amortized over a wider user base.

Early Databases

These advantages were promised by a first generation of database, notably IMS and IDMS, in the 1970s. Unfortunately, they were not realized for several reasons. It became clear that with this technology an enterprise-wide data model needed to be created, complete with a data dictionary. This is time consuming, and individual application developers do not wish to fund it. The database technology was confusing, so that end users could not access their data except with custom programs. In fact, it was harder to access the information in the database than in traditional "flat files." There was a proliferation of "databases," typically one per application, so that the reuse advantage was not attained. The database system deteriorated into a mere access method.

Relational Databases

The relational database, introduced in the 1980s, is based on a solid theoretical foundation. This model specifies data and its access from a user perspective, not by specifying linkages and physical contiguity. This allows an application or user to access information without regard for its location or other physical properties. The view that the application has is abstracted from the real data. Because of this, programs written to access a relational database are flexible. The model allows for reuse and true program independence from the data structure. The SQL language is a standard, allowing the development of heterogeneous systems and third-party tools. The system has a good theoretical foundation, which has served to give it a stability and growth path that previous proprietary ad hoc products generally lacked. The relational database model with SQL is one of the genuine advances made by the software industry. It is a key foundation element for client/server computing.

The systems available are very far from perfect, however. These imperfections will be the basis for many products in the client/server marketplace, so they should be discussed.

SQL

SQL is not the ideal language, as has often been pointed out. Perhaps because of its theoretical limitations, it has been extended by most vendors of SQL databases. These extensions are necessary to do most significant jobs, rendering almost every application nonstandard. This is a variant of the same problem that makes COBOL, UNIX, and other "standards" unsuccessful.

This problem has led to a series of attempts to establish standards for SQL. The history and current situation of these standards is covered in the appropriate chapter; we should be aware that this problem runs fairly deep. On the positive side, it is possible to isolate 90 percent of application code from this problem by employing languages and code libraries that implement the necessary database recognition and manage the differences. On the negative side, this leads to extra cost for gateways, libraries, etc., with which to do this. It can also lead to performance penalties.

The languages and tools that surround each vendor's database have traditionally been proprietary to that vendor. Fortunately, this has changed recently, so that at least in marketing and product strategy the major products can work together.

One problem is less significant than many people think. At one time, the SQL databases were less efficient than the older databases, which were built around explicit pointer constructs so that their programmers were very aware of access paths. This issue is generally solved today by the improvements in database optimization, combined with today's processor performance. After all, relational databases are able to use indexes, memory cache, and data clustering and ordering; they simply hide these details from the application code. This is rather like the comparison between assembler and C languages. Perhaps, theoretically, a person can hand-optimize a piece of code better than the general-purpose efforts of the machine. In practice, however, the best person does not have the time, and the actual code produced is inferior.

A database management system is also a general-purpose problem; if one piece of a system needs outstanding performance, it can be handwritten in any case.

Essentially, any system that can benefit from a database of the hierarchical, network, or relational type at all might as well use a relational one. Vendors of the older database types base their sales case today around the difficulties of converting from the old system, not on their performance. The published TPC numbers bear this out. In 1990/91, we often had a serious argument with the defenders of a proprietary direct-access or memory-based file I/O system, not believing that a relational database could work; by 1993/94, the case has been proven so often that it is no longer an issue.

Object Databases

There is a new type of database, which claims to improve on relational just as relational improved on the older databases. And the analogy has some appeal: Just as object modeling is superseding data modeling, which super-

Chapter 7 • Selecting the Database 153

seded structured design (process modeling), so are object databases superseding relational databases (data oriented), which superseded network databases (process oriented). There are a couple of important differences, however. For one, the object databases have not moved out of the laboratory as rapidly as the relational products did. This is probably tied to the slow penetration of object-oriented languages (these companies are older than you think). For another, the relational vendors have tremendous vigor and seem more likely to adopt new technology to compete than the original network database vendors would. It seems at present that the object databases will succeed in niche areas where they have particular advantages—storing complex information or supporting very long transactions.

Two database products at least offer a hybrid approach, which offers the benefits of SQL combined with those of the object databases. These are UniSQL and Montage. These are worth considering if you need more than a relational database can offer. This might be storage of complex data types or very long (for instance, day-long) transactions. Other complex problems suited to these hybrids include the management of several different database management systems and migration from complex nonrelational databases. The penalty you pay to use these products is their nonstandard nature—for example, the inability to use a range of standard 4GL tools.

COMPARING THE DATABASE PRODUCTS

In this chapter, consistent with the approach of this book, we will consider relational database products that support SQL.

Multiplatform Databases

These products are available on a range of platforms, have been available for several years, and are distributed by large, solid vendors who are not tied to a single line of hardware:

- ORACLE   Oracle
- Sybase   SQL Server
- INFORMIX   Informix
- Computer Associates   Ingres, IDMS, Datacom

These vendors sell from $250 million to over a billion dollars worth per year of database management and related software on a variety of platforms, with no one platform dominating.

Single-Platform Databases

These products are available on one or two platforms from a single vendor, although all these manufacturers have plans to sell the software on competing hardware.

Supplier	Database	Platform
IBM	DB2	MVS
IBM	DB2/2	OS/2
IBM	DB2/6000	AIX
IBM	SQL/DS	VM
IBM	SQL/400	OS/400
DEC	RDB	VAX/VMS
H-P	Allbase	MPE, HP-UX
Micorsoft	SQL Server	Windows NT, OS/2

This categorization between multiple and single platforms is arguably becoming obsolete. Windows NT runs on a lot of different hardware, for example. Since DB2 runs on plug-compatible mainframes, has a wide range of PC-compatibles supporting OS/2, and is planned to support several UNIX variants, it could be said to be as "open" as a product such as Sybase. However, this is still a relatively new approach for DB2, and its long-term continuation will depend on its market success, which is not yet known. Also, although DB2/2 and DB2/6000 share the same code, this is not true of DB2 on MVS. The DB2 line is not as consistent in implementation as ORACLE or Sybase. And each of the above products gets all of its revenue from one single platform or from two (Allbase and DB2/2-6000).

Niche Suppliers

These products have a smaller market share. Some are very new, and the following list may not be complete. In recognition of the commanding market presence of the few major database products listed above, they tend to offer one of two alternative approaches—either an interesting advantage in a particular niche environment or a low price.

- Borland Interbase
- Cincom Supra Server
- Red Brick Warehouse
- Gupta SQLBase

- Btrieve SQL
- Quadbase-SQL
- Raima Database Server
- Watcom/PowerSoft SQL
- XDB

All of these products are relational, although Raima is "born again" from a network database, and all support the standard SQL language. To a large extent, they can be regarded as open because of this. The vendors have a variety of schemes for persuading a customer to lock in to their proprietary extensions, and it is difficult to avoid adopting some. Still, any of these databases can be reached from a good selection of front-end development tools.

BASIC STATISTICS

The largest database vendors are IBM, ORACLE, Sybase, CA, Microsoft, and Informix. Across all platforms, the leading databases in use are ORACLE, DB2, and the CA products. The leaders in current new installations are ORACLE, Sybase, and DB2. Microsoft SQL Server has sold the most copies at small installations. The major trend seems to be towards concentration on a smaller number of suppliers. IBM, ORACLE, and Sybase are growing in share at the expense of the next tier, which includes Ingres and Informix. Some vendors who used to be successful have essentially disappeared from database sales to new customers, and no new names have appeared. For example, there are nine databases, which are installed at 10 percent of large sites, but there are only three planned for future purchase by greater than 10 percent of the sites. The large installed base of nonrelational products, including FOCUS, IDMS, and IMS, is not being replaced. Not coincidentally, the same three databases (Sybase, ORACLE, DB2) seem to be the ones chosen in most client/server strategies. Sybase is the smallest but has the highest rate of growth, as it has for several years.

This overall picture varies in the different markets offered by different operating systems, where different databases show strength. Informix has traditionally been relatively strong in the UNIX world, for example, where it is second to ORACLE in sales and installed base. In the DEC VAX/VMS market, the four leading products are ORACLE, Ingres, RDB, and Sybase. In the OS/2 market, Microsoft SQL Server (based on Sybase) and ORACLE lead. There is a clear trend towards these markets becoming more similar, with the niche players being squeezed by the three larger products again.

Commodity Trend

Another trend could open up the possibilities for new vendors of databases. The proliferation of third-party tools, such as PowerBuilder and Visual Basic, combined with the development of database access standards, such as ODBC, may make the underlying database system purchase decision more of a commodity market. This would presumably be the preference of tool vendors, such as Microsoft and Borland; fear of this development, which is probably inevitable to some degree, is perhaps behind the aggressive moves ORACLE and Sybase are making into other product areas, notably development tools and more general data management strategies. Companies that would like to sell SQL databases by undercutting the current price structure include Microsoft ($99 Access supports SQL, and ODBC defines the API), Borland (desktop database leader and the pioneer of price cutting), and PowerSoft (who offer $100 and $250 development tools with a full SQL database and a $350 small network server), not to mention Gupta, XDB, and Quadbase. At present, it seems most likely that these systems will gain support at the desktop level, for small application software products, and among developers, where price is important, but not in the larger delivery environments where system maturity and vendor stability are more important than price.

Support

This is a changing market. Recent developments include CA's picture of Ingres, Powersoft's purchase of Watcom, and the separation of Microsoft and Sybase.

The above market factors were covered to remind us of the most important thing to consider in a database system, which is the ability of the supplier to maintain the product, support us, and enhance the system over time. Careful consideration of the importance of this may make selection relatively simple. In my experience as a consultant, I have never met a case where the presence or absence of one or two technical features was of critical importance in the course of a system. All features can be developed at some price in application code. I have met several cases where the unreliability of a database project doomed a project and a great many cases where lack of vendor viability over the long term led to the failure or early demise of an otherwise satisfactory product or system.

That having been said, there are many factors to consider when choosing a database server. In selecting a database, we must consider data access, reliability, manageability, and cost.

Pricing

Database management system pricing is a fine art. It is first necessary to consider the cost of a basic system and then that of a fully loaded system, which is one including all necessary unbundled tools:

- network and connectivity software
- performance options
- 4GL tools
- database administration tools, such as load and monitoring tools

Prices of database products vary considerably by platform, not always consistently. UNIX prices are often much higher than OS/2 or NLM, for example. Prices may reflect market size, rather than platform power, and can be affected by politics and timing also, such as the introduction of Windows NT. If you are flexible, there can be deals made here.

DATA ACCESS

The SQL Standard

The original SQL language was developed at IBM. An ANSI specification was developed in the early 1980s. While useful, the ANSI standard covered a subset of the language. A useful system required extensions in several directions. Improvements to the standard were published in 1992, and another version, SQL3, is now in preparation. SQL3 covers structure, branching, flow control, error handling, and object-oriented capabilities. In addition to ANSI, other groups publish database standards. The SQL Access Group (SAG), a consortium of hardware and software vendors, publishes an API and a Relational Data Access standard, and X/Open publishes a Distributed Transaction Processing standard.

It is natural that as each version of the SQL standard is formed, each database vendor provides extensions that will make their product unique. As long as these extensions provide significant enhancements in performance or ease of use, it will be difficult to justify a "least common denominator" approach to standards.

While it is not in the interest of database vendors to support a single standard (other than their own), it is in the interest of application tool vendors and application developers. Recently, several vendors have attempted to set a standard for the database API, or call-level interface. This is important because any tool wanting to access the database in a reasonably efficient manner must employ a call-level interface, and each vendor had developed a completely different one. These standards are based on the SQL Access Group (SAG) model, which, in turn, was based on the Sybase Open Client or DB-Library interface.

Microsoft's ODBC is an implementation of SAG, which has developed into a superset. These standards are for access to the database from tools, allowing these companies' desktop tools to broaden their appeal. The ODBC standard is more widely accepted than the Borland one and is discussed here.

The ODBC standard offers developers who are willing to accept some compromises the option of writing a single set of code that can work with almost all databases in common use. The nature of the necessary compromises is subject to fierce debate; some say it is unacceptable, others that it is minimal. This debate is inevitable, given the vested interests at stake. Agreement on a database access standard will eventually reduce database management systems to a commodity market. In such a market, systems are sold on pure price and performance; this will reduce margins dramatically in that industry, at the same time damaging some vendors of gateway and access library products and reducing the thriving cottage industry consulting on database differences.

The common perception that ODBC is slow is certainly not entirely true. Microsoft tested ODBC against DB-Library, the native API for SQL Server, using a modified TP1 benchmark in a Windows/SQL Server environment, and found ODBC slightly faster. Generally, ODBC is slow when adding functionality to non-SQL systems, such as dBASE, but may not be when performing the same functionality as the proprietary API. Also, ODBC was first available in the middle of 1993, so it is in early stages, and some drivers' performance will likely improve. At present, it is clear that ODBC is a good way to offer connectivity to a wide range of databases without extensive development and that it is adequate for decision support and management information applications.

Database management systems add value with some important proprietary features, especially in the area of stored procedures and triggers. Stored procedures are the best way to exploit the application processing capabilities of server systems and to reduce the network traffic of client/server systems. Triggers are the flexible method to implement data integrity at the server. If an application intends to use ODBC for transactional applications, it would be advisable to prototype and benchmark, and it may be appropriate to use some database-specific code. Because ODBC allows triggers and stored procedures by passing the SQL code through to the back end, use of these efficient options leads to nonportable code. This is still a significant improvement; the nonportable code is isolated to necessary enhancements, which are economically justified.

Other database standards exist. The IBM DRDA standard is a protocol for distributed database implementation. As a result, it is possible, indeed quite a useful idea, to have an ODBC to DRDA gateway. The Object Management Group working group seems to be migrating toward having a common command set—OSQL (Object SQL).

Database Objects

All of the standard data types should be expected. This includes integer, float, decimal, date/time, character, variable character, and a long type used for bit maps, word processing fields, and so on. There are many variants of these. Numbers have many size parameters—small and large ints and floats, for instance, and different precisions for fixed decimal. Data and time are handled with many formats in different databases. Long types may have different size restrictions in different databases and very different implementations from a performance perspective.

Database Functions

Functions operating on fields such as SUBSTR and LENGTH (technically called scalar functions) have inconsistent names between databases. Cursor support varies. Transaction management, including concurrency and deadlock, is managed differently. The outer join function is handled with different extensions in different databases. If you have existing applications written to a given standard, such as DB2, you may need to determine how closely the DB2 data types are supported.

SQL Implementation

The database should provide:
- data validation during insertion/update of data
- entity and referential integrity constraints to be specified
- transaction controls during insert, update, and delete operations
- explicit locking of tables or records
- an outer-join facility

- ability to change access privileges at any time for SQL operations
- implicit temporary tables for intermediate data in a multistatement retrieval
- utilities to load and unload data between the database and flat files
- DB2 compatibility option (e.g., declarative referential integrity)
- support for standard networking protocols and gateways
- support for object-oriented standards as these evolve

Stored Procedures and Triggers

Stored procedures allow us to store application logic on the server. Stored procedures are precompiled units of SQL code, stored in the database, and called by name. They improve both performance and application consistency at the expense of database dependency, because there is no standard for stored procedures.

Triggers are sets of SQL statements that are executed as a result of a database event, such as an update, insert, or delete statement. They usually allow us to execute stored procedures. Triggers are a good basis for centralized dynamic database integrity. For example, a trigger could guarantee that a record in a parent table could not be deleted if the record was related to one or more records in a child table. A trigger can ensure that a foreign key must reference an existing primary key, or be null, and that changes to a primary key must be reflected in all foreign keys referencing it.

Triggers can enforce a set of business rules as well as relational data integrity. By storing these in the server, we ensure that all client programs are subject to the same rules without replicating them. This is particularly useful if client programs may be developed in different languages or business areas; it is less useful if the client programs are more monolithic and must support different databases.

Stored procedures were pioneered in SQL Server but have since become available with other databases. Sybase and ORACLE have full implementations of stored procedures and triggers; the DB2 family does not (except for DB2/2), offering referential integrity through static declarations. Other products vary in offering support and in the details of their implementation. Full support can be quite extensive and should not be taken for granted as a simple checklist item. SQL Server triggers, for example, can occur on update/insert/delete for any table, can be nested, and will access remote servers, although two-phase commit is not supported. ORACLE7 triggers

Chapter 7 • Selecting the Database   **161**

can occur before or after update/insert/delete on tables or rows, leading to 12 trigger types. Other vendors may not support nesting or a full range of types.

Effective use of triggers needs careful management. Triggers should not be too general or try to do too much. Updates to important fields should not involve a cascade of field checking against the database. In practice, it is hard to predict when they will be used.

Through the use of defaults, rules, triggers, and transaction logs, data integrity can be achieved with a high degree of confidence. Defaults are used to specify what to insert into a particular field, if no value is inserted by a user. Rules can be placed on fields to control what data can be entered into the field. The transaction log is a record of every modification made to a database. Since each modification is recorded, the database server can guarantee that each transaction is either completed successfully or is rolled back.

A good stored procedure mechanism is essential to a database.

Declarative Referential Integrity

An alternative approach to triggers for referential integrity was pioneered by IBM DB2. This is a static approach, where the necessary table constraints are part of the database definition. This is less general than the trigger/stored procedure method but much simpler to develop and enforce. ORACLE, Progress, NetWare SQL, and SQLBase also use DB2-style declarative integrity: Sybase did not offer it until System 10, and Microsoft SQL Server does not yet.

The listing below shows an example.

```
CREATE TABLE linitem
(order char(5) not null,
 part char(5) not null,
 quantity int
PRIMARY KEY (order, part)
FOREIGN KEY (order)
    REFERENCES TABLE orders
    ON DELETE CASCADE
FOREIGN KEY (part)
    REFERENCES TABLE part
    ON DELETE RESTRICT)
IN DATABASE ORDER_ENTRY
```

This is a very desirable feature.

Front-End Software Support

It is important to consider what front ends are available for the database server you select. Equally, the database server should be able to exchange information with other database systems—for example, mainframe databases.

Data Dictionary

This should be open and should support distributed and heterogeneous databases.

PERFORMANCE

Performance of client/server database systems is difficult to predict. As with all such performance models, output is not a linear function of the various input parameters but is based on bottlenecks. You must consider the hardware, memory, operating system, network operating system, number of users, network traffic, and so on; then determine which of these is constraining performance. Typically, removal of one constraint provides some improvement and then leads to another, so the results of a performance upgrade are not easily predicted.

Performance sought must be expressed in specifics in these categories:

- throughput (TPS)
- storage capacity (gigabytes)
- response time for updates
- response time for simple queries
- response time for complex queries
- resilience against failure
- recovery time after failure

Design for Performance

Design of a database system for performance is a complex job involving several disciplines: physical design, application design, database design, and database operations. Client/server systems are sensitive to many issues that are sometimes out of their control. On the good side, they are highly amenable to tuning; they are also vulnerable to change.

Physical server configuration is very important. For an individual system with a given set of products, the "three Ms," MIPS of CPU, MEGABYTES of memory, and MILLISECONDS of disk access time, are critical. Main memory is used extensively in relational systems for sorting and caching. This allows optimization of a single thread of access. Once this is done, resource contention is the determining factor for a multiuser system. The database machines should have several disks, with not too many disks on a controller. Frequently accessed files, particularly transaction logs, should reside on a separate disk and controller. Concurrently used objects should be put on separate disks. Disk striping should be used to spread tables across disks.

Client/server performance problems generally show up as complaints about the loading of large tables onto screens. These are not discovered in early tests with smaller databases and show up in volume testing late in development. Unfortunately, most of the development tools do not allow use of the corrective data access tuning techniques without considerable early design work, so thought should be given to the various techniques for addressing this problem early on.

Techniques for improving database access include preloading of data, accessing it asynchronously, or accessing it in stages. Preloading often works in transactional systems, where the next action can be guessed. Asynchronous loading can allow the first screen of a long list to be displayed while further data are retrieved; this may depend on design issues, such as sorting or joining. Staged access is offered by some servers, again allowing an initial screen to proceed while further data are gathered.

Another technique is to distract the users with messages or graphics or simply tell them what's happening. This may be the best option for some applications where genuine ad hoc queries are taking place; queries on the Internet, for example, may be best managed by explaining the complex and unpredictable nature of the network. Of course, if certain queries are common, these results can be stored ahead of time or at least retained after first access. Caching of various forms is very effective; most databases have subsets that are much more active than the rest. This can take the form of database memory caching, local database versus remote (i.e., data replication), or application caching mechanisms.

There are many aspects of database design that improve performance. Use of database stored procedures to reduce transmitted data can be very effective. Overuse, particularly of triggers, may have the opposite effect. Indexing and the use of clustered indexes (i.e., sorting the database) are the best solution for large queries, particularly for nonvolatile databases.

In database operations, the important thing is to update the database statistics. Several databases, including Sybase, ORACLE, Informix, and DB2, have cost-based optimizers that work on these. Use of performance monitoring tools also helps to understand how the database is being used. More performance problems can be addressed with database design than any other area, and this is also the least expensive solution.

Benchmarking

It is important to do your own benchmarks. Many people pay too much attention to the published benchmark performance tests when selecting a database server. Like gas mileage, your mileage will differ from the published numbers. There are many reasons for this. Vendors optimize for the benchmarks, designing table sizes and cache limits with the industry benchmarks in mind. The benchmarks were chosen to be realistic but not to make database technology look bad. Many real-world applications perform much worse than the benchmarks, because they must meet real constraints that cause performance problems. Many of the problems being addressed today are also more demanding than the banking transaction used for the most common database benchmarks.

In client/server systems, every database and application is going to perform differently, even on the same database server; performance is application- and database-specific. No serious system should be built without prior benchmarking. This was easy to forget in a mainframe shop, where there may have been several large implementations in a row with the same hardware and database technology and the same general application behavior. In 1994, the industry is littered with the failure of client/server applications whose authors did not realize the importance of this. Before you commit to a particular platform of database server and operating system, set up a prototype of your major database application. Perform your own benchmark tests on your database and applications to model your application and its database use before you build it.

The goals of an application-specific benchmark are to verify that the technology to be used works and can be afforded, to model throughput and response under typical loads, and to measure degradation and determine breakpoints. This does not require a great amount of coding; it does demand a database and transaction volume that approximates the complete system, an appropriate mix of transaction types (e.g., reports, queries, and data entry), and a sampling of typical on-line and batch activities.

Transaction Processing Benchmarks

An important set of useful published benchmarks for database servers are the TPC series. These stem from the TP1 benchmark, originated at Bank of

America in 1972 and described in *Datamation* in the 1985 article, "A Measure of Transaction Processing Power." The benchmark, based on a real-life problem at the time, models the cash positions of retail bank branches accepting deposit and withdrawal requests. The benchmark scales size to performance, requiring 100,000 accounts for every transaction per second (TPS) claimed. The account records are 100 bytes long with a unique index. A 100-character message is received; account, branch total, teller, and history records are updated; and a 200-byte message written out. Record-level locking and logging are required, subsecond response times are expected, and 15 percent of transactions are not to the local branch.

This defines a useful and realistic application, and the benchmark was very effective for Bank of America. Publishing this benchmark did the industry a good turn. Until this point, hardware and database vendors tended to produce their own self-serving performance figures; afterward, we began to see a series of improving measures.

The initial TP1 measure had essentially two limitations: the benchmark was insufficiently specified, and there was nobody to enforce the specifications and prevent cheating.

A variety of shortcuts were taken by vendors eager to improve their performance. They would leave out parts, such as the error-checking or the history file. They would fail to scale the benchmark as specified, increasing transactions per second without increasing the number of accounts. They would fail to document all the hardware, software, cache sizes, etc., that they used, thus giving misleading impressions of the cost or feasibility of the system. And they would publish comparisons of their latest product to the competitions' previous versions.

The Transaction Processing Council was set up as a body to manage a series of benchmarks based on the original TP1 debit/credit benchmark, which was tightened up and supervised to cut down on cheating. There is a series of TPC benchmarks. TPC Benchmark A (TPC-A) is a version of TP1 for on-line transaction processing systems. TPC-B is a version of TP1 for the DBMS only, and the newest, TPC-C, is an order-entry benchmark introduced in August 1992, which supports a mix of five transaction types.

The TPC numbers must be used with some care. These are three different benchmarks, and it is necessary to compare like with like. Further, TPC-A can be run on a client/server or host/terminal configuration, and this will produce different and noncomparable results.

TPC numbers are published with the relevant cost data. The TPC-A benchmark measures the combination of processor, memory, I/O, terminal, network, and database used in support of the on-line transaction processing.

It is database-dependent, of course. When looking at $K/TPC-A, it is important to compare like configurations. Many companies offer the same processor and disks in different packages (deskside, rack-mounted) at substantially different prices. For example, the IBM RS/6000 models 580 and 980 will have identical performance but cost different amounts.

Portability and Scalability

Portability to other platforms is an important performance issue. This allows selection of more powerful or less expensive systems depending on need and also ensures system viability over time. Portability is more complex than the list of supported systems. We need to check that the latest, full-featured versions are available on these platforms and review the history for consistent support. Platforms that do not sell well are often sponsored by their vendors and are unlikely to remain well supported. Most companies have a porting list, and systems high on the list are supported the best. Different tools may also be sponsored on different platforms; while this may represent appropriate use of a platform's unique capabilities, such as ORACLE support for HyperCard on the Macintosh, it may also make it more difficult for an experienced professional to function, as evidenced by the completely different support tools on Sybase and Microsoft SQL Server.

Scalability is a special case of portability. If the size of the database application or number of users accessing the database could potentially increase, make sure the database server is scalable. You will want to ensure that the database is easily portable to a more powerful platform. This should include availability on small and large platforms with appropriate pricing, performance, and behavior. Some databases were available in the past on DOS, for instance, in greatly scaled-back versions; others demanded expensive and unusual upgrades and still performed poorly. Ideally, a system will be available on a notebook computer under Windows with an adequate price and performance for one user and also run on a data center-class, multiple-processor system with support for many users at a presumably much higher price.

Of course, if portable database standards are followed, we could use different databases for these scenarios without altering the applications; this is another possibility but, as discussed before, not an easy one to implement.

Data Storage

You should review your application database needs and examine the database limits for:

- table size
- database size
- relations/join
- tables/physical file

Sometimes operating system limits are relevant; OS/2 has a 2 GB size limit on files, for example.

MANAGEABILITY

Database manageability issues are key areas of differentiation for the suppliers. Even if we see the data access become a standard, leading to commodity-based performance competition, questions of data management and security will continue to be areas where database suppliers can add value and command a premium. High-performance database servers need to offer high availability, data integrity, and security. They should be able to share and distribute data in a heterogeneous environment and support a reasonable set of paradigms for management of that data.

Database management cannot be separated from other issues of server and distributed system management; this is covered in a later chapter.

The Special Case of DB2

DB2 cannot simply be treated as another relational database. It is a mainframe product; this brings some tremendous advantages along with some considerable liabilities. It is not at all paradoxical that DB2 can be a tremendous enabler of client/server computing. Client/server is about exploiting the benefits of each platform; DB2 offers the benefits of mainframe data and system management, while allowing access to the data from tools running on intelligent workstations. Mainframes, with their high-speed concurrent processing, large storage capacities, multitasking, and multiuser architecture, may provide an ideal platform for some large database servers.

Many workstation-based relational DBMSs are not able to handle heavy loads of structured queries against large volumes of data—for example, a customer needing information about a particular order over a particular period of time. DB2 performs this type of query very well.

DB2 has several effective features for optimizing SQL processing. The two most important for performance are prebound SQL and prefetch.

DB2 prebound SQL packages let the administrator drastically reduce processing requirements during run-time execution. Other database servers may let you send an SQL command from client to server only once but allow this to execute repeatedly on the server, so that it is reoptimized every time.

Prefetch uses the Distributed Relational Database Architecture (DRDA) protocol to allow a client to request the prefetch of data from a server. The client specifies how much data it can receive as a block. The server returns as many rows in the answer set as can be put in the block; the client sends another request after these rows have been exhausted. This approach substantially reduces communications overhead between client and server.

DB2 integrity support includes static referential integrity and a transaction mechanism, which was the model for the SQL standard. The DB2 referential integrity implementation provides for declaration of primary and foreign keys within the table definition. This, together with the support for synonyms and aliases, avoids duplication of effort, inconsistency, and maintenance problems that result when integrity code is scattered throughout applications or stored procedures.

In a nonmainframe site, the economics of DB2 pertaining to the MVS data center and staffing can be very difficult to justify. In a mainframe installation, where those things are already bought and paid for, the strengths of the product may be considered against the incremental cost of additional disk storage. DB2 can be an excellent way to centralize data and create usable information repositories, possibly as a staging area on the way to distributed databases. This type of strategy makes use of gateways and distributed database protocols, which are discussed in a later chapter.

Summary

The SQL database standard is an imperfect one, particularly when examined in detail, but valuable nonetheless. The technology of distributed databases on a variety of platforms is reasonably mature; advances to object-oriented systems in the business arena seem likely to build on this base in an evolutionary manner. Application development can use the relative stability of this component of the architecture to create durable and flexible business systems. Because the data model can be described and built in a stable manner, the point solutions we construct on top can be integrated through the database.

Selection of the database management system for an enterprise seems to have come down to choosing between DB2, ORACLE, and SQL Server from Sybase or Microsoft, with larger organizations often recognizing that they will employ all of them.

8

Selecting Workstations, Development Tools, and Applications

The choice of workstation hardware and software is the most visible decision you can make. Minor variations in this choice can be perceived much more than in middleware, database, or server selections. Because of the many different application possibilities, this is also an area where a single standard is unlikely for any but the smallest corporation. Several tools may be used even for one application.

As we will discuss later, support and training costs are very high in workstation environments and trending higher. One response to this is to select a standard hardware and software configuration, or a set of configurations, recommend and support them, and require their use. Generally, in such an approach, one allows special cases where the users' needs vary substantially from the norm. In the recent past, for example, many corporations have had a standard of Intel/DOS, while supporting the exception of Macintosh for graphical work, such as desktop publishing, and possibly UNIX workstations for some specialty tasks and proprietary terminals for others. When companies adopt e-mail or other forms of workgroup computing, the benefit of this type of standard becomes more compelling, as documents are increasingly exchanged using the formats of the various software packages.

Several new trends have emerged in the tool marketplace; these include the development of integrated suites of applications, the exchange of formats within workgroups, the ability of the scripting languages in applications to be used for application development, and the ability of applications to access data stored in the common workstation and server database systems. This is resulting in a new class of application, which is assembled from component tools with little or no traditional programming. These applications offer tremendous productivity; they also tilt the playing field towards adoption of workgroup standards for office tools. Since most companies consist of interlocking and overlapping workgroups, this tends to encourage company-wide adoption of standard office tools. Although, theoretically, a company might pick "best of breed" tools, at the moment, tool pricing strongly encourages purchase of the "suites" from a single vendor.

SELECTING WORKSTATIONS

When selecting a corporate workstation platform and tools, the choice used to be between volume and standards (IBM PC) and power (Macintosh or UNIX). Now, several available systems all appear to offer an adequate range of power and cost options. With the advent of OS/2 and Windows NT, we are beginning to see several strong contenders for general-purpose office automation platforms that can support specialized, high-powered computing needs as well.

During 1993, several new 32-bit operating systems were introduced to join the 32-bit systems already shipping—SCO Open Desktop and Apple Macintosh System 7. Possible workstation choices are listed in Figure 8.1.

Current versions are:

- Windows 3.11 (later Windows Chicago)
- Windows NT 3.1 and 3.5
- Macintosh System 7.1 and 7.5
- OS/2 2.1 (and later, e.g., Warp)
- UNIX (Solaris, NeXTStep, SCO UNIX, UNIXware, etc.)

Both DOS systems and X terminals have their specialized uses, but neither is an adequate choice for standard workstations.

DOS Limitations

Despite the preeminence of Windows (based on DOS) as the corporate desktop platform, DOS is technically a very poor choice of operating system. It was never intended for its current role. DOS limitations include:

- no security (no logon, authentication, encryption)
- no multitasking (needed for networking and reliable GUI)

Chapter 8 • Selecting Workstations, Development Tools, and Applications

- memory limit (640K)
- segmented Intel memory model

Expanded memory, TSRs, and Windows itself are examples of "kludges" introduced to extend DOS beyond its architectural limits. UNIX and OS/2 are both greatly superior operating systems, designed for use in networked environments.

Microsoft, the purveyor of DOS, is well aware of these defects, and has led the way in pointing them out and trying to correct them. Because of these DOS problems, first OS/2, then Windows NT, and now Windows 4.0 have been developed.

X Terminals

X terminals deliver the beauty of the large-screen graphical interface to an occasional user for less cost and trouble than a dedicated workstation. They have a role as part of the mix for an organization that chooses a UNIX desktop approach. Fundamentally, the X station is defeated as a general solution by the simple fact that the costs of processor and disk, which the X station has less of, have come down much faster than the cost of desktop real estate and large screens, which the X station has. The additional cost of a full workstation over an X station is not much and becomes less each year. A PC with a large screen and a fast graphics processor running X software is more flexible.

- Microsoft Windows
- Macintosh
- OS/2
- UNIX
    - NextStep/OpenStep
    - SCO Open Desktop
    - Solaris, UNIXware, etc.
- Windows NT
- Terminals
    - X or dumb

Figure 8.1 Workstation choices

Availability of applications, now and in the future, is the first thing to consider. In the long term, some of the present platforms may not be viable because there are too many for developers to support. The most reliable way to see what applications will be available in the future is to look at what developers are writing for today. Two or three years ago, new tools and applications were first developed for Macintosh, OS/2, or UNIX more often than for Windows, because these platforms were technically superior. Examples include:

- Aldus PageMaker (Mac)
- Knowledgeware ADW (OS/2)
- Lotus Notes (OS/2)
- Lotus Improv (NeXTStep)
- Framemaker (Solaris/UNIX)

Today, applications are generally developed for the Windows platform first. It is good enough and the market it represents is immense.

Windows/DOS

The corporate graphical user interface market is standardizing on Windows, which has a rapidly rising share—currently over 80 percent. Windows (including Windows 3.1 and Windows for Workgroups 3.11) ships millions of copies a month, far more than any other system. The rest of the market is split about evenly between OS/2, Macintosh, Sun, and other systems. The non-GUI market consists of the more conservative DOS users, who will mostly go to Windows in the next one or two years.

When developing applications, if we include environments like the Power Mac and OS/2, which can run Windows applications well, close to 100 percent of corporate desktops can be reached with Windows applications in the next two years.

Windows NT

The arrival of a solid high-performance Windows NT (Daytona, or 3.5) gives Windows the underlying operating system and hardware platform choices to extend into the territory previously owned by UNIX workstations. The standard system supports fault tolerance and multiprocessing, for instance. This gives the Windows adopter today a migration path for higher performance.

Windows NT requires up to 16M of memory, which has delayed its acceptance as a desktop system.

Although a new operating system, Windows NT has all of the advantages of its familiar interface. It has built-in networking. As a desktop operating system, it will appeal to some power users because it supports high-speed platforms, including the DEC Alpha and MIPS R4400.

Macintosh

The Macintosh was clearly the leading GUI machine by any measure until 1992. It pioneered introduction of all the Xerox PARC inventions in the corporate world: the mouse, windows, icons, easy networking. It brought desktop publishing and graphical interface development into common use and pioneered multimedia. Although in a sense it deserved to become the standard client workstation, it has not done so. The advantages of the early Macintosh have now eroded, so that a commodity PC can perform the same functions. While the Macintosh is still the system of choice for many specific tasks, the future of the Macintosh interface as a mass-market platform now appears to lie in software that can run on a variety of hardware platforms.

OS/2

OS/2 is an operating system with an underlying structure greatly superior to DOS. It is a good system on which to develop, because it is stable and has good basic tools. Unfortunately, the series of delays in development of OS/2 since 1984 has caused it to miss its real window of opportunity as the DOS replacement. It is now a requirement for OS/2 to support Windows applications as well as Windows. This solidifies the guarantee that developers will write for Windows first. Emulations of this type never really succeed (see below).

OS/2 2.1 is a technically good migration path in 1994, since it does support Windows well and can run on systems with reasonable amounts of memory, unlike Windows NT (OS/2 requires 6 to 8M RAM and 40M disk). If you are willing to consider proprietary enhancements, OS/2 also has an attractive user interface (Workplace Shell) and the REXX command language.

There are some questions about the long-term viability of OS/2, since it is very expensive to fund such a system if it cannot sustain a larger share of the market.

UNIX

UNIX is an operating system whose time has been coming for many years. It is certainly a successful server operating system, with more growth to come. Every computer company is selling UNIX-based servers as a primary strategy. However, UNIX operating systems, despite their technical advantages, are not the right general-purpose choice for the desktop. The PC industry model requires a commodity operating system and hardware base, and the UNIX vendors have never organized themselves to deliver this. Despite "open systems" talk, UNIX vendors have historically worked hard to maintain proprietary distinctions between their products. If they come together now, it will be too late. UNIX systems have a diminishing set of advantages over the volume systems, such as Windows NT. The arrival of Intergraph applications on Windows NT is an example of the direction.

There are not enough software choices for UNIX workstations; new desktop software is not written for UNIX. Even when products such as WordPerfect are available for UNIX, they are often out-of-date versions. DOS emulation is always painfully slow and has other problems (see the section on Emulations).

As the price of these systems came down, there was a time when it appeared that they might challenge the PC industry for dominance. Unfortunately, although it appeared that the systems had come down to PC prices, the $4,000 workstation turned out to be a marketing ploy, not a serious system. These inexpensive systems have high processor performance (20–50 SPECint92) but tend to be configured to be of minimal use. Diskless workstations require a network with a server, of course; worse, because UNIX systems use virtual memory, they go to disk a lot. On a diskless networked system, which has a lot of network traffic and poor performance, the UNIX graphical interface for most systems is not mature, so you have to drop into character windows a lot, and these machines have remained difficult to install, administer, and support. The price for a real system, with the necessary large quantities of memory and disk, has never come down much below $15,000 to $20,000. Software and peripherals cost much more than their equivalents on PCs and are much fewer. The functionality of PCs came up faster than the price of workstations came down.

Table 8.1 shows costs of reasonable workstations from the five main vendors, configured with a 19-inch color monitor, 16M of memory, and 400M disk. This is not enough memory or disk for most purposes. These prices are approximate; they change rapidly and can be negotiated.

In the next year, Solaris and NeXTStep will have their last chance to carve out a role as a mass-market operating system. As the two most elegant,

Chapter 8 • Selecting Workstations, Development Tools, and Applications   177

Table 8.1 Low-Cost Workstations

	SPECint92	*SPECfp92*	*Cost*
DEC Alpha AXP300	67	77	$13,000
HP 9000 715/50	37	72	$14,000
IBM RS/6000 355	40	81	$16,000
SGI Indigo	58	60	$17,000
Sun SPARCstation 10 Model 30	45	49	$20,000

well-thought-out systems available, we should wish them well. However, in the Intel marketplace, these are not the strongest or fastest-moving companies, and, as Damon Runyon said, "the race is not always to the swift, nor the battle to the strong, but that is the way to place your bets."

If not the winner in the mass market, UNIX-based desktop operating systems are powerful systems, well-suited to professional knowledge workers. Some early examples of their specific professional use include CASE, desktop publishing, GIS, CAD, and financial trading/analysis; these areas are now dominated by Windows-based systems. UNIX systems have moved on to more computationally intensive work, including scientific computation, digital media, molecular modeling, simulations, visualization, and virtual reality. While the lower-end functions are often possible today with general-purpose Windows systems, the higher-end functions are not, and new uses are invented as the systems become more powerful.

UNIX variants are supported across many hardware architectures. UNIX is still the best development environment, with Solaris and NeXTStep being the best examples of this. And UNIX, as a mature operating system, has many influential supporters in the industry.

UNIX on Intel PCs and X terminals are the other alternatives for low-cost UNIX desktops. Desktop UNIX on Intel is available as:

- Sun Solaris and Interactive
- SCO UNIX (and Xenix)
- Novell UNIXware
- NeXT NeXTStep

UNIXware is a shrink-wrapped UNIX available from Novell. It is based on UNIX SVR4.2, extended with NetWare SPX/IPX protocol support, access to NetWare services, and the Lotus DOS Merge product.

Taligent

The Apple/IBM joint venture offers a fascinating alternative. As stated above, the three alternatives to Windows are the Macintosh, OS/2, and UNIX. This product could integrate all three, or there may be a confusion of offerings, including:

- OS/2 on Intel
- OS/2 on PowerPC
- Mac System 7 on Motorola
- Mac System 7 on PowerPC
- AIX on RS/6000
- AIX on PowerPC

It is too soon to tell. By 1995, the prospects for Taligent will be clearer.

Is There a Case against GUIs?

Many companies today resist the graphical user interface (GUI), although these systems offer many benefits (Figure 8.2). The common objections are that it costs too much and that the users don't want it. There is a good deal of truth in this, but it is almost never a sufficient argument against the interface. GUI systems today cost much less than the original purchase cost of the systems they are replacing, whether dedicated dumb terminals or character-oriented PCs. Those purchases were justified then, and the new systems do everything their replacements did and more. The only computers not able to run Windows today are the older systems in the installed base. A Windows-capable PC can be purchased for less than a thousand dollars. If it is worth hiring an employee and installing a system at all, this cannot be a prohibitive cost.

- ◆ Context switching between tasks
- ◆ Ease of navigation
- ◆ Usable help
- ◆ Consistency of use between applications
- ◆ More attractive, less tiring information presentation
- ◆ Increasingly, access to latest software

Figure 8.2 What a GUI offers the user

Users generally want what they are familiar with. Users specifying a replacement system generally specify what they have with a few bugs fixed. Since many users today have character-oriented screens, that is what they want; however, it is probably not what they need. The graphical screen is best for presenting a variety of information, allowing a user to work on several tasks concurrently or to switch between them. It is, therefore, preferable for all professional work. It is required to present document images, allowing document composition or many other simple clerical tasks. The full GUI technique, with help information, mice, and windows, is ideal where a user interacts with the computer in a variety of ways and does not memorize all of the sequences and possibilities.

It is true that the most noticeable features of a GUI (see Figure 8.3) are not best for employees who perform repetitive tasks, such as order entry, airline reservations, or commodity trading. But there is no requirement to use a mouse or multiple windows; good applications function well with keyboard use. The keyboard is a good device for these people; sometimes a dedicated keypad or other entry device is better. They can be trained to operate a keyboard more rapidly for the limited interactions they perform. However, such employees often can use color or audio confirmation in their regular work, and almost all of these jobs may involve error correction or summary functions, which require standard GUI approaches. As an example, commodities traders spend much of the day entering trades very rapidly. They wish to minimize their keystrokes and see simple screens formatted with a dense array of numbers. They will not use a mouse, demanding a small keyboard with abbreviated character codes. At any time, they wish to be alerted to unexpected movements in prices with color signals, possibly audible alerts. On occasion, they want to see a variety of summaries. They can best navigate the many options offered here with a mouse or touch screen. Some of the summaries are time series displayed as graphs.

- Multiple overlapping windows
- Selection with a pointing device
- Variety of proportional fonts and weights
- Graphics (bit map and line drawing pictures)
- Generally color
- Often sound

Figure 8.3 What a GUI is

To summarize, there is generally not a good reason not to install GUI-capable systems for all users. The difference in cost is too minute to be a concern. It is still useful on occasion to develop applications that do not employ graphical techniques but which still can be deployed on GUI-capable hardware and software.

Emulations

Emulations have been offered for several years, from the beginning of the PC industry. There are several different architectures for emulation, including hardware coprocessors, and a variety of software techniques, including use of processor features designed to assist. The various efforts have one thing in common: They have worked in selected uses but never worked reliably and fast, over a sustained period of time, on a broad range of products.

Early emulators included the very successful CP/M Z80 boards for Apple II systems. Recently, UNIX, OS/2, Apple, and now Windows NT have offered emulators for DOS and then DOS/Windows. These products are very useful, allowing a specialized solution based on, for instance, AIX, while preserving compatibility with corporate e-mail systems or individual legacy DOS applications. They serve a transitional purpose. The limitations include the following.

1. The performance of a fast machine running the emulator is no better than a slow machine without it.

2. The application will be harder to use because of minor incompatibilities in the interface, such as keyboard, screen, mouse, or printer features.

3. The application will be hard to install and support.

4. The latest, best applications for the environment being emulated won't work.

The performance issue means that you are always better off with the cheaper solution, if most of your work is in the emulation environment. You may buy a Sun workstation and enjoy occasional Lotus 1-2-3 use; if you are a power Lotus user, you will run it on a real PC.

Keyboards differ between the IBM PC, Sun, and Apple Macintosh. Screen navigation and mouse control differ between different GUIs. Device support is always an issue for each operating system.

When you install an application on an emulator system, you generally cannot follow the instructions that shipped with the application. Directories and devices will be described differently. When you call the application technical support, they will have no knowledge of the environment you are running. The platform vendor will not know the application.

The latest, best DOS or Windows applications always push the limits of the environment. When DOS emulators were supporting 640K, the best applications were using extended or expanded memory. When emulators supported the 80286 real mode, the best applications were using protected mode. When emulators supported Windows, the best applications used Windows extended mode. Now, the best applications are supporting multimedia device drivers.

Operating systems that offer the API and binary interface of the emulated environment have a better chance of succeeding. Sun WABI or IBM WIN OS/2 support the Windows applications directly; IBM even has the original Windows code running. They still face the problem that the emulated environment, in this case Windows, can change. The latest and best applications will take advantage of changes in the API more quickly than the emulating operating system can support them. This is particularly likely if, as some people have suggested, the vendor of the emulated environment designs and times changes in the API to disrupt the emulation strategy.

Processor Choices

Five years ago, the personal workstation market used to be split between general-purpose PC-DOS systems, based on the Intel 286/386 processor; the Apple Macintosh, based on the Motorola 680x0; and more powerful professional systems (notably Sun, Apollo), based on the Motorola 68030.

With the advent of reduced instruction set computing (RISC), the professional workstation market moved off the Motorola 68000 to the various RISC chips (IBM POWER, HP-PA, Sun SPARC, Motorola 88000, MIPS R3000).

It appears that RISC chips have a sustainable performance edge over the standard Intel series. Since this would give operating systems built for RISC an edge over those stuck on the Intel, there was speculation at one time that UNIX would become the desktop operating system for an increasing group of power users. Instead, what appears to have happened is that as both RISC and Intel processors have increased in speed, the difference between them has seemed less important for most purposes. Intel systems have become very fast, and the general-purpose PC and professional workstation markets have collided. That is why NeXT and Sun have moved their operating sys-

Table 8.2 Processors Supported by Desktop Systems

Vendor	Operating System	Processor
Microsoft	Windows 3.1/Chicago	Intel
IBM	OS/2 2.1	Intel
Microsoft	Windows NT	Intel, Alpha, MIPS, PowerPC, HP-PA
Apple	Mac System 7	Motorola 680x0, PowerPC, SPARC, HP-PA, RS/6000, Intel (with Novell)
IBM	Workplace OS	Intel, PowerPC
...	COSE/UNIX	Intel, Alpha, SPARC, MIPS, HP-PA, ...
Novell	UNIXware	Intel, ...
SunSoft	Solaris	Intel, SPARC, PowerPC
NeXT	NeXTStep	Intel, Motorola 680x0, HP-PA, SPARC
SCO	Open Desktop	Intel, MIPS
IBM	AIX	PowerPC, RS/6000, Intel (version)
H-P	HP-UX	HP-PA
DEC	OSF/1	Alpha

tems to Intel, while Apple, IBM, SCO, and Microsoft have moved theirs to RISC.

The various processors available are compared in Chapter 6. At the moment, it appears that corporate client workstations may standardize even more thoroughly on Intel processors than in the past. More importantly, the same major operating systems will run on Intel Pentium, DEC Alpha, MIPS R4000, and PowerPC. Several will probably also run on HP-PA and SPARC.

GUI OS Choices for the Desktop

Table 8.2 shows the variety of processors supported by advanced desktop operating systems according to announcements and rumors.

SELECTING DEVELOPMENT TOOLS

This section will discuss development tools for the remote database client/server development paradigm. Tools and approaches for the more complex distributed application logic model are covered in the next section. Because of its market dominance, we will focus on Windows tools for the

Chapter 8 • Selecting Workstations, Development Tools, and Applications

Increasing Complexity

High-end toolkits	Trinzic ADS, IEF, FCP, Dynasty, Forte
C++	C++ with Galaxy, Appware, XVT
SmallTalk	VisualWorks, IBM Visual Age, Enfin, PARTS
Traditional 4GLs	Natural, Uniface, Progress
GUI Basic 4GLs	PowerBuilder, VB, SQLWindows, ObjectView
Personal databases	Access, dBASE/FoxPro/Clipper, Paradox
Groupware	Lotus Notes, MS Info Exchange, OBEX
Office tools	MS Office/VBA, SmartSuite, OpenDoc
EIS/DSS tools	Forest and Trees, Lightship, Powerplay
Query/reporting tools	Quest, IQ, Crystal Reports

Figure 8.4 Development tools

client workstation in this book. Many of the tools on other platforms are similar to the Windows tools; some are direct ports.

These application development tools (see Figure 8.4) can be classed on a spectrum from user-oriented to developer-oriented. In selecting front-end tools, we attempt to differentiate them as follows:

- Query and report tools
- EIS tools
- GUI tools for general application development
- PC business tools

In the past year, several of these categories merged into a type of tool that does easy things easily but is sufficiently powerful in the hands of a developer. Where, in early 1993, you could distinguish between PC-heritage tools, such as dBASE and Paradox, and corporate client/server products, such as SQLWindows, competition and acquisition have forced these products to merge into a single category of client/server development tools. The pricing of these tools has been in tremendous flux; it appears to be moving to a tiered structure for desktop and enterprise, with prices based on PC volumes and without a run-time cost component. Single-user desktop tools cost between $100 and $300; workgroup tools cost from $500 to $2,000. This is a tremendous bargain and is likely to reinforce the rapid adoption of these tools. It may lead to an entry barrier for newer tools, which would typically be

Table 8.3 Price Fluctuations in Client/Server Tools, 1993–1994

Product	High	Low
SQLWindows	$2000	$200
ObjectView	$3000	$250
Paradox	$800	$150
Access	$500	$100
PowerBuilder	$3000	$250

priced much more expensively. Table 8.3 shows price fluctuations in client/server tools for 1993 and 1994.

These tools take advantage of the graphical interface to allow object-based development techniques. These tactical GUI development tools are a very strong product category today. However, they do not generally present the benefits of object-oriented development. They do not enforce or require strong methodologies, do not support repositories or shared development well, and do not scale up to larger systems development.

These limitations are addressed by a more expensive and elaborate class of tool, often with a mainframe heritage. Alternatively, the tactical GUI tools can be augmented by add-on methodologies and tools, such as graphical modeling and a central repository. Presumably, these categories, too, will eventually become indistinguishable. At the moment, the "large system" camp includes Knowledgeware (interfacing ADW, ObjectView, and Flashpoint), TI (adding client/server support to IEF), Antares Alliance (with the Huron product, owned by EDS and Amdahl), and Intersolv.

The vendors of AI tools were early supporters of portable applications and the components of client/server architecture. Trinzic, for example, has a set of tools (ADS, KBMS, InfoPump, Forest and Trees), which offers a variety of approaches to client/server development.

The CASE tool and client/server companies are firms in the $25 to $100 million size range. Some have lost money regularly. Microsoft is two orders of magnitude larger than this and wants to be a major player in client/server application development. It pays to consider their tools; they are likely to be there in the long run.

4GL Product Features

A good application development system has always included three important elements: forms, reports, and application navigation. Today, these elements must be supported with the full collection of graphical objects available. Interface design should be accomplished entirely in the native graphical environment. Extensibility with a full-powered programming language and through DLLs is required. Access to the variety of remote databases in a standard manner is also a requirement. The following are key questions to ask of the tools.

What Is the Performance of the Tool?

Does the tool run this type of application with satisfactory performance on the target systems? Developers often have fast machines, such as a 486DX4, while users may still have earlier systems, such as the 386, which will offer marginal performance. Frankly, all the available workstation tools have performance limitations, which must be designed around. These problems usually do not surface until the application and database become production-size. This needs to be tested early for the specific application under consideration.

Some tools offer little control over SQL queries, so that large amounts of network traffic may be repeated. A project management tool I am familiar with was rewritten from a 4GL to C++ because it viewed the same data in several different views, and the default action in that language was to read the data over and over again from the server.

Can Simple Forms Be Built Easily?

Is there an application generator for simple applications, so that basic maintenance functions can be brought up quickly? This is the DataWindow in PowerBuilder, for example, which allows basic forms for navigation and update to be generated instantly from a table or view, then included in more elaborate forms later in development. Can the default format of the forms be customized easily? It should be possible to eliminate or move elements, add or change design elements such as graphics and fonts, and make other changes to the user interface while in a prototyping session. Can all attributes be changed easily?

Does the tool support all elements of window design within the graphical environment? Is the tool an intuitive screen painter, with elements dragged and dropped into place, or is it based on a scripted 4GL? Access to the 4GL script is not necessarily bad; a requirement to work from a script is awkward and usually indicates an old product. Can forms be linked together to support application flow, and is it possible to easily move between forms?

Can a master-detail screen (such as order entry) be built without programming? Can reports with headers, footers, and different levels be built without programming? Systems that can only build the trivial one-table and simple report cases give good demonstrations but offer no real productivity increase, because no real applications are that simple.

Can Complex Applications Be Built at All?

Can procedural code be run from forms? Can a complex business process be programmed with the programming language? Some tools, such as ObjectVision or Approach, do not have a full-power procedural programming language. Today, there are still almost no real applications that do not require full programming logic at some point. Tools that have the language removed, like PowerMaker and Quest, may be acceptable, because the language is available when necessary by purchasing the full product. Support for external DLLS, which can be programmed in C or even in COBOL or other languages, is a requirement, but not a substitute, for an integrated language.

Can data validation be centralized? If this is not possible, trivial edits will proliferate to every field in every form in the system. This is astonishingly difficult to maintain. The product should have a data dictionary, which maintains this information, presumably in the same database used for system data. What provision is there for reusing code, including code libraries, browsers, and inheritance features? Can code be reused with new objects? It must be possible to develop reusable functions; again, without this code, fragments will proliferate into a maintenance nightmare. Some systems will allow management of and search for these pieces well; others will not.

Is there a full-featured debugger, capable of breakpoints, animation, and watch variables? Procedural code development without this eventually runs into asymptotic limits, as bugs become difficult to detect and code must be written just to set breakpoints and watch variables manually.

Is there a multiuser development environment? Several low-end tools are productive for an individual but are difficult to manage in the shared workgroup situation. Using third-generation code, for example COBOL, it was normal to use a library tool that accepted the code and enforced a check-in/check-out protocol. With early 4GLs, there was often no text file to manage in this way. It is not necessary for this support to be built into the tool; integration with a leading third-party tool, such as PVCS, is quite sufficient.

Can the Tool Access Necessary Databases?

If a tool does not offer access to the normal range of SQL databases, it is not viable for serious development. Does it support the specific databases necessary in this environment? Non-SQL databases can present specific problems, necessitating use of gateways.

Is it possible to develop forms that use multiple tables? Many simple languages have serious limitations on table access. Real applications use one or two dozen database tables, accessing many from a single form. A common limitation today is on the number of databases accessed or the types of databases accessed concurrently. In a corporate environment, there may be a need to access several database types and join the data. This is particularly true of decision support systems.

What GUI Environment(s) Is Supported?

An important decision today is whether to use a Windows-specific product or one that supports several environments.

In the past, many large organizations found support of multiple environments essential, because there are different workgroups in the corporation with different standards. There is a class of application, which enables inter-enterprise cooperation, including EDI, where the originating firm cannot dictate the desktop standard. And, of course, product companies would like to appeal to the broadest possible market.

Many tools run only on one platform: Windows, OS/2, or Macintosh. This may be less important now than in the past, when the market dominance of Windows was in question. It is now possible to confine a product to the Windows market with some confidence. However, times change, companies merge, and interfaces change. If portability to non-Windows platforms is a serious concern, the choice of tools becomes much more restricted. The 4GL tools that are available for multiple platforms tend not to support Windows as well as the ones developed for that environment but aimed at a lowest-common denominator. At the moment, the more mature AI-based tools seem to lead other systems in application portability. Enfin, SmallTalk, Aion ADS, and the Neuron Data products run on a variety of platforms.

There are good code libraries that support several GUI environments. There are not yet many good tools written using these libraries. One example is the AI tools, Nexpert Object and Aion ADS. We can expect more such tools in the next one to two years. Some of the Windows tools are being ported; PowerBuilder is being moved to the Macintosh, and SQLWindows should eventually run on OS/2.

The trade-off to be made with the products that support several environments is that they are often not the best for any particular one. They may not be the first to support Windows standards, such as OLE and DDE, or to form alliances with leading vendors of CASE tools for Windows. For products that support several environments, we must ask if the user interface is appropriate to each supported environment and if performance is as good as for a one-environment product. History has shown many cases of general-purpose products being beaten by products that perform better and are better suited to the high-volume target.

If you must support multiple platforms, the following may hold.

Windows and Macintosh C++ is a good choice for this. Microsoft, Borland, and Symantec support cross-development for Windows and the Macintosh using their application frameworks. There are not many strong fourth-generation languages in this category. FoxPro is currently the best choice, at least until PowerBuilder support for the Mac is released.

Windows and OS/2 ObjectView has good support for Windows and OS/2. Borland C++ is a good compiler.

All Platforms (Windows, Macintosh, OS/2, Unix) Smalltalk (Digitalk or ParcPlace) is a good choice. C++ with a portable library is probably the most practical, although you don't generally get the latest frameworks. The library choices include:

- zApp
- Visix Galaxy
- Novell Appware (possibly using Borland OWL)
- Neuron Data Open Interface
- Guild UIM
- Vermont Views
- JYACC Jam

What Windows Features Are Supported?

As already discussed, the great majority of users will be running Microsoft Windows. Tools must be judged on their support for the important Windows communications features. In the past this has included DDE (client or server), OLE (client and server), DLLs, and VBXs.

It is often difficult to determine the true details of support of these protocols being offered. There are two versions of the VBX standard and several different levels. PowerBuilder supports the older Version 1.0 standard, for example. Many products implement client, but not server, versions of the protocols.

In the future, support for the various ingredients of OLE will be necessary. This includes OLE Controls and OLE Automation in particular, and other features such as in-place editing as appropriate.

Since most users will be running Windows, which of the important Windows communication features are supported? This has included DDE (client or server), OLE (client or server), DLLs, and VBXs. In the future, all of these will be included in OLE 2.0. OLE 2.0 support is essential. This includes OLE custom controls, OLE automation, and in-place editing where appropriate.

It is sometimes difficult to unravel all of the details of the various support possibilities discussed above. VBXs have two versions and different levels, and many products implement client, but not server, protocols. The more the better, and, of course, it is necessary to look specifically for any requirement essential to an application (such as VBX support to use a particular library). We will cover the varieties of these protocols in a following chapter.

INFORMATION DISPLAY TOOLS

The common denominator of end-user reporting tools is the display-only capability for custom forms, although most of these tools allow some table-oriented editing. Simpler tools in this category include Crystal Reports from Crystal Services, Quest from Gupta, Q&E Database Editor from Q&E, Microsoft Query, IQ for Windows from IQ Software, and PowerViewer from PowerSoft. These tools cost a few hundred dollars or less, but versions of these reporting tools are often bundled with other development tools.

Crystal Reports is a powerful and easy-to-use report writer. The print engine is a DLL, which can be accessed separately, so that user-developed applications can invoke it.

Q&E Database Editor became well known because a version shipped with Microsoft Excel. It offers wide support for back-end databases through Q&E database libraries. These libraries are so good that the company now is better known for them than the report generator. Q&E has both client and server DDE support, so that it can feed Excel or other front ends. It offers direct coding of SQL statements, query by form, and an interactive query builder. It serves as a report writer and can be used to design forms, including tabular (spreadsheet-like) forms.

Quest is built into the professional version of SQLWindows, or it can be obtained separately. It includes the SQLBase local data engine, so it can be used as a self-contained package or to access other databases. It includes a full two-pass report writer with support for crosstabs. A visual dialog box, "Link Tables," is used to combine related tables. It supports stored queries, direct coding of SQL statements, and query by form. Quest connects to ORACLE, SQL Server, or OS/2 DBM, using the Gupta gateways, and to XBase and Paradox through ODBC.

EIS and Decision Support

More complex tools include EIS packages and more powerful decision support tools such as:

Forest and Trees	Trinzic
Lightship	Pilot
Commander EIS	Comshare
EISToolKit	MicroStrategy
PowerPlay	Cognos
GQL	Andyne

These tools offer graphical representation of results, drill-downs, and spreadsheet-like "what if" calculations. They cost a few hundred dollars and up, depending on the functionality. The true cost in building an EIS is in the custom development, particularly understanding, cleaning, and accessing the support databases. These are good tools for end users and for the specialized functions that they support. The systems support creation of decision support applications, such as sales analysis and financial reporting by business analysts, with little or no programming.

If you are planning to train a general-purpose IT staff, these tools may be less advisable. There is some programming required, but the tools do not support the disciplines of programming on a large scale. You might do better to take your staff up the learning curve of a full-strength tool, which could do these functions and, in addition, do more complex data-entry systems.

On the other hand, these tools include support for the graphical displays and data drill-downs required by these systems, which will take custom programming in normal 4GLs. For some marketing and sales situations, databases, such as those from IRI and IMS, offer powerful decision support with a multidimensional query engine packaged with a database designed for marketing analaysis in particular industries.

Forest and Trees

Forest and Trees is now owned by Trinzic. This program falls between the easy-to-use report writers and the more powerful client/server tools. It offers good connectivity; triggers to execute actions, such as printing a report or calling a program; and multiple views of data using crosstabs and hot spots. SQL statements can be coded directly. It includes a full-power report writer. There is no programming language, which limits the ability of Forest and Trees to build a full-powered application.

Lightship

Lightship is from Pilot, who also sell Command Center, one of the leading large-system EIS packages. It enables easy development of graphical information displays, featuring crosstabs and hot spots, and using Lightship Lens allows connection to a variety of back-end databases.

EISToolKit and the Andyne GQL product are both available for the Mac or Windows. EISToolKit is based on the Informix Wingz spreadsheet and HyperScript, combined with the Q+E libraries and ClearAccess. The Andyne GQL product is available for the Mac, Windows, or UNIX.

GRAPHICAL CLIENT/SERVER 4GLs

This category appears destined to replace COBOL in many corporations, so competition is fierce. The top group offers the necessary features of these tools, previously discussed, while differing in style and additional features. Based on use and adoption in 1993 and 1994, there appear to be five database-independent leaders. They are:

PowerBuilder	PowerSoft
SQLWindows	Gupta
ObjectView	Knowledgeware
Visual Basic	Microsoft
Paradox for Windows	Borland

These products have more similarities than differences. In each one, an application is designed interactively, by "pointing and clicking" or "dragging and dropping" controls on a form. The controls include text, edit areas, buttons, pictures, and more complex objects, such as tables. The database tables are defined interactively, using a tool that can display table relationships graphically and allows definition of all the attributes of tables, keys, and data items, including loading the data.

A simple application can be created without programming using an application generator. This could include data maintenance, master/detail, simple business graphics, and fairly complex reports. More complex programs are developed using a programming language similar to BASIC, with the possible addition of custom or third-party code in the form of DLLs or VBXs, or access to programs using OLE.

All of these products come with an integrated single-user SQL database. They offer, generally at extra cost, access to almost any database—either natively or through one of the driver standards now available.

PowerBuilder and SQLWindows are the market leaders in sales and also provide the best support for inheritance and other object-oriented features that facilitate application development with a large development group and facilitate reuse. ObjectView is a powerful, well-priced tool whose adoption by a larger company may help it in the marketplace. Visual Basic (which shares the Access database engine) and Paradox are backed by the leading development tool companies and have a large base of supporters in smaller companies.

PowerBuilder

PowerBuilder supports a wide range of databases natively and with ODBC. It ships with an integrated database, Watcom SQL, which is now owned by PowerSoft. Using PowerBuilder, everything is done in a Painter. SQL databases are defined and populated using the Database Painter. Applications are defined in the Application Painter, then you create the screens by selecting controls and properties in the Screen Painter. The DataWindows of PowerBuilder are an important feature, pioneered by this product. DataWindows, naturally defined in a Data Window Painter, support tables in a grid or free-form display for use in forms or reports. Programming is done with scripts in the PowerScript language, created in the Script Painter. The PowerScript language, which is similar to BASIC although somewhat C-like in appearance, is coded in a Script Painter accessible from the other painters. The language can be extended, since it supports C function calls, C DLLs, and embedded SQL.

Other Painters support development of functions, libraries, preferences, menus, user objects, and bit-mapped graphics.

PowerBuilder offers good support for code reuse and management for workgroups. Code is checked in and out from object libraries. The company offers links to the Intersolv PVCS version-control software and exchanges data with LBMS and Bachman CASE tools. Object-oriented support is mostly in the GUI environment; PowerBuilder offers inheritance for user-created objects, for instance. A full-power debugger is included.

An extended data dictionary lets you set up column headings, display formats, initial values, and validation routines centrally. Simple charting and graphics are supported. Reporting is done with PowerViewer, a reasonable banded report writer.

The family of PowerSoft products extends from PowerViewer and Power-Maker through PowerBuilder Desktop to PowerBuilder Enterprise. Power-Maker is limited in scope, but PowerBuilder is a very good deal. It allows development of sophisticated applications.

Careful attention must be paid to PowerBuilder performance. As always with this type of product, database design is critical. Particular PowerBuilder issues include keeping the code libraries small and limiting the number of objects and events per screen. Failure to do this leads to asymptotic performance fall-off as applications get larger, often late in the development cycle.

SQLWindows

SQLWindows has been available since 1988. That makes it the pioneer of this class of commercial product by a considerable margin, although the first version was not client/server as we understand it today. Version 4.0 was introduced in spring 1993. SQLWindows can be used with its built-in SQLBase local database engine or connected to a variety of databases directly, via Gupta routers, or through third-party products.

The new version added workgroup support and object-oriented features, to compete with (indeed surpass) PowerBuilder. Workgroup development with TeamWindows includes project management facilities, source code control, and development of reusable templates and storage in a central repository. The repository uses the SQLBase database to store metadata and application templates, supporting check-in, check-out, and change management for data models, specs, and program modules.

Like PowerBuilder, SQLWindows consists of a group of interrelated tools. Outline Windows contains the application main outline. You combine use of the outliner with the various generation tools in combination to develop an application. Report Windows can generate complex reports, such as crosstabs, and store reports as documents (RTF), or Quest can be run within SQLWindows. Forms are designed in Form Windows, then scripts are attached with the programming language SAL (SQL Application Language). Express Windows is used to generate simple applications quickly. Database Browser allows interactive development and reveals database dictionary and design.

The OLE support is both client and server, which is unusual.

The object-oriented features in SQLWindows are in support of the user interface, as with PowerBuilder. They include inheritance, encapsulation, and polymorphism. User-defined window and functional classes and custom window classes, which are created with C and the Windows SDK, are supported. These new features are voluntary; they can be mixed in as required, or development can be performed as previously.

SQLWindows is a strong tool from a small company competing in an aggressive market segment. It could use strong alliances if it is to thrive.

ObjectView

ObjectView is from Knowledgeware, which acquired the original developer Matesys in 1993. It can access a good range of remote databases. A personal SQL data access/report writer version is available, as with its competitors. The single-user version of Object-View is bundled with the Gupta SQLBase database.

ObjectView supports forms, which can include spreadsheets and data panels. Developing an application using ObjectView, you define a form, select tables, draw the relationships (as a data model), select columns, and save the "form definition." This form is generated automatically, including VCR-style controls, and can then be customized and tested in place.

Complex forms, such as header-detail, can be created just as easily using this method. For further customization, you create a script with the programming language ViewScript, which is BASIC-like. This is reasonably easy to do.

The Pinnacle Graphics Server is built into ObjectView to provide business graphics. Reporting tools are inferior to the competition, and database table access must be built up with the script language. A Visual Query Tool for SQL query construction is available.

A powerful debugger similar to CodeView was added recently. In the future, a Work Group Edition with an Object Repository is planned; currently, ObjectView lacks tools for workgroup development and a data dictionary. Despite its name, ObjectView does not support inheritance.

ObjectView has good Windows support, including DDE, OLE, MCI, and a C/C++ API. Unlike PowerBuilder and SQLWindows, ObjectView is available for both Windows and OS/2.

Paradox for Windows

Paradox for Windows, from Borland, is a total rewrite of Paradox using Borland Object Component Architecture (BOCA) and the Interbase database engine using ODAPI. The product accesses XBase and Paradox files natively and accesses a range of remote databases.

To develop an application in Paradox, you create the screen using a data model and then select columns to generate a default window. This can be customized by dragging and dropping objects, then attaching code. The programming language, ObjectPAL, is powerful and has object-oriented features. A high-quality report writer is included. Some business graphics are included.

Paradox is compiled but requires a run-time Paradox environment to operate. This appears to require a copy of Paradox to be purchased for each site.

ObjectVision, also from Borland, was their earliest Windows tool. ObjectVision Pro 2.1 has interesting multimedia support, an unusual graphical development paradigm, and offers connectivity to many databases natively and through ODBC and Q&E/OV. It is one of the few tools available for OS/2. The product had no conventional programming capability and failed to scale to larger applications. A third-party developer is offering a compiled version of the product, but it is now receiving no more development—basically a casualty of Borland's decision to focus on Paradox and dBASE.

The biggest concern with Paradox is that Borland management has made many changes of direction, and may again change emphasis. At the time of writing, dBASE for Windows is close to launch and a new client/server tool is expected shortly.

Visual Basic and Access

Visual Basic is the tool of choice for amateur and small-business Windows programmers and has a tremendous following. With the release of 3.0, supporting the Access database engine and OLE 2.0, and the announcement of Visual Basic for Applications, it is clearly a serious developer's tool. The Professional Edition includes remote database support including ORACLE, SQL Server, and ODBC, and the Crystal Reports report writer. Visual Basic programs require a run-time DLL, but this can be freely distributed.

Visual Basic allows screen painting, in which you can select a variety of controls for inclusion in a form, and development of BASIC code for event handlers tied to the screen. Controls for database access are included. The real strength of Visual Basic is its array of third-party products, supporting everything from TCP/IP to speech recognition to full-text search, as well as the large developer population sharing code on the public networks.

Access attaches, with a live link, to XBase, Paradox, and Btrieve files and through ODBC to SQL Server and other remote databases. It offers forms, queries, reports, charts, query by form, and a powerful two-pass report generator. Access has an excellent user interface. In 1993, it was a new tool and glitches in version 1.0 made it hard to produce complete applications with sufficient control and documentation. With version 2.0, the product is reliable and powerful. Combined with Visual Basic, Access offers an inexpensive and powerful set of tools for client/server development.

FoxPro is a fast tool with cross-platform support (Macintosh and UNIX).

Tools from Database Vendors

The database management system vendors all offer tools that, despite their origins, support competing databases. In practice, they are not treated as vendor-independent but seem to be used entirely by sites that have adopted that database. These tools include the ORACLE Cooperative Development Environment, Accell from Unify, Wingz and other tools from Informix, the Ingres/Windows 4GL from CA, and Gain Momentum and Build Momentum from Sybase.

The best received of these, and probably the best technically, is ORACLE CDE. The ORACLE toolset is very strong and complete. It includes an Information Engineering methodology, CASE tools, and a variety of development tools, which run under Windows.

SmallTalk Tools

Several tools use the SmallTalk language, the original language of Xerox PARC. This is a very powerful language for interface development, and the SmallTalk tools generally offer some portability, at least between Windows

Chapter 8 • Selecting Workstations, Development Tools, and Applications

and OS/2. The promising new IBM tool, Visual Age, is one tool; Enfin from Easel Corporation and the products from Digitalk and Parc Place are others.

Enfin is available for Windows or OS/2 or selected UNIX systems. It is a product of Easel Corporation. It supports SQLBase, ORACLE, Sybase/SQL Server, OS/2 DBM, dBASE, and other databases through the Micro DecisionWare Gateway and DDCS/2. Enfin supports EHLLAPI, which allows access to mainframe applications.

Enfin supports a group of visual programming tools that ultimately generate SmallTalk source code. These tools are unusually powerful, supporting database tables and complex reports, as well as business graphics and financial modeling, and can be linked together.

Enfin is a good tool in the OS/2 environment, supporting the "drag-and-drop" paradigm of CUA '91, similar to Workplace Shell. Programs can be moved between the Windows and OS/2 environments with ease. Like SmallTalk, Enfin applications are interpretive and need an Enfin environment.

VisualWorks, from long-time SmallTalk veteran Parc Place, is a powerful, if expensive, SmallTalk application. This is not easy to learn, but some organizations are going to build large systems with it. It supports Windows, OS/2, Macintosh, and UNIX. An unusual feature allows the display for all target environments to be seen at any development station.

Perhaps the biggest issue with SmallTalk products is the lack of a strong community of developers; it is not easy to find or train productive SmallTalk programmers.

AI Tools

The group of artificial intelligence-based tools includes ADS and KBMS from Trinzic, Level5 Object from Information Builders, and BridgeBuilder (formerly Contessa) from BridgeBuilder. Most of these tools have traditionally been expensive tools with a narrow focus but are being repositioned to compete with the likes of PowerBuilder as powerful general-purpose tools.

Trinzic is a company that appears to be developing a stable of client/server products, including Aion Development System (ADS), KBMS, Forest and Trees, InfoPump, and Intellect. There may be some interesting synergy from these products in the future.

Level5 Object is a product of Information Builders Inc. (IBI), who also make EDA/SQL and FOCUS. While originally positioned as an expert system tool, it is now marketed as an object-oriented tool with optional expert system features. It is interpreted and requires a run-time system to operate. Unlike most client/server tools, Level5 is fully object oriented and supports data encapsulation and multiple inheritance. Each element of the system provides an object-oriented interface for development. Inference engines support backward and forward chaining, procedural and object-oriented programming styles, or hybrids. This is a powerful tool at a reasonable price, but it is not easy to learn for conventional programmers.

More Tools

4-D, originally known as Silver Surfer, and Omnis Seven have been long-standing staples in the Macintosh world. Both can access a variety of databases using DAL. ToolBook, from Asymmetrix, is a good multimedia prototyper, which in our experience is too slow for use in most application development. Novell Appware, developed from their acquisitions, including Serius Developer and STI, is a brand-new object-based development tool.

There are some good tools from the mainframe, minicomputer, and PC worlds that have migrated to client/server. They have considerable power but do not have the intuitive Windows approach or object-based development of the more popular tools. They do have a base of applications, VARs, and customers in their niches. Uniface (a Dutch product now owned by Compuware), Supernova (also Dutch), Empress, and Progress all originate from UNIX. These tools support distributed development on a variety of platforms. DataEase and Revelation were originally on minicomputers, FOCUS and Easytrieve on mainframes. The traditional 4GLs from mainframes are all ported or in process of porting to new client/server versions, including ADS/O, Natural, Ideal, and Cincom.

The numerous XBase PC databases include CA-Clipper from CA, dBASE from Borland, and FoxPro from Microsoft. These products currently lack both the object-based, drag-and-drop development paradigm and the connectivity to SQL databases expected of client/server products. It is hard to see how these products can be made over while retaining any kind of compatibilty with their code and user base. Worse, dBASE and FoxPro appear to be the "second-string" offerings from their vendors.

"Large System" Tools

As noted above, the available 4GL tools do not generally present the benefits of object-oriented development. They do not enforce or require strong methodologies, do not support repositories or shared development well, and do not scale up to larger systems development. If you wish to develop a

Chapter 8 • Selecting Workstations, Development Tools, and Applications

large, complex system for delivery on a heterogeneous distributed network, those tools require a great deal to be added in and integrated.

There are some sophisticated environments for client/server development available today, but they have their limitations. The more expensive environments cost around $8,000 per seat, which is competitive with the traditional CASE packages from which they evolved. They are coming down from the mainframe. Some comprehensive but expensive toolkits are:

Foundation	Andersen Consulting
APS 2.2	Intersolv
PacBase for Client/Server	CGI
IEF Client/Server	TI
Huron	Antares (Amdahl/EDS)

The best established of these is Foundation for Cooperative Computing, from Andersen Consulting. Until recently, it supported only OS/2 clients and CICS servers, but Windows client support and UNIX and VAX servers are now available. The tool is independently marketed, but it seems that very few customers have bought and used this tool independent of Andersen Consulting engagements.

Intersolv APS 2.2, introduced in 1992, builds true client/server applications under MVS/CICS/DB2 and OS/2 with APPC and has just introduced Windows clients. The PacBase I-CASE product supports Windows or OS/2 clients and HP-UX or IBM-AIX servers.

CASE

These tools appeal first to users of their ancestral mainframe versions. They have weak interfaces compared to the tactical products, such as PowerBuilder, but are strong for development of larger systems. They are generally used in structured development.

The CASE tool market focused on IBM mainframes for a long time. It is now moving to client/server, and we can expect to see more effective client/server code generators by 1995, if not before. Knowledgeware, who are integrating ADW, ObjectView, and Flashpoint, and TI, who are adding client/server support to IEF, should be able to do this. At the moment, the leader is ORACLE, whose new line of products includes ORACLE*CASE and a range of graphical interface tools, which operate on a variety of platforms.

At the moment, it seems best to use CASE "in the small" for most client/server systems. This includes products such as System Architect, System

Engineer, ERwin/ERX, SilverRun, and EasyCASE Plus. These tools allow full-scale data models to be produced and used to generate database schemas. System Architect and EasyCASE Plus also support process models and event diagrams, allowing useful system documentation. ERwin/ERX can generate ORACLE7 and Sybase triggers.

Some data exchange facilities between the leading 4GLs and CASE tools are available. LBMS (SE/Open), Popkin, Knowledgeware, and Bachman (Component Designer) all have arrangements with PowerSoft, for instance.

C++

If you wish to develop a substantial open client/server system today, two choices are the 4GLs mentioned above or the CASE-based structured tools. A third choice is to combine a solid relational database, C++ language development, for the core transactional system, supplemented with the 4GL tools from the previous section for information presentation and entry and reporting. This gives the right mix of performance and maintainability. Some systems will be developed entirely in the 4GL, others will have larger C++ components, depending on the requirement for industrial-strength design.

The C++ choices for Windows development on the client workstation include Microsoft Visual C++ (with MFC), Borland C++ (with Application Frameworks), and Watcom C++, or Symantec C++ (with MFC). Symantec also supports the Macintosh. Borland and Microsoft have announced cross-platform strategies. Good C++ compilers are available for the major UNIX systems. Microsoft MFC and Boland OWL are the leading frameworks for development.

PERSONAL WORKSTATION APPLICATIONS

The languages internal to the major personal computer applications are another important category of development tool. This has been true for 10 years; many important applications have been developed with Lotus 1-2-3 macros. These have even been ported to UNIX workstations. Commercial products are available written in Lotus 1-2-3, WordPerfect, and Word macros, among others.

Until recently, the price of the application software for office functions made the development of this type of product unusual. It is difficult to sell an inexpensive product that requires the purchase of a $500 additional component, and there was no guarantee that an individual had any one class of product. There was also the problem that there was no clear standard for development in a product area, so that many versions had to be distributed. The new situation of widespread Windows use combined with less expensive software changes that. It now appears possible to develop an application solution that requires the purchase or prior installation of commercial packages.

Of course, the major trend in office applications in 1993 was the introduction of suites at aggressive prices. The effect of the suites at the user level has been to make the combination of word processor, spreadsheet, and presentation graphics available at the same street price of one of these previously. Where previously users tended to use one, now they have all three installed. Along with this pricing came efforts to integrate the applications at the user interface. Toolbars, menus, and other graphical items have become similar. Application macro languages are changing from product-specific to vendor-specific—for example, Visual Basic for Applications and LotusScript. Because corporate users will probably have one of the three suites installed, this provides a higher-level platform to write to. The application can focus on its added value, instead of worrying about providing table layout and document editing features that are probably inferior to those in the suites.

The object-oriented standards OLE 2.0 and OpenDoc will open up even more possibiliities. Two classes of application appear to be enabled by this. One type will build on top of the commercial products to integrate and offer a solution to end users. Another will serve as a component, based on an individual core competence, which can be accessed from the commercial products.

Groupware

When a suite with its macro language is combined with a powerful client/server development tool, it becomes possible to quickly develop the automation solution for a business area in a well-documented, standardized, professional manner.

One method for integrating the work of a group of people is with the database for consolidation. This is a natural method for client/server today. Documents of various types are filed in the relational database and extracted. However, this is not the only solution. Work-flow solutions see the documents as serial activity, passed from person to person. And many applications are suited to a more free-form type of database, which allows text and other materials to be loosely stored and retrieved.

This leads to the varied set of issues surrounding groupware. Groupware seems to be more a property of many products than a product category. As with graphical interfaces, multimedia, and object orientation, the features will be added to many existing market leaders, while allowing new entrants in areas where the leader is not agile. Many groupware applications are enabled by e-mail; indeed, mail-enabled applications may be a more precisely targeted term. Often, groupware enables professionals to work together. It may facilitate meetings or joint document production.

While there have been several early examples of groupware, such as NCR Cooperation, the early market leader is clearly Lotus Notes. Notes is an integrated product based around an innovative distributed replicated database engine. It combines e-mail and bulletin board abilities with application development. Most importantly, all this works over both local and wide area networks on a variety of computers. This enables workgroups to be formed and cooperate regardless of location.

Lotus Notes, or similar products as they become available, provides an infrastructure for information collection, sharing, and storage. Once in place, additional applications can be added at a low incremental cost. The result is improved control over our information storage, access, change history, and routing. A large company can gain much of the "look and feel" of a smaller company by using this technology.

The following are good candidate systems for this type of product:

- mailing list and telephone directory
- project summary system
- distribution of memos and newsletters
- means for publishing company standards, experts list
- technical conferencing
- working party communication tool
- proposal boilerplate, joint development
- management of multilocation projects, joint development of client deliverables
- sharing information on multilocation clients (e.g., national accounts)
- sales/management time and activity reporting.

The critical success factors for this tool are senior management support; excellent training and support in use of the tool, requiring selected communications using the tool to create a "critical mass"; and development of a body of enthusiastic users who will use the tool for voluntary communications.

Summary

There is a confusing variety of tools to choose from in this category. The leading tools today, PowerBuilder, Visual C++, and Visual Basic did not exist three years ago. It seems certain that there is a great deal of change still to come. Many of today's tools will not survive, and those that do will change. One good place to start is that the databases developed with these tools will continue to be accessible in the future. This is true even if we transition to new database types; the object-oriented databases can access relational systems. So it is critical to build on a sound data model.

Much of the application code built in 4GLs may not survive. The tools do not enforce maintainability or reuse, and many programmers with these tools do not have the training or any incentive to be concerned. For simple solutions, this is quite acceptable. For larger systems, we must be aware that we are building the legacy systems of the future.

Smalltalk is an interesting language which can provide great productivity and supports the client/server model well. Unfortunately, we have never seen the "critical mass" of developers which would make this language more than a niche product. The same problem applies to the AI tools, CASE, and other expensive solutions. They never break out of a few systems integrators and corporations and achieve real sales volume.

For components which will see extensive use, one answer is professional development with object-oriented methods and C++. But C++ is still a language which is hard to learn and not very productive. It cannot replace COBOL as the language of business programming. A more useful answer is to move to a component model of software development and integration, based around emerging standards clustered on OLE2, OpenDoc, and CORBA. The practical forerunner of this approach today is the VBX. There is a thriving third-party market today in VBXs which is practical reusable code.

Several 4GLs will probably survive and thrive as the tools for business development.

In the future, we will be looking for graphical tools which integrate applications and components into solutions which serve the needs of the enterprise. For the moment, we must build solutions with these components using a careful framework.

9
Building a New Automated System

OVERVIEW

As we have discussed, business cycles are shorter today, and computer systems are less expensive, more flexible, and more immediately apparent. For all of these reasons, we would like to build systems today much more rapidly than in the past. There are countervailing tendencies; the more distributed systems with richer user interfaces are actually much more complex than those of the past. Fortunately, there has been progress in development tools and methods.

To achieve rapid development, we cannot expect to simply work harder or smarter. We need tools and methods that enable this. There are three fundamental justifications for a radically shortened development life cycle.

1. Investment: use of integrated CASE (I-CASE) tools and an organized methodology to develop large systems with sizable components of generated code
2. Limited scope: use of client/server development tools to develop smaller systems with controlled scope
3. Reuse: use of previously written and tested chunks of code

Option 1 is the RAD methodology of the Information Engineering school, popularized by James Martin. Until recently, it was the best model for successful development and is still the only choice for large transactional systems. Option 2 is the methodology for rapid application development outlined here. It is based upon the use of a client/server architecture and a toolset based on relational database technology. This is the type of system discussed throughout this book and is best used to develop information-intensive applications. Option 3 is the component model that is enabled by a market in component parts and a method for integrating them. This is an emerging methodology, which will probably become the dominant model in years to come.

Before starting on a rapid methodology, or any other development, we should understand that the business area of the problem is well bounded and understood. The architectures for development, data management, and production should have been defined. This is a process for developing a fully operational system and placing it into production. Some professionals may have used prototyping within the requirements analysis phase of a more traditional system development life-cycle methodology. The difference here is simply that we can use the developed interface code without reimplementation.

Senior management and end users should be involved throughout the project. Include at least one senior executive as well as representatives of the user community and IT staff who will support the product. This review board will participate in the review of the project plan and will review key deliverables throughout the project. End-user involvement at all stages is imperative.

Manage the project closely. Establish an agreed project information set supported with a project management tool. Get agreement on the objectives, scope, and plan and formally monitor all changes. The project management information includes:

- project objectives and scope
- key external groups and projects
- critical deadlines
- project costs and benefits
- risk
- quality
- people, tasks, and schedules

The new development tools can produce one large gain for the management of projects; the scale of the effort is reduced, so that smaller teams must be managed. Against this, the teams are more varied, using tools and methods that are less familiar. Many of the techniques are performed with

Chapter 9 • Building a New Automated System

the users, which can have the effect of working in a fishbowl. The goals of a project team that includes end users and reports across business functions can be hard to establish and maintain.

Contemporary projects involve the concurrent introduction of new business ideas, new systems supporting them, new technology supporting the systems, and new or retrained staff supporting the technology (see Figure 9.1). The fundamental principle of RAD is to use parallel activities to compress the development cycle time. JRP and JAD replace serial interviews and reviews with group (parallel) sessions. The development is broken into multiple parallel design/construction activities occurring in parallel. To monitor this, an accurate, complete data model and good project management are needed. Projects must be planned, tracked, and reviewed in an iterative real-time manner.

It is important to use good staff and the right methodology. The methodology, which should be specifically designed for rapid development of client/server systems, ensures that:

- project objectives are well defined and understood by all project staff
- tasks are fully defined and assigned to staff with the appropriate skill set
- quality reviews are conducted throughout each phase of the project

In the beginning of the project, standards for system development are established. Throughout the project, all staff should have access to a project plan that allows them to review the project objectives, their assignment, and

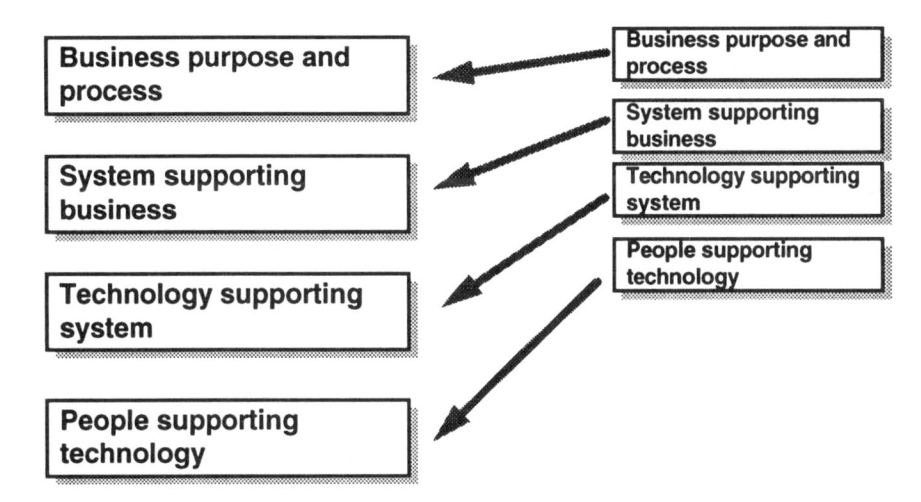

Figure 9.1 Concurrent change

the quality review criteria established for the tasks to which they are assigned.

You should maintain and publish a data model. Use of a shared data model from the early stages of the project ensures that key business and data models are well understood by all members of the project team. Some small systems will allow the limited models available in a tool such as Paradox or PowerBuilder; most will require use of a CASE tool such as Erwin or System Architect.

The rapid application development methodology uses evolutionary prototyping (see Figure 9.2). The problem of creeping functionality, which is common with prototyping, is handled with a "timebox" approach. The goal is to produce an initial version that delivers 60 to 80 percent of the solution in 20 percent of the time.

The methodology has six phases:

- selection and planning
- requirements
- design
- construction
- host
- cutover

Cutover is handled separately later.

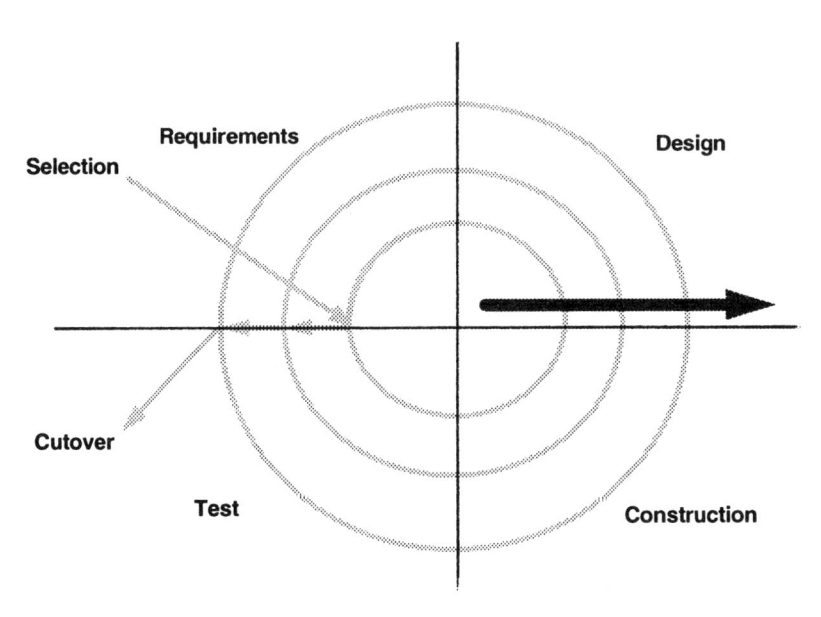

Figure 9.2 The evolutionary development spiral

Each phase of the methodology feeds the next, but this is not a rigid process. Scope is frozen early on but requirements and design are not. Detailed changes can be made fairly late in the process. In fact, the users are involved throughout. The project plan and documents evolve throughout the development.

It is important to follow some standard project management rules.

1. Know who the client is. There may be a business and a system sponsor, and they may not agree.
2. Document formal meetings with minutes.
3. Remain familiar with the project plan at all times.
4. Scope changes must be recognized and dealt with through change control procedures.

ESTABLISH PROJECT PLAN

The purpose of this stage is to organize the project so that it can be successfully accomplished. In addition to establishing the project, the major deliverable is the detailed project plan. Let's review the project business case we met earlier.

Project Business Case

We will develop this document in this phase. Initially, we should review available internal documents, such as reports, current system documentation, and any plans relevant to the area. Then, working with the highest-level end users, we should confirm:

- scope (what business problems are to be solved)
- objectives (what the functions of the system should be)
- the level of senior management commitment to the project
- the components of the application
- the functions to be delivered first

This can be a series of interviews or facilitated sessions, depending on availability.

Next, we establish the issue management process—in other words, the steps to follow when things go wrong. We create the Advisory (business-level) and Technical Steering Committees, to which the project will report. Finally, this work is summarized in a project announcement.

> - Evolutionary prototyping
> - Timebox to control creep
> - Concept -> Content -> Process prototype
> - Parallelize activities
> - Use data model as integration vehicle
> - Deliver 80% solution in 20% time
> - *Not suitable for all systems*

Figure 9.3 Rapid client/server development

Development Environment

We should establish the complete development technology platform at this stage (see Figure 9.3). We assume that an overall architecture has been chosen for the enterprise already, so this effort should be a "menu," selecting the right technology from the preapproved choices. The platform will include:

- hardware/operating systems
- development languages/tools
- database management
- networks, system and network management software
- connectivity needs
- utilities, such as editors and testing tools
- facilities
- documentation standards
- configuration management

Then, the project team is organized and the project initiated.

ESTABLISH BUSINESS REQUIREMENTS

The business requirements are established in a series of Joint Requirements Planning (JRP) sessions. The JRP session is a facilitated workshop similar to the better-known JAD but involves different participants and produces different results. The JRP attendees have the power to introduce a new system, rather than only having knowledge of the details. There are many advantages to facilitated workshops (see Figure 9.4).

- ◆ Builds team consensus and develops shared vision
  - Cuts across organizational barriers
  - Can resolve conflicts
- ◆ Collects details about operations
  - Enlists knowledge of business users
  - Produces hands-on, visual results
- ◆ Reduces time for solution
  - Reduces interview and design time
  - Reduces propagation effort at back end

Figure 9.4 Facilitated workshop advantages

Facilitated Session: Joint Requirements Planning

Purpose

The purpose of the Joint Requirements Planning session is to develop the business requirements for the system, achieving a consensus between all the affected parties.

Objectives

1. Nail down the business requirements, particularly scope and objectives.
2. Link the system plan for the project to the goals and critical success factors of the enterprise.
3. Understand and form a consensus on management objectives for the project.

Participants

The participants should include senior people from each affected area of the organization. This is where top executives are brought into the planning. The Executive Sponsor must be present. There may be one or more key players, whose approval (not to mention enthusiastic commitment) is needed for the system to succeed. They must be present. The attendees must be prepared and capable of brainstorming the system functions.

Preparation

The executive sponsor and key user executives must be established and prepared. The facilitator researches the application area, reviews the participants, and prepares a "straw man" document. A custom agenda is created and distributed. The overall scope and objectives of the project are detailed. Any known contentious issues should be reviewed with a sufficiently high-level executive sponsor and the ground for resolution prepared. The logistics of the meeting are performed.

Session Steps

1. Explain the concepts of the session and the ground rules for the session (such as no criticism of ideas).
2. Introduce and review the "straw man" document.
3. Determine the functions of the system as a whole.
4. Guide the participants through the business processes in an orderly way to produce the deliverables listed below.
5. Agree on status of project and next steps.

Key Deliverables/Work Products Created

1. List of affected business operations (departments, sites, external bodies)
2. Business problems addressed by the system
3. System objectives
4. System functions, with benefits and priorities
5. Process decomposition and flow
6. Essential data model
7. Unresolved issues with action plans for resolution
8. Project phase deadlines

Postsession Activity

Complete the documentation of the deliverables. Present the results to the Executive Sponsor and get a decision on movement to the application design.

Comments/Suggestions

1. All attendees must be present full time. This is not easy with the higher-level people, but any time lost is multiplied by the lost consensus and the need to catch up. If the time cannot be given, consider off-site locations and weekend days. If it still cannot be given, consider abandoning the project.
2. Thorough preparation is essential. This includes similar systems at the enterprise, benchmarking information, results of prior business process analysis, and possibly technical information on enabling technologies.
3. Leave your status at the door; all team members are equal.
4. The following should be considered:
   - What are the strategic business opportunities?
   - What constraints and assumptions affect the project?
   - How can technology be applied to the business?
   - What functions are being performed?
   - What information do you need to make that decision?
   - How can this information make this step more effective?
   - Can this decision be made at a different place?
5. The facilitator should promote interaction and consensus. The facilitator directs the scribe in producing the final report.
6. The material becomes the Project Business Case, which is updated throughout the remaining phases.

The Structured Workshop Facility

Structured workshop sessions, such as JRP or JAD, are best conducted in a comfortable facility with a large meeting table, chairs, and plenty of wall space.

Flip charts with pens should be available; one alternative is the large static clinging sheets for wall attachment. A large white board with colored pens is essential; if possible, a board that allows copies to be produced directly. Possibly, large Post-it notes and wool or string for brainstorming and process diagrams could be used.

For any session that goes into substantial detail, a PC with data modeling and prototyping tools is required. Some early management sessions may not

- ◆ Full commitment
  - Senior management support
  - Every essential person attends full-time
  - Everyone leaves status at the door
  - Commitment continues before, during, and after sessions
- ◆ Full support
  - Experienced facilitators
  - Tools for business modeling and prototyping
  - Appropriate goals
  - Thorough preparation

Figure 9.5 Facilitated workshop success factors

require this. For larger groups, a large-screen monitor, BARCO-type projector, or LCD panel and overhead projector is the best way to display PC output. Sometimes a small group can gather around the PC screen.

Access to copier and printer facilities should be available. This facility should be undisturbed—with no telephones and a minimum of urgent messages. Refreshments should be provided. Figure 9.5 summarizes critical success factors.

APPLICATION DESIGN

In the application design phase, we will prototype the external interfaces and application content, as well as develop data, event, and process models of the system.

Initially, we establish scope and architecture. The purpose of this stage is to define the core components of the application and establish which functionality will be developed as the first implementation of the evolving application. The following data should be available at the start of the project or must be collected as a separate step:

- significant business events
- major business processes
- critical information needs

Prioritize the functionality to be developed. First, prioritize the business processes. Then, identify the required data entities and supporting work and select the first process(es) to be supported. Because of commonality of data (as often documented in a CRUD, or Change/Read/Update/Delete, matrix) and the possibility of higher workload, the first few processes may not all be of the highest priority.

As part of this prioritization, identify architectural components that must be developed. There may be infrastructure development—for instance, remote data access or security. Identify manual and/or temporary solutions; there may be some support data not initially available (to be loaded from spreadsheets, etc.).

PROTOTYPING USING JAD

We use prototyping to replace external design documents in the iterative development stages. The documents on screen and report layouts and dialog flow will be produced automatically after the design is complete, to the extent that they are needed. Often, the prototypes can be produced faster than the design documents. Almost always, they are more complete and more accurate.

A good prototype can be built easily and quickly; the effort can be reused in the production system, the limitations are clearly explained to the users, and the system is changeable and expandable.

A prototype is needed when all details of the system are not defined, the end user has an interest in the operation of the system, and the system is sufficiently complex to need modeling. The clearest exception is where the system is a wholesale replacement of an existing one—in which case, the old system serves this function.

The entire system is not modeled in a prototype. The most suitable components for prototyping are those with the most end-user interaction: data entry and edits, reporting, and dialog flow.

The least suitable components are those in which the important design decisions are not visible to the user or not within their power to control:

- access to legacy systems
- exchange of data with other applications
- calculations
- protocols
- external business rules, such as accounting and tax

In this method, we are building iteratively, maintaining work for the production system without throwing effort away. The prototype should be built in the production tool. In the past, we often employed prototyping tools that were different from the production system. This should not be necessary today for client/server business systems.

There are some pros and cons to prototyping. On the positive side:

- users receive an early deliverable
- it helps users visualize benefits ("shares the vision")
- it helps "sell" the system internally
- users own the system because they worked on the design
- user expertise can help and is more effective because it can visualize the system better than paper documents
- can be quicker and less expensive than paper design
- poor design is caught much earlier in the development cycle
- good way to give specs to programmers
- can be training tools

On the negative side:

- use of prototypes has led to many problems of mismatched expectations
- user can be confused as to the cost and time for the real system
- the details of production systems can be forgotten
- can lead to a premature focus on details
- some systems get trapped in a cycle of continual change
- some users do not get involved

The Timebox

The timebox idea is an attempt to tackle some of the problems of iterative prototyping. The biggest problem is that you don't know when you've finished. The timebox simply sets a firm deadline, which must be honored. If the system is slipping, functionality is dropped, but the deadline must still be met.

Ideally, a system will be completed on time with the expected functionality. In the real world, as we know, this does not always happen. First, it is often better to have a working, but incomplete, system on the expected date than a more complete one at some later date. Second, the knowledge that

Chapter 9 • Building a New Automated System

this method is being employed puts a different pressure on users, rewarding them for being efficient in their efforts. The cooperative user gets more function within the time allotted.

A typical time period for the timebox is three months.

Types of Prototype

There are different types of prototype. A *proof of concept* may be employed during the requirements phase. This is a "toy" system used for sales or demonstration purposes, showing the major features of the system. Sometimes, one of these systems will be available at the beginning of the development project, as a "straw man."

The prototypes used in this methodology include the following:

1. Content: user interface only, generally accompanied by data model and other design activity
2. Process: user interface backed by limited data access, generally somewhat limited in function and not optimized for production performance
3. Production: functional application, often about 80 percent of necessary function, with acceptable full-volume production performance.

While the production prototype is expected to have the necessary completeness and user friendliness, there is still a further institutionalization phase, where the system is completed after the experience of a few months of full-time use.

We will often employ a performance prototype early on, to confirm the feasibility of the architecture. That is covered elsewhere.

Content Prototype

The purpose of this stage is to prototype the external interface between the user and application, although this is expected to be at a demonstration level.

Acquire the relevant information sources. Interview selected business users to gain insight into their critical information needs and to identify preliminary performance measures and critical success factors. Based on the interviews, develop an application prototype using samples of actual data.

Using JAD sessions, develop the screens, menus, and dialogs that make up the external interface of the system.

Confirm this content prototype by demonstrating it to the end users and identifying activities to complete content prototype. This will almost certainly be a JAD session that results in one or more iterations.

Obtain management approval to proceed to the functional prototype. This is an interactive process—repeatedly performing activities in this stage until management approval is obtained.

Advantages of JAD

JAD both establishes end-user commitment to the system and draws upon their knowledge to improve its quality. It produces visual documentation and hands-on prototypes, which users can understand, as opposed to technical documentation, which they cannot. It introduces IT techniques, such as prototyping and data modeling, to end users.

It can cross organizational boundaries and resolve conflicts, whether political or substantive, between different user groups or between users and the system development staff. If we cannot resolve conflict, at least we are made aware of it early in the process and can take steps to manage it.

The JAD technique develops a design in a much shorter elapsed time than traditional interview-based system analysis, because the interviewing is parallellized. It can also use less resources when performed well, but it may not optimize the time of some important individuals. It can waste resources, if the sessions are not well prepared and structured (there is a high burn rate). Running a JAD session is like renting an expensive power tool; you must plan ahead, then use it effectively and with skill.

There are usually a series of JAD sessions. A common duration is about a week. They often run late into the night; when they do not, there are often subgroup meetings, which do. A follow-on one- or two-day session is used to review and confirm the results. If a system is very large, it should be broken into subsystems that can be addressed in week-long JAD sessions.

Facilitated Session: Joint Application Design

Purpose

The purpose of the Joint Application Design session is to develop the design documents for the system, achieving a consensus between all the affected parties.

Chapter 9 • Building a New Automated System

Objectives

The objective of this session is to document the work flow, essential data model, screens, and reports for the important functional aspects of the new system.

Participants

A facilitator and scribe are needed. People from each affected area of the organization should be present, including managers and workers. Attendees must have the authority to commit their area. If possible, get the "informal leaders" of the organization involved, as well as the creative thinkers and a combination of old hands and new employees (preferably those coming from other companies with a different perspective). The key players are the end users who want the system. Keep the total to 10 or 12.

Preparation

The facilitator should perform necessary logistics, review the participants, and prepare a "straw man" document. The purpose and constraints of the project should be detailed. The work flow should be covered in a structured manner with sufficient detail to develop screens and database models.

Session Steps

1. Explain the concepts of application design and the ground rules for the session (such as no criticism of ideas).
2. Guide the participants through the system requirements in an orderly way, following the work flow, to produce the deliverables listed below.

Key Deliverables/Work Products Created

1. Purpose, scope, and limits of system
2. Business problems addressed by the system
3. System interfaces
4. Functional decomposition
5. Process model, including essential events
6. Data model, including essential attributes
7. Screen and report layouts
8. Operating requirements and procedures

Comments/Suggestions

1. All attendees must be present full time. This is not easy with the higher-level people, but any time lost is multiplied by the lost consensus and the need to catch up. If the time cannot be given, consider off-site locations and weekend days. If it still cannot be given, consider abandoning the project.
2. Leave your status at the door; all team members are equal.
3. Without good people, the session will fail.
4. Ask questions about the following.
   - How do users plan or assign work; what is coming and when?
   - How is work received? How are resources received?
   - How is receipt tracked and reported?
   - How is work monitored?
   - How is work processed?
   - What events can occur and how are they recorded?
   - What reporting takes place? Which is event-driven or periodic?
   - Where is work sent after completion?
   - What management information (summaries, exceptions, trends, budgets, objectives) is required?
5. The facilitator should promote interaction and consensus. The facilitator directs the scribe in producing the final report.

Estimating the JAD Session

Triage the screens, reports, and process routines into complex, medium, or simple. This is informal but can use the function point guidelines as a starting point. Four to eight functions can be tackled in a day:

Complex: 4/session/day
Medium: 6/session/day
Small: 8/session/day

Add one kickoff day for every three days. If the total activity sums to over six days, consider partitioning into smaller sessions.

Add four days per session day for draft report preparation. Add prototype development time and document review. A second JAD to review the work should be scheduled as one day, if the first session was up to three days; otherwise, two days should be selected.

Example JAD Estimate

5 complex, 7 medium, 12 small routines:
5/4 + 7/6 + 12/8 = 4 session days
Add 2 kickoff days = 6-day JAD
16 days to prepare report
Second JAD: 2 days

DATA MODELING

If we are building systems with small teams in short time frames, there would appear to be limits to the systems that can be constructed. To some extent, this is true; this methodology is limited to a subset of all systems, tending to the smaller and less mission-critical. However, large systems can be built by developing several smaller efforts in parallel and coordinating them with a consolidated model.

In information engineering, data and process models are prepared. For the type of system employed here, the data model is the essential work. While the data model is probably always the single most useful map of a system, this is especially true for decision support and operational control systems. Many of these systems are driven by user requests for information, not by incoming events. Thus, while a full information model would have these four components:

- event modeling
- process modeling
- data modeling
- entity life-cycle analysis

we develop the data model to more detail, using the others to gain a view of the business.

Another reason for emphasis on the data model is that it is *stable*. Processes change much more often than data. An essential data model is stable within a company over time, across companies in the same industry, and between similar functional areas in different industries. A process model is not.

If a data model has already been created for the business area, it should be used. If it has not, one should be built for the processes under development.

The data model for the system evolves during the phases.

In the requirements phase, the preliminary data model represents the types of data maintained by the business and the interrelations and interdependencies of that data. The senior users produce this as they define and prioritize their goals and objectives in the requirements planning phase. This model is used along with the goals and objectives. It defines the scope of the project in terms of information necessary to support the targeted business area as well as interaction with external agents.

In the application design phase, essential data, process, and event models are built concurrently with the content prototype. These allow a thorough and clear understanding of the business area, all current problems associated with the business area, and appropriate data sources.

In the development phase, the models are expanded and refined to incorporate implementation-specific requirements and to include additional detail.

There are many CASE tools available for building data models. The most natural for a client/server environment is the Windows-based "small CASE" tools. While not having the integrated code-generation features of products such as IEF and ADW, these tools can be purchased for one or two thousand dollars. They are more than simple drawing tools; they have repositories that can be used for reporting, and they will generate database schemas from the diagrams. The three leading tools of this type are:

- System Architect
- ERwin
- EasyCASE Plus

Building a Data Model

A data model, often called an entity/relationship diagram, documents the static relationship between entities. By developing this model, we produce a system design that is likely to remain stable over time. If, instead, we define database files around process needs, we find a tendency to introduce ad hoc changes as user needs evolve.

The downside to a system based on a data model is that it has more database tables than a system with files in support of the major applications. In particular, the normalization process (see the Data Normalization subsection) breaks complex tables into smaller units. This is not a problem if using a full relational database, which allows easy navigation through these tables and definition of views. It is a problem with some low-end database products.

In the past, this proliferation of tables could cause performance problems, and tables would be "denormalized." This is less common now, thanks to improved database and hardware performance. As a result of these problems, many experienced database developers are not as comfortable with normalized relational database design as we would wish.

After the design is complete, an entity is roughly equivalent to a database table (or file) and an attribute to a column (or field).

An entity is a group of data that can be uniquely identified and described by a number of facts (attributes). An entity could be a physical thing, an idea, or an activity. The data model describes the entities, their attributes, and the relationships between them.

Data models can be developed top down or bottom up, or using a combination. A generic data model can often be employed based on experience in a similar business. Data models are much more portable between businesses than process models. If we can see the entities directly, with or without a generic data model, we should ask the following for each application.

1. What entities are in this application?
2. What attributes does each entity have that are relevant to this application?

In other systems, the best way to do this is bottom up. We collect all forms, screens, reports, files, and other documents or data stores, cull the attributes from this information and classify them into groups, and then integrate them into the model and normalize them into entities. These approaches should lead to the same result.

Relationships are the reasons that two entities are associated. They are very often represented by verbs:

- has a
- supervises
- is composed of
- ships to

These can usually be expressed in both directions (supervises . . . is supervised by). Relationships can theoretically be one to one (1:1), one to many (1:M), or many to many (M:M). Many to many relationships are in practice expressed as two 1:Ms with an associative entity, since it is necessary to identify which relationship is which.

1:1	guest is booked	hotel room
1:M	order contains	line items

M:M	student is taught by	teacher
1:M, M:1	student is taught	class is taught by teacher

Additionally, two entities can have a zero to one or zero to many relationship.

0:M   employee has degree

Data Normalization

The objective of data normalization is to remove redundancies and inconsistencies in the data, arriving at a model that is stable, flexible, and complete. This is accomplished through a series of logical steps.

In a normalized model, every attribute is dependent on the key, the whole key, and nothing but the key. This is accomplished with three rules.

1. No repeating groups
2. All nonkey items are dependent on the primary key
3. All nonkey items are independent of each other

Example of Data Normalization

This example is taken from a system that maintains records of employee skills, so that we can search and find an employee capable of performing a particular job. The original employee-record file is seen as it might be in a typical COBOL or dBASE program.

Not Normalized

Employee-Record

Employee ID
Employee Name
Employee Number
Employee Address
Skill [occurs 1 to 20]
Skill Description
Skill Level

This file is of variable length. We have an arbitrary limit on the number of skills. We must program access to the skills in a manner different from other records.

Chapter 9 • Building a New Automated System

First Normal Form (1NF)

Remove the repeating group skill from the record, adding an item skill ID to identify it.

Employee

> *Employee ID*
> Employee Name
> Employee Number
> Employee Address

Employee Skill

> *Employee ID*
> *Skill ID*
> Skill Description
> Skill Level

There are still problems with this layout. For instance, there is no easy way to list the available skills. If a skill is added, deleted, or changed, we will have to scan the entire employee file.

Second Normal Form (2NF)

Skill description is dependent on skill ID alone, not employee and skill.

Employee

> *Employee ID*
> Employee Name
> Employee Number
> Employee Address

Employee Skill

> *Employee ID*
> *Skill ID*
> Skill Level

Skill

> *Skill ID*
> Skill Description

TEAM COMPOSITION

Figure 9.6 illustrates the hierarchy of the project team.

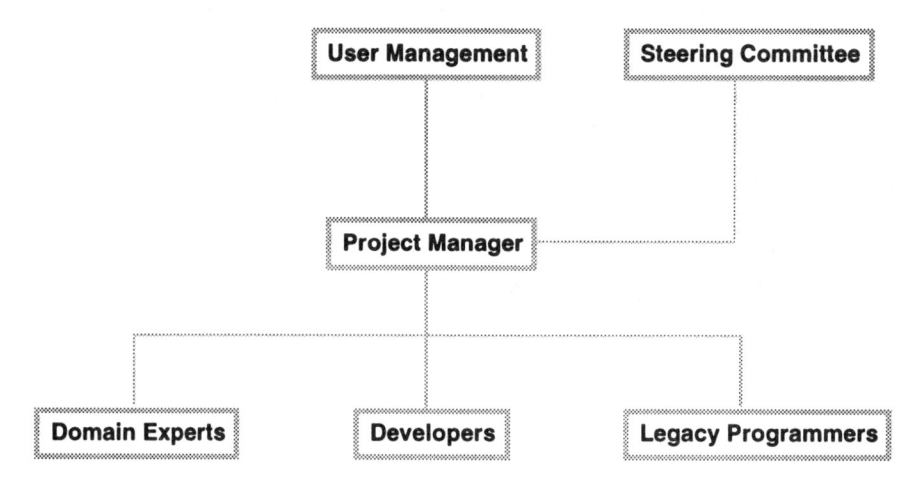

Figure 9.6 Project team

Summary

The critical success factors for rapid application development are:

- management and end-user commitment and participation
- good project management
- motivated, skilled staff using an appropriate methodology
- shared data model

The emphasis on these systems is less on procedural coding, more on person-to-person interactions. It is important that the team reflects this. This is not to say that conventional programmers cannot do this work—only that those who were drawn to programming because they would not have to deal with people may be in trouble. Similarly, database and network design require a consideration of other applications in a way that older systems did not need. The emphasis is shifting from closed problem solving to a more open process.

10

The Old and the New: Porting and Bridging Systems

"If we start today to build all our new applications using open systems tools, we will still be using most of our current applications in fifteen years."

— Paul Pinson (Dupont)

There is a tremendous investment in existing systems. As the quote above points out, this will be with us for many years even if we were deliberately trying to replace all the systems. In fact, we are not actually trying to replace all of the old technology; we cannot afford to, and, as pointed out earlier, it is still the best for many applications. Worse, this is not a one-time transition; it is likely that many systems being built today will be seen as obsolete within a few years. This is the "legacy system" problem; at any time, most of our data are stored in systems that we would not choose if beginning anew. We will speak mostly about IBM mainframe systems as the "legacy," because that is the most common case and because this book is about "downsizing." However, much of the same commentary applies to other mainframes, such as Unisys, or to systems that were not regarded as mainframes. A lot of companies are facing the legacy system problem with their XBase code; this is very often "spaghetti code" without documentation or a comprehensible data model.

If we recognize that much of our data will be stored on older systems for the next few years, we need a strategy for accessing these data. The choices come down to using middleware, such as gateways or other techniques, to

- Solution often different for transactional and information systems
- Transactional:
  - Two-way traffic
  - Update data quality and auditability
  - Generally gateway strategy
- Informational:
  - One-way traffic
  - Generally replication strategy
  - Information warehouse
- Legacy data is very difficult to use

Figure 10.1 Legacy systems

access the systems in real time or replicating the data to "data warehouses." This is the division between transactional and information systems (Figure 10.1). As usual, most complex environments will employ a strategy that mixes both approaches.

We once might have thought that distributed database would be implemented in an enterprise from a single data model in a predesigned, top-down manner, often on a homogeneous technical platform. It turns out that the real world of distributed database is very different: ad hoc, designed after the fact, based on access by application or workgroup, built on multiple data models, and generally based on a heterogeneous platform.

Basic connectivity to legacy systems is achieved with two major approaches. The front-end system approaches the host looking like something it expects, or the host is changed to recognize the front end as what it is. The most common example of approaching on the host terms is traditional SNA. Examples of loading client/server software on the host include TCP/IP, OSI, Novell, and more recent versions of SNA.

MAINFRAME CONNECTIVITY WITH SNA

The staple of communication with IBM mainframes is 3270 terminal emulation. This is available on almost every platform in a range of alternatives.

Chapter 10 • The Old and the New: Porting and Bridging Systems

SNA communication at the hardware level is done with a confusing variety of choices and is often best left to a specialist. The following indicates the principles involved. In one set of scenarios, the host is left unaltered and the front-end system replaces some components of the expected system. Basically, the most common mainframe situation is the tiered 3270/3x74 system. The mainframe communicates by fast serial connection to the 3x74 controller, which communicates with the terminals over either coaxial cable or Token Ring. The front-end system then replaces some component of this.

Scenario 1: The front-end system replaces 3x74 and uses serial RS-232 to communicate with the host front-end processor.

Scenario 2: The front-end system replaces the terminal and is connected by coax to the 3x74 and through this to the host.

Scenario 3: The front-end system replaces the terminal and is connected by Token Ring to the 3174 controller and through this to the host.

Good Windows products support multiple sessions and offer a programming interface. The top sellers are AttachMate Extra! and Wall Data Rumba.

In the terminal emulation environment, file transfer is generally accomplished with the IBM IND$FILE program, which runs under TSO or CMS. However, 3270 terminal emulation is not an efficient way to transfer large quantities of data. For this, a Remote Job Entry (RJE) protocol is required. The 20-year-old IBM 2780/3780 standard is commonly used.

Two programming APIs are included in SNA. The peer-to-peer application programming interface CPI-C, based on the LU6.2 protocol, requires programming at both ends. By contrast, in the EHLLAPI interface, the mainframe deals with a terminal stream and the front-end system operates on that.

MAINFRAME CONNECTIVITY WITH OPEN SYSTEMS

As an alternative, non-SNA software, which recognizes the front-end systems as what they are, can be installed on the host. For example, the front-end system can run NetWare and be connected by LAN to Novell NetWare for SAA, which runs on the host. Similarly, the front end can run TCP/IP and communicate by LAN or by serial connection using a 3172 controller with a host supporting TCP/IP.

Using this approach, the mainframe really does look like a large reliable server. Using TCP/IP, for instance, standard facilities such as FTP and NFS are used for file transfer, and the peer-to-peer programming interface is TCP/IP sockets or one of the RPC standards layered on this.

USING MIDDLEWARE TO ACCESS LEGACY SYSTEMS

The various components that are called middleware are used to connect front-end systems to the back end—the back end generally, but not always, being a database. This is more than a legacy system access issue. An important issue of client/server application design is making access to the database transparent to the end user. Middleware can help us do this; ideally, the end user developers, whether using a query tool or development language, do not need to concern themselves with the details of access to the specific back-end platform, in particular the network protocols or the low-level database subroutine calls. In most cases, the network protocol used by the application should be able to be changed without requiring modification of the application. The database access can be written in SQL. For example, middleware for accessing an ORACLE database can translate client SQL commands into ORACLE Call Interface (OCI) calls that actually access the database.

Middleware can run on any combination of machines. The different strategies are often related to the alliances of the vendor, and to their theories on the future of gateway functionality.

Figure 10.2 shows a three-tier gateway design from Micro Decisionware Inc., now a division of Sybase, who are second only to IBM as one of the leading mainframe gateway vendors. The MDI gateway runs on a dedicated machine and accesses a mainframe component. The desktop system is running no special software and is actually not aware that it is not accessing Sybase SQL Server. The system easily supports many desktop systems. The MDI products allow desktop software written to the Sybase DB-LIB or Microsoft ODBC APIs to access many databases on host systems. The dedicated gateway offers the opportunity to access different databases transparently, and to manage data transfer or other systems management functions. On the other hand, the mainframe component is usually expensive in this architecture.

Figure 10.3 shows a two-tier gateway. Here, a gateway component runs on the workstation. This eliminates the additional gateway, and its associated management and acquisition costs. As illustrated, there is still an expensive mainframe component. Of course, if the workstation software costs very much and there are a lot of users, costs can still be high. The direct ODBC

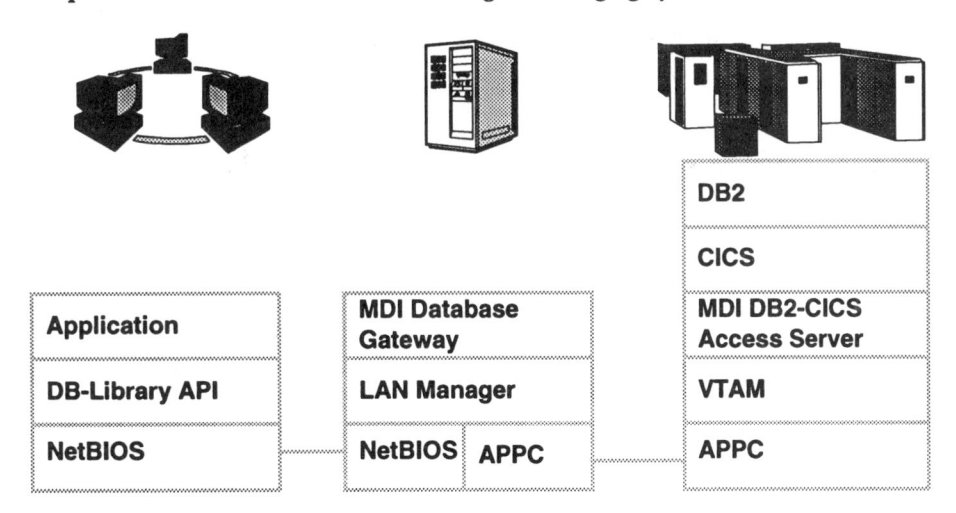

Chapter 10 • The Old and the New: Porting and Bridging Systems

Application	MDI Database Gateway	MDI DB2-CICS Access Server
DB-Library API	LAN Manager	VTAM
NetBIOS	NetBIOS / APPC	APPC

Above workstation column: (none)
Above middle column: (none)
Above host column: DB2 / CICS

Figure 10.2 Three-tier gateway

strategy is an example of a two-tier strategy with software only at the workstation. Again, costs are high if there are many workstations, and there may be performance limitations, but for situations where a few workstations need data access, this is very effective. In general, two-tier strategies work best accessing a single host database.

Application	DB2
Gateway component	CICS
NetBIOS or APPC or TCP/IP	Gateway component
	NetBIOS or APPC or TCP/IP

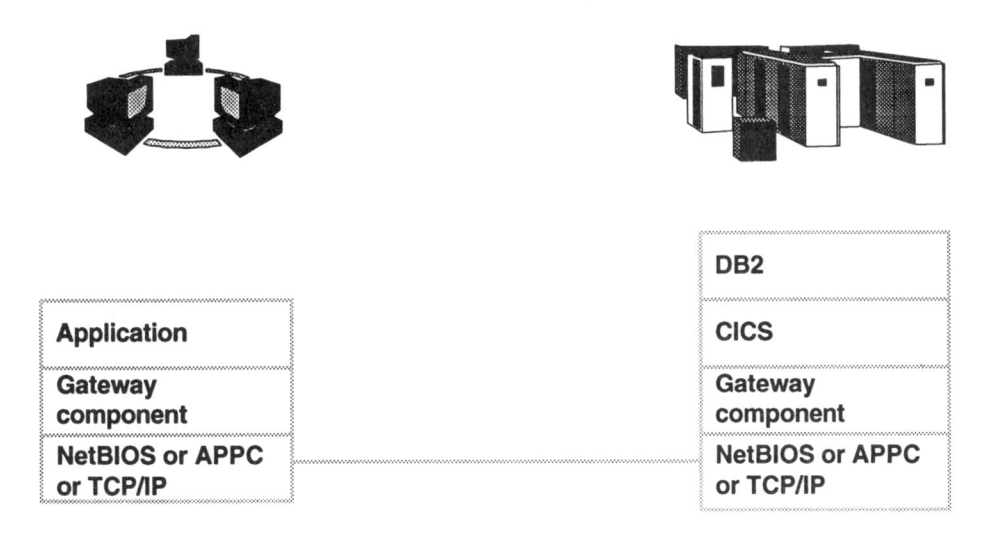

Figure 10.3 Two-tier gateway

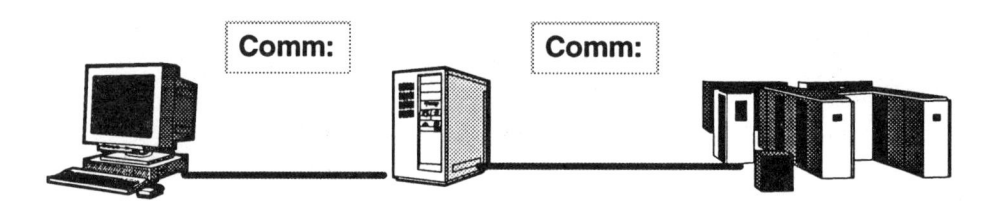

Figure 10.4 Accessing legacy systems

Figure 10.4 is a form which can be used to record the environment an application is being developed or installed in. Figure 10.5 is the same form filled out for a particular environment. Typically, there may not be a database at the workstation or user interface at the server.

Middleware issues include:

- legacy system complexity
- access to SQL databases
- access to non-SQL databases
- nondatabase (transactional) access

Legacy System Complexity

The job of accessing data on disparate systems is not as simple as it might appear. First, SQL was designed to be a consistent and conceptually simple way to access data. The flat file and network and hierarchical systems that preceded relational databases are more difficult to access. Systems with flat files have no data dictionary, so until one is created there is no way to know what data are actually stored in them other than reading the programs that maintain them. Flat-file systems also generally have tremendous redundancy, being designed around individual application needs. Often, a file is processed through a series of algorithms with incremental changes to data

Chapter 10 • The Old and the New: Porting and Bridging Systems

UI:	*Windows*	UI:		UI:	*CICS*
Tool:	*PowerBuilder*	Tool:	*C*	Tool:	*PL/I*
DB:		DB:	*SQL Server*	DB:	*DB2*
OS:	*DOS*	OS:	*OS/2*	OS:	*MVS*

Comm: *Novell*   **Comm:** *MDI Gateway*

Figure 10.5 Accessing legacy systems

elements. There is no single place with "the right data." Older databases are often no different; IMS systems, in particular, often treated the databases like files, with multiple redundant copies. These systems also use complex algorithmic data storage techniques; the contents of the record depend on fields within the record indicating types or numbers of occurrences in ways that are not cataloged but embedded in application code. Some systems will not have standard "copybooks" describing the data; those that do will often not explain the timing issues—for instance, a field may not have contents until a particular program is run. Furthermore, legacy systems have a strong application orientation. In case after case, these systems resulted from management's tendency to opt for the local over the global and the quick fix over the long-term solution.

Not only were these systems inherently complex, they have often become more so with maintenance and obsolescence. Data on production systems are typically accessed through layers of code, which navigate and also hide details. As an example, suppose you wish to query the average salary of an employee. Further, suppose that using a gateway, you can access the master employee file (which is VSAM) with an SQL query something like "SELECT AVG(EMPSAL) FROM EMPLOYEE." Many problems can arise here. Perhaps employees are not deleted from the file but marked with various codes for their departure. Possibly some employee salaries are not known; these may be stored as zero. Some record numbers may be not employees but subcontractors, with special code written in COBOL to exclude them from employee processing. The salary field may be limited to five digits, and, because of the difficulty of changing field lengths in the old files, salaries over $100,000 are indicated with a special flag, which the code reads. Typically, these types of problems are common. They are never well documented. For this reason, we should recognize that this type of access will generally be labor-intensive, involving careful design and review of the existing systems. Some companies have instigated lengthy database cleanup operations, usually including migration to DB2 combined with exhaustive redesign to make the database tables clean and consistent.

Access to SQL Databases

If the legacy data are in a relational database, our problems are lessened greatly. Perhaps, if the data are in a relational database, we should not call it a legacy system—at least not in 1994.

Access to SQL databases is simpler than to other types but not as simple as it should be, because SQL is not a sufficiently encompassing standard. New standards for database access are being promoted but are not, in practice, ready yet for most situations. Some form of middleware is generally necessary.

There have been SQL standards for several years now, and essentially all the SQL databases of any significance were produced in the same few square miles of Silicon Valley. Despite this, there are significant functionality and dialect differences between implementations. These occur occasionally in basics, such as syntax (such as the use of INTO in INSERT); semantics, such as allowing nulls in CREATE; and data types other than the most basic five (such as BLOBs). Beyond this, the divergencies accumulate. There is no common format for system catalog tables, although the SQL2 standard will help. The SQL2 standard also has standards for the return code SQLCODE, which currently varies.

Call-level APIs have been totally different. Data encoding, such as collating sequences, varies. SQL gateways are products that resolve these differences, translating into the specifics of each implementation. The need for a standard to provide a common API for database access has been recognized for some time, but 1993 was the year that workable standards were introduced. While there are competing standards, the ones with market acceptance seem to be the Microsoft standard, ODBC, and the IBM standard, DRDA.

Open Database Connectivity (ODBC) allows an application developmernt tool to use a single SQL-based standard and is supported by many software companies, including Lotus, Gupta, Apple, and Q+E. It is an implementation of the SQL Access Group Call Level Interface draft standard (CLI). This standard is largely based on the Sybase DB-LIB (Open Client) API, as discussed earlier.

The IBM standard, DRDA, is implemented by the IBM product DDCS/2 and by other products, such as the DRDA version of the Sybase/Micro Decisionware Database Gateway. A DRDA gateway does not have a mainframe component at all. This is essentially a protocol that allows a database to access remote DB2 databases, allowing the various IBM DB2 versions, including DB2/2, DB2/6000, DB2/400, and DB2/MVS, to work together seamlessly. In the future, we can expect other databases to support DRDA also.

These two standards are not mutually exclusive. Several vendors support ODBC access to DRDA.

There are alternatives to DRDA when accessing DB2. These generally resolve front-end requests using a special mainframe component, the host transaction server, which obtains data from DB2 and returns it, together with any messages, to the gateway. Unfortunately, although vendors try to optimize their mainframe component, gateways offer significant tuning concerns in their effect on DB2 performance and overall MVS resource contention. Some host components of gateways run as CICS transactions, some as MVS startup tasks. MVS tasks help shops minimize additional system overhead but cannot execute remote procedure calls (RPCs) and, therefore, cannot support static SQL. This directly impacts DB2 performance and also allows a very limited number of concurrent DB2 connections. A gateway can run short or long transactions. Long transactions supply complete transaction integrity; however, this option may affect concurrency. Short transactions release DB2 resources, such as locks, once an SQL statement is executed, but they do not let you roll back any undesirable updates. In short, a successful DB2 client/server implementation depends on effective DB2-gateway interaction. Perhaps DRDA is the simplest choice.

Access to Non-SQL Databases

It is now possible to access nonrelational databases with SQL. This is a partial answer to the problem, unfortunately. First, the problems of data access to old files remain, as mentioned above. Second, there are complexities in the systems, which make some data inaccessible through these gateways. Third, there are significant issues of performance.

Where this access makes the most sense is for prototyping or for analytical systems. While the alternative, the construction of data warehouses, may be theoretically sounder, use of a gateway can be a good adjunct to the warehouse, allowing code to load the database to be written in a familiar language.

The best-known products that offer dynamic SQL access to nonrelational data are EDA/SQL from Information Builders and InfoHub from Trinzic. EDA/SQL, developed by IBI and sponsored by IBM in its Information Warehouse program, supports over 100 front-end tools and 50 databases, which is the largest number of different database and file formats. This is not an inexpensive product, but it should be considered when a variety of databases have to be accessed.

Another approach is to allow SQL queries to be translated into a user-developed programmatic access routine, or Remote Stored Procedure. This has the obvious major disadvantage that each SQL query must be hand-coded in COBOL, FOCUS, or some such mainframe language. The advantage is that because the access is hand-coded, it can be as efficient and complex as necessary. The best-known example of this approach has long been the Database Gateway from Micro Decisionware, now a division of Sybase, although EDA/SQL offers a similar facility. The Sybase OmniSQL Gateway, introduced in early 1993, supports DEC RMS and IBM ISAM, VSAM, and AS/400 in addition to the major SQL systems. Presumably, this product will be merged with the MDI Database Gateway.

Using the Database Gateway, a client application written to the SQL Server application programming interface (DB-LIB or Open Client) or to ODBC is capable of accessing DB2 for read and write operations.

Further products in this category include Cross Access and CA Visual Express Host. Sybase, Information Builders, and Computer Associates all have available ODBC drivers. Thus, any application supporting ODBC can use these products to access all of the databases they support.

Q+E Software, based in North Carolina and now owned by Intersolv, began selling Q+E Database Editor, which accessed a variety of databases, several years ago. While the editor is still a viable database reporting tool, the support libraries have evolved into a product in their own right. Using the Q+E Libraries, a front-end tool can communicate with a variety of databases. The company supports IDAPI, ODBC, and DRDA. These drivers are used in products from vendors such as WordPerfect (Office), Lotus (Improv), Computer Associates, Intersolv, and Delrina. Special versions are sold for ObjectVision and Visual Basic.

Q+E supports a huge range of databases—essentially, all SQL databases; the non-SQL PC databases Progress, Btrieve, dBASE, Paradox, and Excel; and the SQL gateways from IBM (DDCS/2) and Sybase (Micro Decisionware and OmniSQL).

The middleware area is more complicated than this. Most database vendors offer middleware specifically for their products. ORACLE (SQL*NET) and Informix (I-NET), for instance, both provide vendor-specific middleware that can be used effectively with their own development tools. These tools are practical and usable with third-party products.

ORACLE has been very open in publishing specifications for the SQL*NET API. Many independent middleware vendors, such as Q+E Software (Q+E Database Editor and Q+E Database Library), and development tools vendors, such as PowerBuilder and SQLWindows, support SQL*NET. ORACLE Glue supports ORACLE, DB2, ORACLE Mail, and the Sharp Wizard. It can be accessed from Visual Basic, Ami Pro, Microsoft Word, Microsoft Excel, and Lotus 1-2-3. Support for MAPI, ODBC, DAL, and SQL Server is due soon.

Informix support has recently been added or announced for some of these tools. Gupta SQLNetworks offers gateways to the best-known SQL databases. Other products available to deal with mixed vendor environments include Sybase's Open Server API.

In the Macintosh arena, Apple's Data Access Language (licensed to Blyth Software for Windows and other implementations) is an important middleware product that is tightly integrated with the System 7 operating system.

REPLICATION STRATEGIES AND DATA WAREHOUSES

A data warehouse is a decision support data model, implemented on a relational DBMS, representing the information an enterprise needs to make strategic decisions, allowing easy access to the information for business analysis. It should be integrated and organized around subject areas, which may be stored in separate "warehouses." While the idea seems to have originated in association with mainframes and DB2, it is actually a very good application for the new technology of relational database and client/server tools.

The information warehouse does not make the issues of accessing legacy data easier, but it does recognize the problem and provide a structure to deal with it. In this model, you recognize that substantial time and effort will be devoted to cleaning up the situation and that an enterprise-wide or at least substantial data model will be carefully designed.

In terms of efficiency and for many other reasons, a traditional mainframe is a better choice than new technology for many transaction-processing environments. In that situation, removing the decision support data and processing from the operational systems, including reports, ad hoc analysis, extracts to the workstation environment, and downloads to the client/server environment, can give the best of both worlds—a more effective operational system and a more responsive informational system. This removes a large amount of historical data from the operational system. It reduces the maintenance burden; the decision support world is full of people who constantly change their minds. It removes many intricate dependencies of data and processing. It streamlines and simplifies the workload. No longer will some users want transaction response time and other users want massive reports from the same legacy environment. By removing massive reporting needs and old, historical data out of the legacy environment, the resulting environment is optimal for transactional, high-response, updated processing.

The products that support this architecture are many and varied, including entries from every large vendor. ORACLE and Sybase have their various replication mechanisms. IBM, H-P, and DEC have architectures with a variety of internal and third-party products. AT&T has their massively parallel database engine inherited from Teradata. And there are the smaller companies, such as Bill Inmon's Prism Solutions, Red Brick Warehouse, Trinzic with their InfoPump, Tools & Techniques with Data Junction, and Evolutionary Technologies' Extract.

Summary

This is a complex subject, and this chapter only scratched the surface. There are many specific problems to be solved in this area and generally several tools and vendors attempting to address each one. There is also a general problem, which is simply the old one of software maintenance. That is a deep and complex problem with no simple solution in sight. Sometimes, we can be carried away by the announcement of a simple tool and forget that these tools only address selected specifics, not the general issue. There is no substitute for understanding and hard work.

11

Implementing and Managing the New Systems

TECHNICAL PROBLEMS WITH CLIENT/SERVER SYSTEMS

The single biggest problem with open client/server systems at this time is not developing them but managing them. This is likely to be true for some time. There are a range of problem areas (see Figure 11.1). Although many of the problems of managing open systems are the result of their immaturity, others are not. It is useful to compare this situation to the replacement of railroads for most purposes by the automobile and road system earlier in the century. The automobile system has higher expenses than the railroad and much greater risks of damage to property, injury, and death. We accept these problems because we desire the responsiveness and freedom that automobiles offer. These risks are not inherent in the technologies of, for instance, internal combustion engines or pneumatic tires but follow from the way we use them. Similarly, while microprocessor and network technologies can be deployed to create secure and tightly managed systems, people will often choose to create systems where performance and availability cannot be guaranteed.

The biggest problem in corporations at the moment is simply lack of expertise in the new systems. This is largely a problem of transition, since we are undergoing a paradigm shift involving several related new systems. For example, there are clearly shortages of skills in areas such as UNIX, Win-

- Lack of expertise with new systems
- Security of open systems
- Data integrity of distributed systems
- Performance
- System management
  - Job scheduling, printing, resource allocation
  - Storage management, backup strategies
  - Software version control
- Support of remote systems
- Integration of products from several vendors
- Batch processing

Figure 11.1 Client/server problems

dows, relational databases, and various development languages. It is also true that there will be more disparate systems in the future, so that training and support will be permanently more important than they used to be.

Another set of problems is in the area of systems management. Security, backup, data integrity, and software version control all raise specific issues. This is both a transitional problem, reflecting lack of expertise and a temporary lack of products, and a permanent one, reflecting the greater complexity of these issues in enterprise-wide distributed systems.

The OSI Systems Management model defines five areas as components of systems and network management.

1. Performance, which deals with control and tuning of system resources in order to monitor satisfactory service levels and with planning for future system resource needs
2. Configuration, which focuses on the control of system and network device configurations
3. Accounting, which tracks systems resource utilization, including job accounting
4. Security, which defines how to protect the system, network, and its components from unauthorized intrusion or surveillance
5. Fault Management, which provides the ability to quickly identify, diagnose, and recover from system and network problems

In addition to these five, we must consider two further activities: operations management and storage management.

PERFORMANCE MANAGEMENT

Performance management includes fault and performance diagnostics, capacity planning and system modeling, problem tracking, and the collection and reporting of statistics.

A good system should provide for the collection of extensive performance data, including user response time, per user resource utilization, per terminal resource utilization, per process resource utilization, file system I/O, and many other system parameters. Facilities should be provided for both analyzing the performance data and optimizing system performance.

On mainframe MVS systems, reasonably comprehensive data are available through the Resource Management Facility (RMF) and the System Management Facility (SMF). UNIX systems offer similar facilities, but with no ability to save long-term historical data, and poor facilities for automated collection and integration of data from different systems. Without additional tools, understanding UNIX performance data is a rare skill. In practice, each UNIX vendor offers a combination of proprietary and third-party tools.

Hewlett-Packard, for example, has several performance management tools of its own as optional supplements to the capabilities of HP-UX. GlancePlus/UX is an on-line tool for viewing a snapshot of current system activity. CPU, memory, swap space, and disk utilization can be monitored by the system administrator, allowing the system's performance to be characterized and managed. Problems can be identified and resolved either on the host or from across the network using "rlogin." LaserRX/UX combines historic performance data collected on an on-going basis from the kernel with graphical analysis software to analyze system performance and activity over time. It can be used to identify system bottlenecks, perform load balancing, and locate potential performance problems. LaserRX/UX can work across the network to analyze all supported systems. Building on the data collected by LaserRX/UX is a capacity-planning tool called RXForecast/UX. This product builds on the historical performance data from the current system configuration to forecast performance under future loading. It uses a variety of statistical forecasting tools to perform this analysis, and the documentation takes users through the analysis so they can make informed forecasts of future requirements.

HP PerfView is designed for managing a large number of systems in a distributed environment, including servers and workstations, rather than a few large data center-class machines. PerfView has two components: the Motif-based performance analysis software runs on H-P servers and is integrated with OpenView to provide a graphical map of the system environment. The performance collection software runs on all HP 9000s and other workstation systems, including the Sun. PerfView uses management by exception to spot and resolve both actual and potential problems before they affect users.

CONFIGURATION MANAGEMENT

Configuration management includes:

- network inventory and topology
- device configuration
- change control
- update/install management
- network configuration
- software licenses

Large data centers, with thousands of users spread over many sites and hundreds of gigabytes of data being backed up and archived almost constantly, require capabilities built into the system as well as tools to manage their configurations. Tools for assisting with capacity planning, for managing the installation of new equipment, and for hardware and software updates, as well as for all of the tasks involved with network configuration and management, are critically important.

Software distribution and installation is a critical area, which is not well managed on distributed systems today. It includes the capability to push upgrades out to distributed users from a central licensing source as well as to allow users to pull installations from a server. This category also includes tracking software licenses, not only for the data center, but for all products that are supported centrally and used throughout the enterprise.

System management is handled by tools such as HP System Administration Manager (SAM) and IBM System Management Interface Tool (SMIT), which are screen-oriented system administration environments that hide details of the UNIX administration scripts and files. These systems now have graphical interfaces but do not handle networked systems very well.

Network management is provided through a variety of tools, including HP OpenView, licensed by IBM as NetView/6000, and by third-party solutions, including Tivoli Systems' products.

ACCOUNTING MANAGEMENT

Chargeback of costs from the data center is standard in virtually all companies. The system must maintain extensive statistics on usage and must support overhead allocation, split charges, discounting, and credits based on a wide variety of parameters. Even within companies that are simplifying their chargeback, for example, on the basis of average usage, those statistics still need to be maintained.

SECURITY MANAGEMENT

> "There's no such thing as meaningful security. Nothing is at all in any sense secure."
> — Peter Neumann, principal scientist, SRI computer lab, quoted in *Byte*, May 1993.

The risks that a computer system faces are of several types. The most common causes of losses are the physical issues of fire and water damage or power problems, rather than manmade threats. The manmade threats, in order of likelihood, are:

- programming errors
- curious outsiders
- hostile insiders
- hostile outsiders

It is estimated that $1 billion in losses occur annually from computer network break-ins. More than 85 percent of these are committed by insiders.

In the client/server environment, particularly the mixed vendor environment, security management becomes increasingly complex. Systems are distributed, so are less likely to sustain a single catastrophic loss from a physical problem but are much more likely to sustain a series of small ones. The power available to distributed systems is often unconditioned and likely to "brown out" or spike, causing failure of electronic parts. There is a considerable growth industry supplying uninterruptable power supplies to purchasers of distributed systems.

A disaster recovery plan appropriate to the level of system being secured is an essential management responsibility.

There is an inherent trade-off between usability and security. Just as locked doors are less easy to use than open doors, secure systems are less easy to use than insecure ones. Client/server architectures are generally associated with more widespread interactive access to data in at least two respects. First, there is more physical access—when 10 systems with single-function terminals are replaced by full-function workstations on a LAN, there is a tenfold increase in the physical access points to each system. If a public network is used, there may be an almost infinite number of access points. Second, access from each point is simpler. The security of a mainframe system in the old days lay in its difficulty of use. If a terminal were accessed, data were not accessible except with obscure programming languages and access to system documentation. Today, that system can perhaps be dialed to from a laptop computer anywhere in the world, and the databases can be browsed with graphical query tools designed for nontechnical end users.

Security on client/server systems involves paying attention to the same key security ideas used for any system, recognizing that the dangers are more acute because of the wide distribution and ease of use of this type of system. The key ideas are:

- identify and authenticate users
- restrict access to logical resources based on user ID
- audit access to logical resources based on user ID
- physically control access to physical resources
- use encryption whenever data leave the secure area

The extent to which we apply these ideas is a trade-off between the importance of the data to be protected and the cost of protecting it, bearing in mind the quote at the beginning of this section.

Identify and Authenticate Users

Identification is simply the ability to put a name to the user. On a secure system, virtually all access to resources should be from named users. There are few exceptions to this simple idea—an example is public access systems, such as multimedia displays in the building lobby. A system could allow some data or other resources to be accessed by the "nobody" user to support this.

Chapter 11 • Implementing and Managing the New Systems

An obvious problem is that some operating systems, such as DOS and OS/2, do not support the user ID requirement. It is then necessary to require user ID entry before allowing access to the network resources. This is done by the network operating system (Novell, DCE), the file-sharing system (PC-NFS, PCI/AADU), the database (ORACLE, etc.), or the client/server application, since DOS does not support it directly, and this can lead to a proliferation of passwords and logon prompts today. This problem is also a concern when designing client/server applications that might store data or perform processing on the client system, since DOS systems are insecure.

Authentication is confirming that the named users are who they say they are. This is almost always done today with passwords, which is perhaps unfortunate since people do not use passwords well. A research study conducted by Robert Morris at Bell Labs found that some passwords on most multiuser systems could be cracked by use of the system dictionary and a relatively simple set of algorithms.

Since passwords are what we have, the best advice is to:

- change the passwords regularly (e.g., once a month)
- encrypt the passwords on the system wherever they are stored (beware of remote systems)
- discourage user recording of passwords, whether on paper or as automatic logons (such as macros in communications or keyboard recorder programs)
- prevent passwords that are too simple, too short, or otherwise guessable (dictionary words are bad, two words separated by a special character is good)

In many situations, users are indifferent to risk. It is worth examining the password files for trivial passwords (there are programs available to do this, which are essentially "cracker" programs) and for invalid users, such as people who have left the company.

Because of the many problems of passwords, a physical security device, such as a smart card, may be justified in some systems.

Control of the "superuser" passwords, which some systems have, is particularly important. UNIX and Novell allow a "superuser" access to everything on the system. For many systems in an enterprise, access at this level to one system will get you into many related systems. The particular problem is that many activities require this superuser password, including some routine activities that may have to be performed when the main administrator of a system is not around. The "word" tends to get around further than it should. Better systems break up the "superuser" function into several less-powerful roles.

At a higher level of security, a system will not let the system administrator read all files. At present, this is unusual. If files must be defended from the system manager, they must be encrypted, which is usually the responsibility of the individual user.

Restrict Access to Resources

Access to all system resources should be considered and explicitly allowed or denied. The basic UNIX scheme, which identifies each resource with read or write and execute access by users, groups, or the world, is a good beginning. The system should also allow an access list detailing individual accesses for each individual resource. Resources that can be secured include applications, databases, and physical systems. The standards for ACLs are known, but unfortunately each manufacturer tends to have its own implementation, which makes things difficult to administer.

At a finer level of granularity, individual application functions and database objects can be secured. An ideal system would allow physical systems, databases, applications, and individual objects to be secured from a single management point for the enterprise; today, for a distributed system, there may be several management points and several managers. The database is the most reliable central security point for most database client/server applications. A good DBMS allows server-, database-, table-, and row/column-level security. Row/column-level security may be achieved through views.

In many systems, the dividing line between development and production systems is unclear. Because of immaturity, this is often the case in client/server systems. The movie *Jurassic Park* illustrates, among other things, the danger of giving developers uncontrolled access to the live system.

Database Security

Security and authorization must be complete and standard. Security on database servers is generally handled by two different mechanisms: through permissions and through views. Each user has a logon ID and password. In addition, each user is granted permission to access the data in the databases. These permissions can be placed down to the column level of a table in a database. The other main security feature of database servers is views. Views are used to restrict access to a subset of rows or columns of a table or group of tables. Security checking is, therefore, handled in a central place in the database, so that the access privileges of users do not depend upon whether they use SQL, a program, or a form. The lowest level of access control may be fields, records, tables, or database. Other features to be looked for include hierarchical security levels, time periods for access, and audit trails. Most DBMSs use their own login passwords rather than the standard login procedure of, say, the network operating system.

Audit Access to Resources

A full resource access log has the problem of "Big Brother" in 1984. If every action is videotaped, there is simply too much activity to monitor. In response to this problem, the audit of access is used to support two different approaches to managing this volume. We can run batch scans of the data, or simply "eyeball" sorted lists, looking for unusual patterns, or we can conduct a retroactive search after a crime has been found to discover evidence.

The information kept by the audit is which user used which resource, including any files read or altered, and which IDs were used from where. Use of this type of log is amusingly documented in *The Cuckoo's Egg* by Clifford Stahl, who used UNIX system resources and a great deal of hard work and ingenuity to catch an international network penetrator.

Most UNIX systems keep audit logs, but there is no real standard on this. Novell 3.11 does not keep audit logs.

Physically Control Access

Physical security, where possible, is preferable because we have a long history of success at maintaining it. Physical resource security includes all physical entities that hold or access data. It includes shredding paper, clearing data from disks and tapes, and locking terminals and buildings.

Unless systems are behind a locked door, users should log off or lock workstations before leaving them. To assist in this, terminals should be automatically disconnected after a period of disuse. However, because ease-of-use considerations keep the automatic period at five minutes or so, it is a user responsibility to log off each time.

Disks are an increasing problem now that a small drive can hold so much data. A programmer can leave a building with 10 man-years of work on a tiny tape or floppy disk. A stolen notebook computer can contain vast amounts of information, or it may have the passwords needed to access even more.

Communication lines are a problem to secure: Many organizations monitor for a wiretap; others encase the lines in a layer of inert gas so that any leak rings an alarm. Dial-back or caller ID systems can be used to validate the terminal at the other end of the line.

Viruses are also a physical security issue, in the sense that they are physically introduced through an infected disk. Highly secure systems must enforce rules on use of external software; less secure ones will recognize that users will do whatever they want on their PC systems and will run virus checks regularly.

Use Encryption to Secure Communications

Communications that may need to be encrypted include all public networks, particularly the Internet; wireless communication; and most local area networks. An alternative to encryption is installation of private wide area networks and physical security of LANs. The problem with public networks and wireless communication should be apparent. Anyone sending unencrypted files over these networks should be aware of the risks. The problem with LANs is that all traffic goes to all systems. LAN monitor software can read this traffic; there are public-domain programs for PCs that can read network traffic intended for other computers. Network traffic includes unencrypted passwords; for example, UNIX and Novell 3.11 system passwords travel in the clear during login from a remote workstation. It is easy to monitor the contents of messages on Ethernet using a PC with an Ethernet card and public-domain software.

Secure versions are available for many operating systems. These meet the B-level of the DoD standards, or *Orange Book*. Standard security enhancements to UNIX operating systems include a protected password database; access control lists; auditing of events, such as file creation, deletion, open, and close; process operations; logins and logouts; and others.

FAULT MANAGEMENT

Fault management includes:

- network status
- filtering alarms
- determining source and cause of problems
- administering trouble tickets

Chapter 11 • Implementing and Managing the New Systems

- running tests
- operating a help-desk

Capabilities in fault management include automatic problem detection, automatic notification, automated diagnostics, and failure recovery. The ability to run lights out or to run 24 × 7 (24 hours a day, 7 days a week) depends very heavily on fault management. Many vendors have service offerings that supplement the various notification mechanisms they have built into their systems. Few can support other vendors' systems yet because of the differences in interfaces. With the eventual introduction of OSF/DME, that should begin to change.

Help-desk facilities provide support for the interaction between users and systems managers. Help-desk capabilities help maintain logs of problem reports, track how those problems are being addressed, and when and how they are resolved.

Enhancements to the operating system prevent many system outages caused by defective hardware or software, thereby providing reliability. The extended file system and on-line peripheral diagnostics provide availability by reducing the amount of system downtime required for operational maintenance. Improvements in binary maintenance support tools and error detection capabilities enhance serviceability of the operating system.

OPERATIONS MANAGEMENT

Operations management includes:

- console management
- job scheduling
- output spooling

In many ways, the data center is the heartbeat of the enterprise. The operations staff needs proper tools, including those for workload planning, scheduling, and execution. Facilities for logging system events must be provided so that operations can be evaluated and monitored, and the log must be able to be searched and analyzed as well as to be archived for historical analysis.

While UNIX provides "cron" and "at" utilities, data centers require much more sophisticated job scheduling and queue management capabilities. Running a job according to a date/time event is easy. Running a series of jobs that have sequencing requirements because one job relies on the output of another is difficult. Scheduling has to be able to be event based, so that, in these cases, a job runs only if another job has run and has run successfully.

Job scheduling is offered by the Event Control Server for the LAN environment. CA-Unicenter, which is available for several environments, provides scheduling capabilities comparable to its mainframe products. In addition, solutions are available from AIM Technology (Santa Clara, California), which has Job Scheduler; Software Clearing House (Cincinnati, Ohio), which has Qbatch for UNIX; and Maestro from Unison (Sunnyvale, California).

Console management interfaces should provide an integrated environment for managing all aspects of system performance and operation. Remote console is becoming increasingly important for 24 × 7 operations and lights-out operations.

Output management capability, including devices such as printers, plotters, and fax servers, is a data center requirement. Users, as well as administrators, should have the ability to view the status of their jobs and to start and stop their jobs. Also required are queue management capabilities for administrators, including the ability to start and stop queues, reprioritize jobs in the queue, delete jobs in the queue, and transfer jobs from one queue to another. Included in this area are the ability to archive and retrieve queues for future output and the management of report distribution. Forms management, enabling data to be merged with predefined forms at print time, is also an important aspect of this area.

Output management and production scheduling come under the area of operations control. Print spooling beyond that offered in UNIX is provided by the MIT Palladium Print System for HP-UX and Solaris. Version 2 of this product is part of OSF DME. The product allows establishment of print priorities, viewing and changing requests; provides form and font management; and supplies templates for repetitive tasks, single-point administration, and security.

STORAGE MANAGEMENT

Storage management includes:

- disk management
- media (tape) management
- backup/restore

Chapter 11 • Implementing and Managing the New Systems

The system must provide integrated, system-level support for large-capacity mass storage, 500 GB as a minimum, and control of backup and restore, both attended and unattended. The ability to span physical disks with logical volumes and to manage those logical volumes is key. Related capabilities are the ability to mirror drives to protect data and other data integrity features, such as RAID support. Support for automatic retrieval and hierarchical storage management helps optimize the use of on-line, near-line, and off-line devices, making certain that required data are available as needed. UniTree from General Atomics is a distributed hierarchical storage management system, which provides an information management solution for large enterprises.

The OSF Logical Volume Manager (LVM) adds disk-spanning capabilities and error-recovery features to UNIX. This includes a mirroring component, which supports up to three-way mirroring, with on-line backup while maintaining mirroring. It is transparent to applications and can be brought into operation while applications are running. RAID arrays are a useful data integrity option. Tape management solutions are primarily obtained from third parties, such as SCH's REELlibrarian, REELbackup, and REELexchange.

Database administration includes a variety of backup, recovery, and loading tools and other utilities. Most of the products include some tools for this, but there is also a thriving third-party market. The better-selling databases tend to have the third-party tools, which can provide convenience and ease of use; DB2 in particular has a variety of third-party tools available, with Sybase and ORACLE being the next most popular. For example, Desktop DBA from Datura, which supports SQL Server and ORACLE, monitors database space, suggests tuning, creates and drops tables, and creates and stores SQL scripts. SQLWatch, from PACE Systems for SQL Server, gives detailed information on CPU usage, I/O, processes, and locks available; sorts and filters data as needed; charts performance; and stores messages from applications. DBA*Monitor, from MITI for ORACLE, is a database performance monitor and analyst, which recommends actions. Remote database administration allows staff reductions and supports true distribution of the database. True support for distributed databases is complex.

Backup

One of the simplest (but most important) procedures in supporting a database server is backing up the databases on a regular basis. Typically, a batch file of some sort can be written to perform these backups on a regular basis. Some database servers even offer dynamic backups, so that users can continue to use the system while the database is being backed up. Dynamic database backup should support on-line system backup and fast recovery.

A data center quality network backup management system should offer automated central backup and recovery. Ideally, backup and restore should be on-line, i.e., while the system and applications are operational. Backup and restore over the network are also important, allowing centralized backup of distributed systems. It should provide unattended backup/recovery with a variety of media, including magnetic tape, DAT, or rewritable optical disk.

Network Management Products

Other than basic fault management, the other items must be managed by a mixture of third-party products.

SNMP

SNMP consists of:

- a simple communications protocol based on TCP/IP
- a set of agents (an agent runs on network components and implements a virtual database called the Management Information Base [MIB])
- managers that receive data from the agents using the protocol in response to events or queries

SNMP allows a single workstation running SNMP management software to monitor all of the devices on a network. The less intelligent components are supported by a proxy feature. The leading SNMP management workstations are:

- HP OpenView and IBM NetView/6000
- SunConnect SunNetManager
- Cabletron Spectrum

DME

Looking into the future, to 1995 and beyond, we see that customers will be able to buy products that fit into OSF's Distributed Management Environment (DME) framework. System and network management applications, running on top of this distributed, object-oriented framework, will allow customers to mix and match management applications in different functional areas provided by different vendors, all of which will share a consistent, integrated management interface. The experience UNIX vendors are gaining providing data center-class systems today will undoubtedly improve the quality and breadth of DME-based products in the future.

H-P's umbrella for system and network management is OpenView. Several components of OpenView were selected as parts of the Open Software Foundation's DME, and it is H-P's plan to move OpenView to fully support DME as it evolves. H-P supplied the OpenView Network Management Server, Network License System, and Software Distribution Utilities to DME and also worked with Bull on the Consolidated Management API (CM-API). OpenView will also be the vehicle for integrating third-party management applications on H-P platforms. Central System Manager (CSM) sits on top of the OpenView services. It is an interface and integrating platform, which is being developed by H-P within its open management framework, and it will allow both H-P and third-party management applications built on top of the framework to share common screen, event notification, and event-handling facilities. It will also allow users to predefine actions to be taken in response to system events.

MAINFRAME VENDORS OFFERING UNIX TOOLS

Many third-party applications are reincarnations of similar products marketed by the same vendors on IBM mainframe platforms. The mainframe data center relied very heavily on layered software products from IBM and third parties. The market for third-party data center applications was significant, and, as the market for mainframe software slows down, these ISVs are flocking in droves to UNIX. It seems to be a safe assumption that virtually all software that is currently running only in the MVS environment but is specific to the IBM hardware or operating system environment will be available on UNIX within two years. Those who begin planning today to migrate their data center operations to UNIX will have a much broader selection of products available to them by the time they are actually ready to bring systems into production. In the interim, applications will be ported and/or developed, performance will be characterized, and policies and procedures for managing the new environments will be developed. Large users in particular are in a position to establish strategic relationships with data center software providers to help guide their efforts in bringing product to market. That work can enable those ISVs to ship products that meet customer requirements.

Legent offers Paramount Astex, NetSpy, LANSpy, Mics DASD Space Analyzer/Space Collector, Mics SNA Analyzer, and OptiModel. Legent has a minority stake in Tivoli Systems and has licensed the Tivoli Management Framework. Boole & Babbage is developing a strong client/server position. We will cover Computer Associates separately below.

Computer Associates' CA-Unicenter

Computer Associates has used its experience in mainframe systems management to bring that functionality to UNIX. The concept behind CA-Unicenter is to provide the management capabilities that data center managers have come to expect on mainframes, give them a contemporary graphical user interface, and eventually allow the management of networks of heterogeneous systems. Computer Associates has promised to migrate CA-Unicenter over time to integrate with OSF's Distributed Management Environment, but it chose to develop the product rather than wait for DME.

CA-Unicenter is an integrated system including console and workload management, security and report distribution control, spool and automated storage management, performance monitoring, resource accounting, and system administration. It is designed to manage environments of mixed UNIX systems and of non-UNIX environments, including AS/400, VMS, and MVS. It has the anchor points to participate with all of the environments Computer Associates will support. When the non-UNIX Computer Associates' management products are enabled in future releases, a data center manager will be able to manage any participating system from any Unicenter console. Security will be the first area to have the heterogeneous UNIX capability, followed by storage management; other areas and other platforms will follow in future releases for each platform. HP-UX was the first platform for CA-Unicenter, but Computer Associates has announced intentions to port CA-Unicenter to most other commercial UNIX offerings, including Solaris, Pyramid, Sequent, and OSF/1, as well as Windows NT.

CA-Unicenter offers some distributed management capability; in effect, it takes advantage of the strength of the UNIX distributed environment, giving the data center manager the power of mainframe-class management tools. Although the GUI-based environment of Unicenter may take some getting used to on the part of data center system managers accustomed to character

Chapter 11 • Implementing and Managing the New Systems

interfaces, the benefits will far outweigh the pain of moving up the learning curve.

CA-Unicenter functionality is focused on five areas.

1. Security, Control, and Audit (SCA)
2. Automated Storage Management (ASM)
3. Automated Production Control (APC)
4. Performance Management and Accounting
5. Data Center Administration

The five areas are unified with a graphical user interface based on Motif, but a command line interface is available as well for administering and monitoring CA-Unicenter.

SCA provides integrated, single-point sign-on coupled with the native security for either a single machine or a network of UNIX systems. It provides global enforcement of both user access controls and resources access controls and sets policy-based security definitions, thereby simplifying security management. SCA manages user registration, user and resource auditing, and monitoring of system integrity. It provides support for enforcing policies for system entry, asset access control, periodic user password change, account suspension, and security for all systems management functions. SCA uses standard UNIX administration tools integrated with the security offering to administer user accounts and file access controls. Passwords are kept in a secure, encrypted database instead of a text file. Among the policies it allows to be enforced are preventing users from changing IDs once they've logged on and allowing the UNIX superuser authority to be controlled and limited by management.

ASM addresses the extended data and media management requirements of the complete data cycle, including backup, archive, restore, transparent restore, recovery, movement, maintenance, retention, and monitoring. It automates virtually every aspect of disk and tape operations. Users can retrieve files they need without help from the systems administrator.

APC addresses workload management, including automated workload balancing, batch queue management, console management, and report management. APC organizes and controls production workloads in a flexible manner, adjusting to dynamically changing requirements. It allows the system administrator to specify criteria for job scheduling, including checking whether key preceding jobs have run successfully. Sets of jobs can also be scheduled to run on a wide variety of event triggers. It includes workload policy definition and real-time tracking, as well as workload scheduling.

Both calendar- and event-based criteria can be defined in advance to ensure that jobs are run in the right order. This module is central to overcoming UNIX's traditional shortcomings in scheduling batch jobs.

The Automated Production Control module includes Console Management, which automates the handling of common console messages from local as well as remote systems. The message/action parameters can alter, suppress, or reply to messages. It can also initiate other actions based on the content, frequency, or certain other characteristics of the messages. The console GUI can be customized to produce site-specific operator console dialogs and can allow consoles to be tailored to specific tasks.

The spool management facility makes it easier to move print files from CPUs to printers and to assess their status and contents. It allows print queues to be viewed, manipulated, and prioritized. Since the spool facility is integrated with the file system, queues can be off-loaded and stored on other media, either for archiving, reprinting, or retrieving of archived data.

Report distribution control facilities allow finer-grained control over what is printed and distributed. Different users can get different subsets of reports, and reports can be delivered either in printed form or via e-mail.

Performance Management and Accounting

The Performance Management and Accounting module reports how system resources are being used—for instance, how memory is being used, which devices are in use, and how processes are running. This is all communicated through graphical windows. In addition to being helpful in tuning system performance, this information can be useful in billing and chargeback functions. Users or departments can be aggregated in straightforward, readable statements. Accounting structures can be customized depending on customer policy.

Data Center Administration

The Data Center Administration module supports help-desk functions as well as problem management. The problem manager provides a problem-tracking and -reporting system that can be customized by the user. It facilitates communication so that user requests can be responded to in a timely basis. Problems can be entered into the system manually or automatically when exception events occur. Automatic priority escalation can be set up, and a help-desk facility is provided, which allows the user to track progress toward solving problems and to track vendors' responsiveness in solving problems.

HOW PRACTICAL IS UNIX?

UNIX is a very old operating system. In the past, it has been justly criticized for many inadequacies. Many of these have been addressed by now, so that UNIX can be considered a viable commercial operating system for use from the desktop to the data center.

Security

The issues of UNIX security are well publicized but not well understood. The tradition of UNIX was that it was an academic operating system, developed and distributed in universities and research institutes. It was open, networked, and had a great deal of dial-in traffic by customers, including Usenet and the Internet. Some of the basic UNIX operating system code is in the public domain, and much of it is known in considerable detail.

Because of the open nature of the UNIX community, its bugs have been discussed at length. While other operating systems may have similar weak points, they have not been so thoroughly examined and exposed. This may arguably have made the system more secure.

All of the serious UNIX vendors have tested their systems and enhanced them in the security area. A particular problem is that these enhancements have led to a lack of standards, so that the sum of several systems may be less than the parts. As an example, the IBM RS/6000 is one of a number of UNIX systems that is enhanced by separating the encrypted password into a separate file. This is done to defeat a "Robert Morris" attack, which guesses passwords, encrypts them, and compares them to the encrypted passwords in the readable system file /etc/passwd. Sun Systems has improved system security with their Network Information System (formerly Yellow Pages), which allows a range of user IDs to be snychronized over a network. The Sun system was initially introduced to defeat a security exposure in NFS. The RS/6000 supports NIS for compatibility with Sun. If NIS is used, the advantage of the password protection is lost. If it is not used, the NFS exposure remains.

Similar problems await the user of multiple UNIX systems when reviewing auditing, ACLs, and many other detailed issues.

There are a number of companies offering add-in security functions for UNIX systems. These vary from simple one-function utilities through suites of shell scripts, which examine your configuration for known glitches (UNIX gurus on a disk, as it were), to the two leading UNIX systems management products:

- CA-Unicenter
- Tivoli Management Environment

Neither of these products is complete at the time of writing, but both offer a significant set of functions to the platforms they support.

System Administration

UNIX system administration used to be a skilled task requiring hand-editing entries in a variety of configuration files and developing scripts in the eccentric "shell" programming language. All the good UNIX systems now offer menu-driven tools, such as the AIX SMIT, to take care of this problem. Until recently, UNIX systems had a tendency to "panic" in the face of rather ordinary conditions, such as lack of file space, but newer kernels have answered that.

Unix queuing and printing, while elegant, is too simple in concept and overtechnical in execution compared to an MVS system. It is not suited to concurrently handling a variety of jobs from many users.

Job scheduling is still performed with the rather crude "cron" program, which requires extensive shell programming to support automated conditional job execution.

UNIX storage management is now very good. Newer systems offer the ability to span disk volumes, mirror and stripe disks, and manage backups with automated tape jukeboxes. The old problems with file system crashes and fixups are long gone.

SERVICE AND SUPPORT OF HETEROGENOUS SYSTEMS

Real Decisions conducts benchmarking of the costs of automated systems, including mainframe data centers and distributed systems. A major finding from this work, conducted at a diverse client base, is that whereas on mainframe systems the largest cost is hardware, then system software, in distributed environments the major cost is support.

Typically, 60 percent of the total cost of a distributed system is support cost. These costs are incurred at several levels: local, divisional, corporate, and third-party (product vendors or outsourced).

These costs seem to be a consequence of several things. The distributed environment is very dynamic, with many new tools, vendors, and types of systems becoming available. Even within one product, new versions arrive annually, so that training is continuous. It is new, so that the channels for this support have not matured and settled. It is also much richer, so that users are being trained and helped with work functions they never performed before. Much of this may settle with time, lowering the costs.

It is also the case that as hardware costs dwindle to the vanishing point, the cost of support will loom larger even if we do stabilize it. If hardware and software were free, support costs would be 100 percent.

It is clear that there is a very large business in addressing this market and driving down these costs. In the next few years, every corporation will need to examine its support costs, probably outsourcing its help-desk, training, and technical support except where a core business system is being addressed.

Summary

If you plan to develop a few client/server systems to add to a backbone mainframe system or to downsize from a mainframe in a centralized $500 million company, the management of the systems can be a problem for professionals, but there is no reason to panic. If you plan to support a large worldwide network of mission-critical applications, you are on the leading edge of the technology. This is being done in applications from Desert Storm to international finance to global automobile manufacture, but it is a complex engineering problem at this time.

The years from 1993 to 1995 are clearly the time of transition to a fully manageable distributed paradigm for business systems. The major product vendors are in first releases of platform ports in mid-1994. Those who need this now are serving as the beta test sites; those who can wait are developing systems now for rollout in a year or two.

The lowest risk strategy would seem to be system development now for distributed system introduction in 1995 and 1996, combined with training of operations and support staff, reengineering of operations and support procedures, and outsourcing of legacy system networks and computers preparatory to the transition.

12
The Human Side of the New Technology

The tools and techniques discussed so far constitute a paradigm shift, or complete change in viewpoint, for the staff who develop and maintain systems. Existing organizational structures and job roles will not in general survive this, although individuals can. The barriers for individuals include not only the amount of new information and techniques to be absorbed but also the differences in salary and work-habits associated with the new systems. Some people may have entered the field for the opportunity to perform purely technical work, for instance, and now find that they are expected to get involved with the business.

Because mainframe systems are centralized, certain problems were endemic. Almost every MIS department has developed a multiyear maintenance backlog over the years, so that it cannot respond to even small user needs rapidly. The costs of development are high. And because the development staff serves and juggles many users, it is difficult to align development priorities with the needs of the business.

COSTS

We have argued before that new systems offer far more power for less cost. Because we exploit the power, the costs of a complete new distributed system may not be less than the old. But they are more acceptable, because of the

Figure 12.1 Trains and automobiles

way they are incurred. Trains are less expensive than automobiles for most transportation purposes, but they have been replaced. The costs of the automobile and highway system are high, but they are distributed. The automobile is more responsive, and its limitations are accepted in ways which would not occur for a shared system. (See Figure 12.1.)

Meanwhile, centralized computing is developing cost savings of its own. Outsourcing puts competitive pressure on the data center to meet market costs. Large companies are consolidating data centers. IBM and other companies are using microprocessor technology to reduce the cost of mainframe systems.

FUNCTIONS TO CENTRALIZE

In the past, IS staff were responsible for a central system. Now, the same tasks must be performed on systems that are dispersed into user areas. The tasks include:

- configuration management
- management of software development and maintenance
- performance and tuning
- backup and recovery

The workload shifts as end users take on more functions, including application development and maintenance in some instances. The boundary

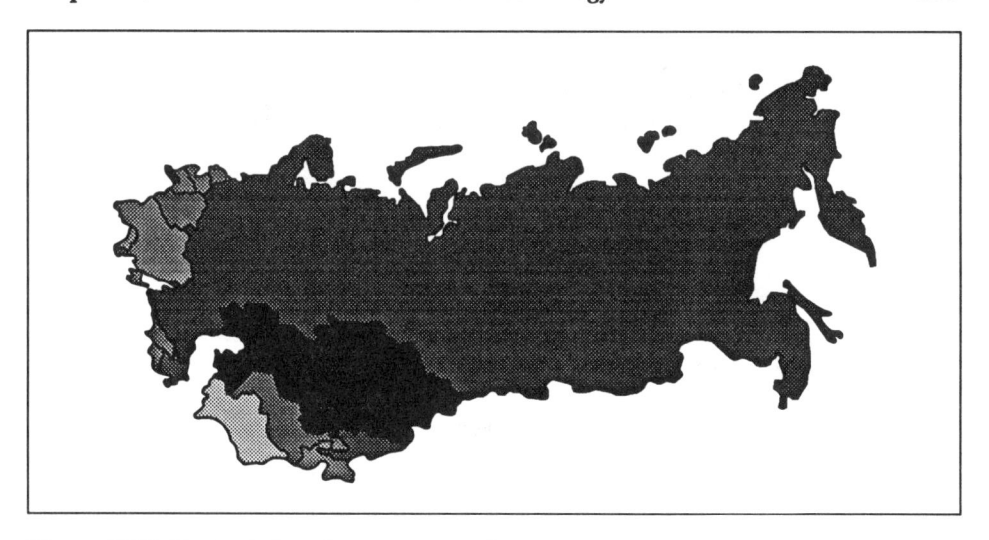

Figure 12.2 Central planning versus market

between centralized and distributed functions must be redrawn for client/server systems. Some management functions can be distributed to departments. Much development responsibility can revert to the business user, as was the pattern in the early days of business computing, in the 1960s and 1970s. There will be centralized functions in the future. Among them are:

- enterprise planning
- data and database administration
- help desk and training
- network management

For many large organizations, these central functions may need a staff half or less the size of the current IS staff.

Business changes today are affecting enterprises continuously at global and microscopic levels. Because of this constant change, the central planning of older IS departments is now as obsolete as it was in the Soviet Union (see Figure 12.2). Planning must now allow for constant change.

TRAINING

Training must occur not only in the new application development technology but in discovery and prototyping methods, end-user support, and network support.

The emphasis is increasingly on reusable code. Partly, this involves the procedures for creating reusable pieces of code. More often, more time is spent finding and integrating prewritten code. This conflicts with the "not invented here" philosophy of many MIS departments. There is an increasing third-party market for code; this market is expanding in variety and speeding up in production. Programming in an event-driven, object-based, graphical style takes months to learn and is inherently more complex than traditional procedural programming. This is increasingly true as it meets the object models and the speed and variety of the product market.

In many ways, today's IT professional has grown up with a single infrastructure and set of standards: COBOL, MVS, TSO, SNA, and SAA/CUA. This is being replaced—not with a single new set of standards (for example PowerBuilder, UNIX, Windows) but with a series of new products. There will be more change in the future.

Teams in this environment include end users working with technology experts and addressing business concerns concurrently with systems issues. The development team is ultimately involved in defining, designing, and developing solutions to high-level business problems. Team members must have a foundation in business terminology, practices, and principles. As my former AGS colleague John Hutchinson said, "IT must cease to be the 'performing bear' and start dancing to the music of the business." (See Figure 12.3.)

Figure 12.3 The dancing bear

The new development style requires a different set of skills, with more of an emphasis on teamwork. The overlapping of development phases, the generally faster pace, and the atmosphere of working "in a fishbowl" can lead to a more stressful environment than the more measured atmosphere of old-fashioned structured development. Developers must interact well with a variety of people. They must be equally at ease in the boardroom, a manager's office, or a data-entry operator's cubicle. You might say that the ideal developer must assume the roles of teacher, salesperson, detective, and diplomat. A toleration for ambiguity is also important; effective developers need to be patient with the trial-and-error prototyping approach of defining business user information needs. Requirements are often vague, and the target is in perpetual motion. In addition, developers must be insightful and creative. They must be able to translate hunches and suggestions into real user interfaces. They must also be willing to throw away a week's worth of programming when the targeted business user group changes its mind.

Not all of the current programmer/analysts will make the transition to the new development paradigm. This combination of business, technical, and interpersonal skills differs from the old programming personality. An old rule of thumb is that one-third will teach themselves (by now, most already have), one-third will be taught successfully, and one-third will not be economically trainable. Fortunately for those who will not be trainable, there continues to be a need for legacy system skills, although not at the higher salary levels of the past. This training is expensive, not so much in training fees as in the cost of salary and benefits during months of unproductive time.

The downsized environment lacks the integrated tools for system management and security that are normal around mainframes. These things must be accomplished with a number of tools and products as building blocks. The UNIX system programmer or system administrator is more resourceful and empowered than his or her IBM counterpart; this is a big shift in mindset.

A program for change begins with the establishment of performance metrics based on user satisfaction. Then, maintenance of old systems is cut back to a minimum, and new development tools are adopted for all development projects. Programmers are retrained and new programmers hired. You must plan to bring in 10 to 20 percent new staff, consultants or full-time, who have solid experience. Those who do not wish to or cannot learn the new tools are concentrated in the maintenance area. As applications are transferred, there will be an excess of old application and maintenance staff. Some organizations outsource their maintenance to avoid facing this problem.

Skills transfer can be deliberately encouraged in the course of development projects. The project team structure must be designed to encourage the diffusion of technology and methodology. The members of the project team must include a number of individuals who readily adapt to new ways of operation, as well as possibly some who are more conservative. The early adopters will provide the support and enthusiasm needed to get the project under way.

Summary

For those who can embrace the next wave of systems with enthusiasm, it is an exciting time. Using the new products of computer technology, we are delivering systems faster—systems that are closer to the needs of the business and have less defects and systems that can adapt over time to changes in the business or new developments in technology. Living in "interesting times" has its problems, too—constant change and high standards, for example. But there is no turning back.

Index

A

Access, restriction to resources and, 246
Accounting management, 240, 243, 256
Activity identification, and business process analysis, 86–87
Adabas/Natural, 24–25
Adobe, 16
AI, tools for, 197–198
AI systems, 3
Aldus, 16
APC (Automated Production Control), 255
Apple Computer, 16, 121
Application Logic Layer, 99, 114–116
Application servers, 127
Applications. *See* Software.
Architecture. *See* Client/server architecture.
ARCnet, 114
ASK ManMan, 23
ASM. *See* Storage management.
Assembler language, 11
ATM (Asynchronous Transfer Mode), 118–119
Authentication, security and, 245
Automated Production Control (APC), 255
Automated Storage Management (ASM), 255
Automated systems, 205–226
 application design, 214–215
 business requirements, 210–213
 data modeling, 221–225
 JAD prototyping, 215–221
 project plan, 209–210
 team composition, 226
Automation, and downsizing, 35–37
Avalon Manufacturing, 23

B

Backup procedures, 251–252
 fault tolerance and, 135–136
Bandwidth
 ATM and, 118–119
 technological solutions, 7
Banyan Vines, 121, 123
Batch systems, 96–97
Benchmarking, 90–91
 of database systems, 164
 transaction processing, 164–166
Borland Interbase, 154
Brainstorming, 91–93
Btrieve SQL, 155

Business computing
   and automated systems, 205–226
   changing needs, 19
   cost/benefit analysis, 55–64
   distributed processing, 100–104
   history of, 5–9
   Joint Requirements Planning (JRP), 207, 210–212
   needs assessment, 45–47
   processor power, 9–10
   technology assessment, 47–49
   See also Downsizing
Business modeling, 84–86
Business transformation, 72–74

C

C++, 200
CASE tools, 3, 222
   I-CASE tools, 11, 199
CA systems, 24–25
   CA-IDMS/ADS/PC, 25
   CA-Unicenter, 254–256
CDDI (Copper Distributed Data Interface), 117
CD-ROMs, 16–18, 127
Cell relay (SMDS), 119
Centralization, of management, 262–264
Central System Manager (CSM), 253
CICS options, 26–27, 99–100
Cincom Supra Server, 154
Cincom tools, 106
Client/server architecture, 95–123
   distributed database, 102, 104
   distributed presentation, 100–101
   distributed processing, 102–103
   interfaces, 97–99
   languages, 96–98
   remote data access, 103–104
   remote presentation, 101–102
   scalability and, 136
Client/server systems, 1–20
   accounting management, 240, 243, 256
   advantages of, 10–13
   communications protocols, 120–121
   configuration management, 242–243
   cost factors, 9–11, 55–64
   data normalization, 224–226
   definitions of, 1–2
   disk storage, 134–135
   distributed, 100–101
   fault management, 248–249
   fault tolerance, 135–136
   graphical, 191–200
   mainframe integration, 39
   network hardware, 114–120
   network operating systems, 121–123
   operations management, 249–250
   performance management, 241–242
   portability, 109–110
   pyramid, 37
   S-curve, 4–5
   security management, 240, 243–248
   standards, 110–113
   storage management, 250–253
   technical problems, 239–241
   user interfaces, 15–19
   See also Automated systems
CM-API (Consolidated Management API), 253
COBOL, 3, 25–26

Index

Code conversion, 27–28
  recovery tools, 31–32
Collier-Jackson, 23
Command Technology, 26
Commodity trends, and database systems, 156
Communications protocols, 120–121
  ATM, 118–119
  CDDI, 117
  DECnet, 114, 120
  Ethernet, 113–116
  FDDI, 117
  IPX/SPX, 120
  Novell NetWare, 121–122, 132
  Novell NLM, 120, 140
  SNA, 15, 39, 228–229
  SNMP, 252
  TCP/IP, 14–15, 18, 102, 109–111, 120, 122
  wireless LANs, 119
  XNS protocol, 120
Computer Associates. *See* CA systems.
Configuration management, of client/server systems, 240, 242–243
Console management. *See* Operations management.
Costs
  and client/server environment, 9–10
  cost/benefit analysis, 55–64
  of database systems, 157
  migration costs, 51–52
  payback measurements, 60–61
  PC-class servers, 130–131
CSM (Central System Manager), 253
Customer need, 70

D

D&B software, 23
Database servers, 127
Database systems
  and client/server environment, 2
  commodity trend, 156
  data access, 157–162
  data dictionary, 162
  data normalization, 224–226
  data storage, 167
  functions, 159
  history of, 150–151
  I/O processing, 38–39
  legacy system, 230–234
  manageability, 167–168
  multiplatform, 153
  niche suppliers, 154
  object databases, 152
  objects, 159
  performance measurements, 162–162
  pricing, 157
  refurbishing, 29–30
  relational databases, 151
  security, 246–247
  single-platform, 154
  SQL, 151, 157, 159
  SQL bridging, 234–236
  stored procedures, 160
  support, 156
  system size, 38
  triggers, 160
Data Center Administration, 256–257
Datacom, 24–25
Data dictionary, 162
Data Management Layer, 99
Data modeling, 84–86, 221–225
Data normalization, 224–226

DB2, 167–168, 251
Decision-making, and control of process, 69
Declarative referential integrity, 161
DEC servers, 144–1456
DEC systems
 Alpha, 7
 DECnet, 114
 minicomputers, 5
 OpenVMS, 128
 System 10, 42
Department of Defense, security standards, 248
Deskside servers, 130–131
Desktop DBA, 251
Development cycle. *See* Automated systems.
Development methodologies, and client/server environment, 2–3
Disk management, 250–253
Disk storage. *See* Storage management.
Distributed computing, 100–104
Distributed databases, 102–104
Distributed Management Environment (DME), 252–253
Distributed presentation, 100–101
DIX specification, 115
DIX (Xerox), 114
DME. *See* Distributed Management Environment.
DOS
 limitations of, 172–174
 peer-to-peer LANs for, 123
 security considerations, 245–246
Downsizing
 automation and, 35–37
 business assessment, 45–47
 candidate assessment, 37–45
 and client/server environment, 2
 code conversion, 27–28
 cost/benefit analysis, 55–64
 critical factors, 66–72
 emulation versus conversion, 27
 payback analysis, 60–61
 risk assessment, 52–54
 software modifications, 23–31
 strategies of, 21–33
 technology assessment, 47–52
 See also Networks

E
Easel system, 29, 101
ECC memory, 132
Education, and business process analysis, 86
EIS packages, 190–191
Empowerment, and downsizing, 35–37
Emulation
 CICS options, 26–27
 and workstation selection, 180–181
Encryption, for security, 248
Enterprise information, access to, 14–15
Ethernet, 113–116
 fast Ethernet, 117–118
 switched Ethernet, 118
Event Control Server, 250
Evolutionary Technologies (ETI), 28
Extended High-Level Language Application Programming Interface (EHLLAPI), 100
Extract Tool Suite, 28

F
Fast Ethernet, 117–118
Fault management, of client/server systems, 240, 248–249

Index

Fault tolerance, 135–136
Fax machines, 16–17
FDDI (Fiber Distributed Data Interface), 117
Fiber optics, FDDI, 117
File servers, 126–127
First normal form (1NF), 225
Flow charts, guidelines, 89
FOCUS, 11
Forest and Trees, 191
FORTRAN, 25, 138–139
Fourgen software, 23
Fourth-generation language (4GL), 24, 109, 184–189
Fourth wave, definition of, 6
Frame relay, 119
Front-end support, in databases, 162
Functions, and database systems, 159

G

Galaxy, 102
Gateways, connectivity, 230–232
Geographically dispersed resources, 68
GlancePlus/UX, 241
Groupware, 201–203
GUI systems, 178–180
 and client/server environment, 2
 for desktop, 182
 graphical client/server systems, 191–200
Gupta SQLBase, 154

H

Hammer, Mike, 66
Hardware
 386/486 systems, 10
 See also Servers

Hewlett-Packard systems, 6, 7
 9000 UNIX systems, 12
 PA-7100, 7
 performance management, 241
 servers, 143–144
 System Administrator Manager (SAM), 242
High-speed LANs, 116–119
HP. *See* Hewlett-Packard systems.
Hutchinson, John, 264

I

IBI systems, 24–25
IBM systems
 360/370, 5
 3090-class mainframes, 39
 EHLLAPI interface, 100
 ES/9000, 55
 PC, 5
 RS/6000, 12, 40, 257
 Series/1, 42
 servers, 144
 System Management Interface Tool (SMIT), 242
I-CASE, 11
Identification, of users, 244–245
ID requirements, security and, 245–247
IEF systems, 24–25
Information display tools, 189–191
Intel
 386/486 systems, 10, 127
 P6 chip, 10
Interfaces
 development of, 96–99
 distributed presentation, 100–101
 improved, user interface, 15–18
Internet, 18
IPX/SPX protocol, 120

ISDN. *See* Communications protocols.
ISPF/PC, 26

J
Job Scheduler, 250
Joint Application Design (JAD), 215–221
  advantages of, 218
Joint Requirements Planning (JRP), 207, 210–212

K
KEDIT, 26
Knowledgeware, 194–195
Knowledgeware Flashpoint, 29

L
Languages, development of, 96–99
LANs. *See* Networks
LaserRX/UX, 241
Lawson software, 23
Layers, OSI model, 112–116, 240–241
Legacy system, 230–234
Lightship, 191
Loading modules, NLM, 120, 122, 140
Logical Volume Manager (LVM), 251

M
Macintosh, 121, 175
Maestro, 250
Mainframe computers
  future of, 19–20
  integration of, 39
  SNA connectivity, 228–229
  UNIX vendors, 253–257

Manageability, and database systems, 167–168
Mansfield Software, 26
Martin, James, 205
Media management, 250–253
Metcalf, Robert, 114
  See also Ethernet
Micro Focus
  application-to-application interface, 29
  COBOL, 26, 106
Microprocessors. *See* Processors.
Microsoft LAN Manager, 123
Middleware, 230–237
Migration costs, analysis of, 51–52
MIPS, definition of, 138
MIT Palladium Print System, 250
Modeling, 84–86, 221–225
Modems. *See* Communications protocols.
Morris, Robert, 245
Mosaic software, 18
Mozart system, 29, 101
Multimedia computing, 16–18, 127
Multiplatform databases, 153
MVS operating system, 15

N
NetWare. *See* Novell NetWare.
Networks
  bandwidth and, 7
  and client/server environment, 2
  communications protocols, 120–121
  configuration management, 242–243
  encryption and, 248
  Ethernet connections, 113–116
  hardware, 114–120

Index

high-speed LANs, 116
operating systems, 121–123
peer-to-peer LANs, 123
security factors, 244–246
UTP (unshielded twisted-pair wire), 119
WANs (Wide Area Networks), 119–120
wireless LANs, 119
See also Client/server systems; Standards
Niche suppliers, and database systems, 154
Novell
NetWare, 121–122, 132, 135, 140
NLM (loading modules), 120, 122, 140–141

O

Object databases, 152
Objects, and database systems, 159
ObjectView, 194–195
OCI (ORACLE Call Interface), 230–231
Online systems, 96–97
Open systems
advantages of, 10–13
definition of, 1–2
enterprise information and, 14–15
groupware, 201–203
limiting factors, 7
mainframe connectivity, 229–231
OSF, 112
portability, 12, 109–110
See also Client/server systems
OpenView, 242–43, 253
OpenVMS, 128
Operating systems, 121–123, 140–147
Novell NLM, 140
OS/2, 141–142
security considerations, 245–246
in servers, 140–144
UNIX, 142, 145–146
Windows NT, 142
See also UNIX
Operations management, of client/server systems, 249–250
ORACLE, 13, 24–25, 107–108, 251
Orange Book, 248
OS/2, 25, 141–142, 175
OSF (Open Software Foundation), 112
OSI model, 14, 112–116, 240–241
Outcome analysis, versus task analysis, 66–67
Output management, 250

P

Pacbase, 24–25
Paradox (Windows), 195
Parallel activities, linking of, 68
Passwords, 245–247
Payback analysis, and downsizing, 60–61
PC-class computing
COBOL and, 25–26
costs of, 130–131
selection criteria, 132–135
types of servers, 125–136
Peer-to-peer LANs, 123
Pen-based systems, 16
Pentium, 13
Peoplesoft, 24
Performance management, of client/server systems, 240–242

Performance measurements
  of database systems, 162–167
  of server systems, 139–140
PerfView, 242
Pilot Systems, 191
Pinnacle Graphics Server, 194–195
PL/1, 25
Portability, 12, 109–110
POSIX, 14
PowerBuilder, 127, 192–193
PowerPC, 13
Presentation layer, 114–115
  data access, 103–104
  distributed presentation, 100–101
  remote presentation, 101
Pricing. *See* Costs.
Printers, selection of, 127
Process analysis, 86–89
  flow chart guidelines, 89
  JAD and JRP, 215–221
Process design, 89–92
  and automated systems, 205–221
Processors
  benchmarks, 137–139
  power of, 9–10
  RISC, 6–7, 137–138
  and server selection, 133–134
  SMPs (symmetric multiprocessors), 128
  and workstation selection, 181–182
Process selection, 74–84
Product development, cycle time, 70–72
Protocols. *See* Communications protocols.
Prototypes, 217–219
  types of, 217

Q
Quadbase-SQL, 155

R
RAD systems, 205–209
RAID arrays, 134–135, 251
Raima Database Server, 155
Red Brick Warehouse, 154
Reengineering, 65–93
  benefits of, 74–75
  modeling, 84–86
  principles of, 65–72
  process analysis and design, 86–92
  process selection, 74–84
Referential integrity, 161
Relational databases, 2, 150–151
  See also Database systems
Remote data access, 103–105
Remote presentation, 101
Resource Management Facility (RMF), 241
Resource servers, 127
RISC processors, 137–138
  RISC/UNIX systems, 6–7
Risk assessment, and downsizing, 52–54
Ross Financials, 24
RXForecast/UX, 241

S
SAM (System Administrator Manager), 242
SAP R3, 24
SAS, 11
SAS systems, 24–25
SCADA systems, 12
SCA (Security, Control, Audit), 255
Scalability, 136

Index

Scheduling, and business process analysis, 86
SCO Open Desktop, 172
S-curve, 4–5
Second normal form (2NF), 225–226
Security management
  of client/server systems, 240, 243–248
  of UNIX systems, 257–258
Sequent WinServer, 132
Servers
  DEC servers, 144–146
  disk storage, 134–135
  hardware considerations, 127–131
  H-P servers, 143–144
  IBM servers, 144
  SUN servers, 144
  types of, 125–130
  UNIX servers, 145–146
Session layer, 113–116
Single-platform databases, 154
SLED (single large expensive disk), 134
SmallTalk tools, 197–197
SMIT (System Management Interface Tool), 242
SMPs (symmetric multiprocessors), 128
SNA connectivity, mainframes and, 228–229
SNA networks, 15, 39
SNMP, 252
Software
  code conversion, 27–28
  decomposing applications, 99–100
  downsizing and, 23–31
  emulation versus conversion, 27
  front-end database, 162
  operating systems, 121–123, 140–147
  portability, 12, 109–110
  See also specific software by name
Software development
  and client/server environment, 2–3
  RAD methodology, 205–206
Solaris system, 250
SONET. *See* Communications protocols.
SPARC, 13
Speech recognition, 16
SQL databases, 151, 157, 159, 234–235
  storage management, 251–253
SQL Windows, 107, 193–194
Standards, 14, 110–113
  OSF (Open Software Foundation), 112
Storage management, 250–253
  ASM, 255
  and database systems, 167
  disk storage, 134–135
  SLED, 134
Stored procedures, in database systems, 160
Striping, definition of, 134
Sun systems
  servers, 127, 144, 257
  SPARC, 28
Superservers, 131–132
Superuser passwords, 245–246
Support
  and database systems, 156
  and server systems, 136–137
  UNIX systems, 258–259

Supra/Mantis, 24–25
Switched Ethernet, 118
Sybase, 13, 107–108
Symmetric multiprocessors (SMPs), 128
System Administrator Manager (SAM), 242
System Management Facility (SMF), 241
System Management Interface Tool (SMIT), 242

T
Taligent, 178
Task analysis
  and business process analysis, 86–87
  versus outcome analysis, 66–67
TCP/IP, 14–15, 18, 102, 109–111, 122
Technical problems, with client/server systems, 239–241
Technology
  and downsizing, 47–52
  S-curve, 4–5
  stages of acceptance, 7–9
Timebox, uses of, 216–217
TI systems, 24–25
Token ring, 114–116
Tools
  for AI, 197–198
  CASE, 3, 11, 199, 222
  Cincom, 106
  evaluating, 106–109
  Extract suite, 28
  information display tools, 189–191
  recovery, 31–32

SmallTalk, 197–197
SMIT, 242
Training, 263–264
Transaction processing, 164–166
  systems pyramid, 37
Transport layer, 113–116
Tricord PowerFrame, 132
Triggers, in database systems, 160
Trinzic systems, 191

U
Ubiquitous computing, 19
UNIX, 127, 142, 145–146, 176–178
  CA-Unicenter, 254–256
  mainframe vendors, 253–257
  market factors, 11
  performance management, 241
  portability, 109–110
  practicality of, 257–259
  resource access restrictions, 246
  security considerations, 245–247, 257–258
  servers, 145–146
  standards, 109–111
UPS (Uninterruptible Power Supply), 135–136
User interface, 15–18, 244–245
  refurbishing, 28–29
User interface layer, 99
UTP (unshielded twisted-pair wire), 119

V
VAX/VMX operating systems, 15
Video processing, 16–18
Virtual reality, 16
Visual Basic, 195
Voice processing, 16

Index

W
Wall Data Rumba, 29
Wang computers, 127
Watcom/PowerSoft SQL, 155
Western Data Systems, 24
Wide Area Networks, 119–120
Windows, 176–190
   costs factors, 61–63
   DOS versus, 174
   SQL Windows, 193–194
   Windows NT, 121, 129, 142, 174
Wireless LANs, 119
Word processing, 16

Workstations
   cost/benefit analysis, 61–63
   selecting, 172–182
   See also Servers
WorldWide Web (WWW), 18

X
X.25 protocol. *See* Communications protocols.
XDB, 155
Xerox Computer Services, 24
   DIX, 114
XNS protocol, 120
X terminals, 173–174